3—

PRAISE FOR GENE STONE'S
LITTLE GIRL FLY AWAY

"A compelling true-life thriller . . . The plot twist is a stunner."

—Digby Diehl, *Playboy*

"Stone fascinatingly reconstructs this unusual case, following Finley through five years of psychotherapy. . . . An empathetic portrait of a severely traumatized woman . . ."

—Sue-Ellen Beauregard, *Booklist*

"*LITTLE GIRL FLY AWAY* is a mesmerizing tale—a vivid psychological thriller—clear and well-written and impossible to put down."

—Patricia Bosworth, author of
Diane Arbus: A Biography and *Montgomery Clift*

"Compelling reading of a woman's courageous struggle to confront her demons and reclaim her true identity."

—Barbara Gordon, author of
I'm Dancing as Fast as I Can

"Highly recommended . . . This is an unusual and compelling story written in a style that pulls the reader in. Both readers of true crime and psychological accounts will enjoy this book."

—Lisa J. Cochenet, *Library Journal*

"This deeply moving account re-creates not only the supposed crime but also the successful psychotherapy which followed. . . ."

—*Publishers Weekly*

D0173280

For orders other than by individual consumers, Pocket Books grants a discount on the purchase of **10 or more** copies of single titles for special markets or premium use. For further details, please write to the Vice-President of Special Markets, Pocket Books, 1230 Avenue of the Americas, New York, NY 10020.

For information on how individual consumers can place orders, please write to Mail Order Department, Paramount Publishing, 200 Old Tappan Road, Old Tappan, NJ 07675.

RC
569.5
.M8
S76
1994

LITTLE GIRL
FLY AWAY

GENE STONE

POCKET STAR BOOKS

New York   London   Toronto   Sydney   Tokyo   Singapore

The sale of this book without its cover is unauthorized. If you purchased
this book without a cover, you should be aware that it was reported to
the publisher as "unsold and destroyed." Neither the author nor the
publisher has received payment for the sale of this "stripped book."

 A Pocket Star Book published by
POCKET BOOKS, a division of Simon & Schuster Inc.
1230 Avenue of the Americas, New York, NY 10020

Copyright © 1994 by Gene Stone

All rights reserved, including the right to reproduce
this book or portions thereof in any form whatsoever.
For information address Simon & Schuster Inc.,
1230 Avenue of the Americas, New York, NY 10020

ISBN: 0-671-51952-2

First Pocket Books printing February 1995

10 9 8 7 6 5 4 3 2 1

POCKET STAR BOOKS and colophon are registered
trademarks of Simon & Schuster Inc.

Cover design by Corsillo/Manzone
Cover photo by Fred George

Printed in the U.S.A.

LITTLE GIRL
FLY AWAY

*Ruth in Richards, Missouri,
at age four*

Ruth in Fort Scott at 18

*The Wichita police sketch
of the Poet*

Ed at 55

Ruth in her early 50s

Dr. Pickens

PART 1

The Poet

1

ON A HOT JUNE AFTERNOON IN WICHITA, KANSAS, 1977, Edward J. Finley was resting indoors after a day of building a back yard patio when he lit a cigarette and keeled over, unconscious. His last memory was of the lit head flying off the matchstick like a tiny firecracker.

Ruth, his wife, had been sitting with him on their sofa. She immediately tried to revive Ed, whose body was now lying prone on the floor, but she couldn't, so she ran to the telephone and called for an ambulance. Twenty-five minutes later Ed was in the emergency room, where he recovered consciousness and spent the rest of the day undergoing examinations.

Both Finleys assumed Ed had suffered a heart attack from the day's strenuous work, although anxiety and concern for each other prevented them from saying the words out loud. By the end of the day, however, the doctors had no conclusive diagnosis, so Ruth promised her husband she would return the next morning, said good-bye, and drove back home alone.

Ruth, at forty-seven, was attractive, with wide brown eyes, dark hair, and a square face. Neither thin nor fat, tall nor short, pale nor ruddy, she wore clothes that were as unexceptional as her demeanor, opting for jeans and shorts on the weekends, and unpretentious suits and dresses at work, where she was the secretary to the district marketing manager at Southwestern Bell. All in all, Ruth's appearance of a quiet, respectable woman with a shy smile and accommodating manners was precisely the image she wished to convey.

Ed Finley was an accountant and secretary-treasurer of a small construction firm. He was forty-nine years old, tall, lean, with similarly unremarkable features except for his scalp, which was completely bald. Ed had lost the hair on the top of his head decades earlier and now shaved the sides and back. Otherwise, like his wife, he chose to present himself as a modest, unassuming man—subdued clothes, little jewelry, no display. Ed and Ruth were very concerned about how they were perceived by others, but their hope was that no one thought less of them rather than that anyone thought more; they both felt a life well led was led without notice.

Ruth parked the family's black 1977 Oldsmobile in the garage—Ed also owned a Ford pickup, which Ruth seldom drove—and went inside to the kitchen. Besides building the patio, the Finleys were installing a new front sidewalk and steps, and their living room window was covered by an enormous, dark tarpaulin that prevented bits of concrete from hitting the glass. However, the tarp also retained heat, and although it was now late, the temperature hadn't dropped much below seventy-five degrees, making the house stuffy. Ruth turned up the air-conditioning and went downstairs to make phone calls in the basement, where the Finleys spent most of their spare time, either watching television or working on their hobbies. Ruth's was ceramics, and the house was filled with vases, ginger jars, and pastel tableaus of animals or small children. But most of all Ruth liked to create dogs, for whom, throughout her life, she had felt a special compassion. Currently she owned an English bulldog named Sherman, short for Sherman Tank, who now lay at her feet.

Ruth's ceramics equipment was located in the basement's far left corner. Most Wichita houses were built over similarly furnished rooms, reflecting the area's pragmatism: why not add a second layer to a house when it costs so little? But a basement was also considered desirable in a city where temporary housing built during World War II was constructed on a concrete slab. The severe local weather was an additional factor: Wichita lies in the middle of tornado country.

Another downstairs corner was devoted to Ed's hobby, painting; the house's most common decorative objects after Ruth's ceramics were Ed's large, dusky acrylic landscapes of midwestern farms, bridges, and rivers. Also in the Finley basement, which was the size of the entire daylight floor, was the family entertainment area, with a color television, a stereo system, a sofa, and several lounge chairs. Otherwise the one-story house was compact: two bedrooms, one bath, a narrow living room with wall-to-wall brown sculptured carpeting, a kitchen, and a dining room that had been recently created by knocking down a wall between a third bedroom and a small dinette. (The two Finley sons were now grown and had moved to other cities.) A ten-piece antique dining room set inherited from Ed's parents was the only valuable furniture in the house. The rest of the furnishings were relatively new and without any particular scheme or design. Everything was, like Ruth and Ed, quiet and unassuming, including the street on which the house was situated, East Indianapolis, a placid dead-end block in a conservative, white, middle-class neighborhood.

Both Ruth and Ed were midwesterners. Ruth was born on February 1, 1930, on a farm in Richards, Missouri (population one hundred), to Carl and Effie (Faye) Smock. She lived at home until she was sixteen, when she moved to the nearby city of Fort Scott, Kansas, where she attended a larger high school and worked part-time for the phone company. A few years later she met Ed who, back from a stint in the Navy, had enrolled at Fort Scott Junior College. The two liked each other, dated, and were married on June 1, 1950. Ed received his B.A. from nearby Pittsburg State Teachers College, and then he and Ruth moved to Wichita, where Ed took a job at Beech Aircraft. Ruth accepted another position with the phone company and stayed there until 1952, when she took time off to raise two sons. In 1957 the family moved to the home on East Indianapolis, and when the boys reached their teens, Ruth returned to work.

Faye Smock now lived in Wichita, but Ruth's father had died of a heart attack five years earlier while being treated in the hospital for emphysema. Ruth also had one brother, Carl Morris Smock, who was a year older, and a sister, Jean Jones, four years younger; both were married and lived in Wichita with their families. Ruth had five nieces and nephews.

When she finished making her phone calls, Ruth watched a little television and then listened to the radio; the BTK Strangler, Wichita's first serial killer, was the major news event. BTK's initials stood for Bind, Torture, and Kill, which was what the man had recently done to his seventh victim on Wichita's east side, where the Finleys lived. Ruth found this kind of lurid story uninteresting, however, and switched the radio to her favorite kind of music—easy listening. Outside the house, a strong wind from the west was causing the tarpaulin to flap repeatedly against the front of the house, making Ruth nervous. She turned the radio off and watched some more television.

Around ten thirty that night Ruth was walking upstairs for a glass of water when the telephone rang. The sound startled her. None of their friends ever called so late, and Ruth immediately feared Ed's health had deteriorated. She continued to the kitchen and picked up the receiver.

"Hello?" she said.

"Is this Ruth Smock from Fort Scott, Kansas?" asked an unfamiliar male voice.

"Yes, it is," Ruth said. Few people knew her maiden name, or that she had once lived in Fort Scott, so she assumed the man was an old acquaintance or a relative.

The man then asked Ruth several personal questions about her past and particularly about an apartment house in which she had lived when she was sixteen. Ruth became agitated. She didn't want to sound rude or hang up, but she gave increasingly vague replies, which seemed to antagonize the man. "Look," he said, "I know all about that night."

"You do?" Ruth asked, more surprised than curious. But she immediately guessed what night the man meant.

"I do," he said. He started reading an article from a 1946 edition of the *Fort Scott Tribune:* " 'Branded on both thighs by a hot flat-iron, apparently used by a sex maniac, Ruth Smock, sixteen-year-old Fort Scott High school girl and part-time employee at the local exchange of the Bell Telephone company, was resting today at the home of her parents, Mr. and Mrs. Carl Smock of Richards, following an attack upon her early last night by a man whom Fort Scott police called a "sex maniac." Miss Smock said the intruder placed a bottle under her nose (chloroform or some other anaesthetic) and she failed to recollect any other happening of the evening until she regained consciousness and found herself lying on the kitchen floor, blood oozing from one leg. . . . She faintly remembers seeing the man heating flat-irons on the stove . . .' ''

Ruth was bewildered. The incident described in the article had been so incongruous with her everyday life that she seldom gave it any thought. No permanent damage had been done. Her assailant had disappeared after branding her body, and the burns had healed years ago. Why in the world, Ruth wondered, would anyone care about an isolated event so long ago?

"I work for a construction company," the man suddenly said. "We've been tearing down buildings and I found a bunch of old papers." Apparently he had found potentially embarrassing stories about three people, and he was planning to call them all. Ruth was the first. The man then said he would keep quiet if Ruth sent him some money. "I know where you work. If you don't do what I want I just might leave that article where everyone can see it . . ."

At that point Ruth hung up the phone. She was frightened, her head ached, and she felt a powerful desire to rest, although she thought she should stay up in case the man drove past the house or knocked on the door. But when she lay down in her bed, she closed her eyes for just a moment, and her next conscious thought was to wonder why the bedroom was so extraordinarily bright. She had fallen asleep for ten hours.

Ruth dressed, ate breakfast, and drove to the hospital to see Ed, who was sitting up in bed. According to the tests, an injury from a car accident the previous Christmas Eve wasn't as minor as Ed had thought: the cartilage between two ribs had separated. While working on the patio he had reinjured the shoulder and had later passed out from intense pain. His heart was in excellent condition, however, and he was in good health.

Still, the doctors asked Ed to stay in the hospital a few more days, and Ruth again drove home by herself. Since her marriage she hadn't spent any significant time alone, and this feeling of isolation, compounded by her fear of another call, unsettled her. Every night that week she stayed up late, cringing when the tarpaulin slapped against the front of the house or when the telephone rang. But the man didn't call again, and after Ed returned home, Ruth tried to forget the incident.

A little less than a month later, in early July, Ruth was sitting at her desk at Southwestern Bell, sorting through the day's mail. It was, as usual, all business, and mostly for her boss, but one cheap, brown envelope fell out of the bundle and onto her desk. Ruth looked at it and was surprised to see her name scrawled across the top in childlike lettering. There was no title, room number, or address, and Ruth wasn't sure how the letter could have found her.

She opened the envelope and a yellowed piece of newspaper fluttered out. "Oh, my God," she thought.

She wasn't sure why, but she was frightened, and she quickly shoved the piece of newspaper in a drawer, even though no one else was in the room. A few minutes later, however, she grew curious and took the paper out again. Her sense of foreboding was justified: someone had sent her the banner headline from the old *Fort Scott Tribune* concerning her attack. She hadn't seen it since she was sixteen. Unnerved, she ripped it up, crammed the pieces back into the envelope, and threw it all into the trash.

Ruth then tried to return to work, but her head hurt too much to concentrate. Throughout her life she had suffered from debilitating headaches that struck randomly, usually without apparent relation to stress or work, and nothing—not aspirin, sleep, or home remedies—relieved the pain. The headaches had recently become worse, but Ruth had never mentioned them to Ed. Nor did she tell him about the letter. She had been taught as a child that personal problems were best kept private.

But the man wouldn't go away. Over the next few months Ruth received six more calls; each time she hung up before the man could say anything except her name. During the same period Ed also answered the phone several times and heard only a dial tone. He assumed the calls were just some kids' prank, and Ruth didn't correct him.

2

WICHITA IN THE 1970S WAS A REMOTE CITY. BUILT
on an unfluctuating midwestern plain, it misses major
east-west interstate highways by hundreds of miles
and is so distant from Kansas City and Oklahoma
City, the nearest major population centers, that its police chief once called it "an island in a sea of wheat
fields." Local boosters liked to say that Wichita, with
a population of just under three hundred thousand,
combined the best qualities of a small city and a large
town. The city's detractors, however, found it guilty
of the opposite.

One of the problems Wichita shared with the rest of
urban America was its core degeneration, caused by
newly constructed industrial parks and shopping malls
on the city's edges. By 1977 only three large department stores remained downtown—Macy's, Henry's,
and J. C. Penney—and it seemed to Ruth that fewer
pedestrians walked about the streets every day. But
both Finleys worked in the city's center and, since
their schedules were similar, they drove in together,

for the companionship and to save gas. Because Ruth usually finished work first, she often window-shopped while she waited for Ed.

In mid-August Ruth was on the corner of Broadway and Douglas when the light turned and a man started walking alongside her. Ruth didn't pay him much attention.

"You've done a good job at work this week," the man said abruptly. "You can take the weekend off."

Then he started to talk about pictures. "The camera reflects the true quality of one's soul," he said.

The man next mentioned that he liked to gamble in Las Vegas. Ruth now took a sideways glance. The man was of medium height and weight, and he wore jeans, a plain shirt, and tennis shoes. Ruth thought, who is this jerk? By this time she had reached the windows of Henry's department store and stopped, pretending to look at the display, but the man kept on walking and chatting until he realized Ruth was no longer beside him. He then came back to Henry's, where Ruth was still standing.

"I'm waiting for my husband," Ruth said, hoping the man could take a hint.

But he didn't. "Are you still married?" he asked. Ruth refused to respond. The man then said in a threatening tone that he would remember her face, and he left. By the time Ed arrived, he had disappeared from sight, but Ruth was rattled enough to mention the incident. "Oh," Ed said, "he was probably just some guy looking for a last-minute weekend date." Ruth wondered, however, if he might be the man who had been calling her. She wasn't quite afraid of him, but she thought the situation was potentially embarrassing. What would her friends think if they found out a stranger was harassing her?

But to Ruth's great relief she didn't see the man again for almost a year. Then in July of 1978, while she was window-shopping on her lunch hour, someone grabbed her wrist as she passed an alley. She looked up: the man was back.

"Ruth, you stupid bitch!" he yelled. Ruth broke loose from his grip and ran across the street into Macy's, where she rushed to the escalator and rode it to the top before she felt calm enough to make a plan. She then went down to the ground floor, found a pay phone, and called Ed.

"Will you come meet me?" she asked. "Right now?"

"Of course," he said. When he arrived at the store, Ruth finally told him about the phone calls, and Ed, upset, decided he should go to the police. First he returned to his office to ask if anyone had a connection on the police force who could help. No one did. So Ed went to the station by himself and met with an officer who dutifully took down all the information. Neither Ed nor Ruth heard from this policeman again.

Three months later on a chilly autumn weekend, Ruth, an accomplished pastry cook, was in the kitchen making pumpkin and apple pies for her church bake sale when Sherman rolled over on his back and waved his front paws, the dog's announcement that the mailman had arrived. Ruth wiped her hands and went out to the front porch.

The mail was mostly bills and advertisements, but among the fliers was an envelope with Ruth's name printed on it in large block letters. Ruth stared at it, then returned to the kitchen, poured herself a cup of coffee, sat down, and opened the envelope.

Inside was a single piece of lined yellow paper. On

13

the top were the words "Fuck you. Fuck the police. Fuck the telephone company." The letter was written in the same childlike scrawl as the envelope, and its message rambled over both sides of the paper. The writer demanded money from Ruth and threatened to hurt her if she didn't comply. Ruth studied the letter for a moment; the grammar and the spelling were poor, although the vocabulary was occasionally advanced. Then she pushed it away and paced the house until Ed, who was out doing some errands, came home. He read the letter and shook his head slowly. "This is bad," he said. "I think we should go to the police again."

On November 6, during their lunch hour, Ed and Ruth drove downtown to the police department, where a receptionist sent them up to the fifth floor to see Lieutenant Bernie Drowatzky. The office faced west and sunlight flooded the room as the Finleys entered, making Ed squint. "Well, what do you know," he thought. "Boston Blackie is alive and working for the Wichita police." Boston Blackie was the hero of a 1940s film series starring Chester Morris as a tough, wiry detective with black hair slicked back over his head; Bernie Drowatzky at fifty-five was older than Morris and had less hair. Born in Wichita, he had been a cop since 1954, first for a dozen years in Oklahoma and then back in Wichita, where he worked his way up through narcotics, homicide, and robbery to become a lieutenant in 1977. His most celebrated case had sent a sociopathic murderer to the Kansas state penitentiary with four back-to-back life sentences.

Ruth and Ed weren't sure why they had been referred to the major crimes division, but they guessed that it was because of the slight similarity their complaint bore to the case of the BTK Strangler, who had also been writing letters.

The BTK Strangler had made his first appearance on the morning of January 15, 1974, at a small Wichita house belonging to a mechanic named Joseph Otero. All four members of the family home that morning— Joseph, his wife Julie, and two of their five children— were strangled. Eleven-year-old Josephine was also tortured; the man gagged her, took her to the basement, cut off her bra, and pulled her panties down around her legs. He next placed a rope around the girl's neck and hanged her until she almost choked; then he relieved the pressure and allowed her to breathe before hanging her again. The police estimated that the man had repeated this as many as a dozen times before he finally killed her. He then masturbated into some fabric that he left on the site.

The police found neither leads nor motives. All they had was a description from neighbors of a slight, brown-haired stranger seen wandering the area that morning, and their only potential suspects were two brothers who were repeated sex-crime delinquents. A beat officer had once found one of them in a car attempting sexual intercourse with a duck; the man was apprehended when the officer overheard the duck trying to escape. However, an anonymous tip led the police to a letter hidden at the Wichita Public Library, in which the writer said he didn't want anyone else taking credit for his murders. He added, "P.S. Since sex criminals do not change their M.O. or by nature cannot do so, I will not change mine. The code words for me will be . . . Bind them, toture [sic] them, kill them, B.T.K."

BTK reappeared on March 17, 1977, in the home of

twenty-six-year-old Shirley Vian and her three pre-teenage children. First he locked the kids in the bathroom, and then he strangled their mother and masturbated into her night clothes. The children saw BTK's face—he never wore a mask—but neither psychologists nor hypnotists could break through their trauma for a description.

The next BTK victim was twenty-five-year-old Nancy Jo Fox on December 8, 1977; once more, after choking Fox to death, BTK masturbated into a negligee and laid it neatly by her head. He then sent his second letter, to KAKE-TV, a local ABC affiliate, in which he described the Fox and Vian murders in detail and claimed that he had killed seven people, not six. The police conjectured that the seventh victim was a twenty-one-year-old college student named Kathryn Bright. At that murder a witness, Kathryn's brother Kevin, had been present. However, before he fled, BTK shot Kevin in the head, causing enough brain damage to prevent him from helping the police. BTK never learned the condition of the witness because the police hadn't given that information to the media.

BTK also noted the lack of media coverage of his first letter. "A little paragraph in the newspaper would have been enough," he complained. And a third note, sent to the local newspaper, the *Wichita Eagle-Beacon,* was a poem on a three-by-five index card. It began "Shirleylocks, Shirleylocks," and went on for seven rhymed lines. The BTK Strangler added, "A poem for Fox is next."

Wichita hadn't seen such homicide for over a century. "Wichita resembles a brevet hell after sundown," a St. Louis reporter wrote in 1873. "Brass bands whooping it up, harlots and hack drivers yelling and cursing . . . saloons open wide their doors, and gayly attired females thump and drum up pianos, and in dulcet tones and mocking smiles invite the boys in and night is commenced in earnest." But the town grew prosperous and tranquil, and through the twentieth century predominantly middle-class Wichita lagged behind other American cities in crime—until BTK. Now for the first time in Wichita's history people locked their doors when they went out and drew their curtains at night. Psychologists quoted in the *Eagle-Beacon* said BTK was probably a functioning member of society, a regular guy "like you or me," which meant he could be almost anyone in the area, and calls to the police hot line reported constant sightings of thin, brown-haired men.

Ruth, however, had her own predicament to describe to Lieutenant Drowatzky. "I've been getting some threatening phone calls," she told him and another policeman, Detective Richard Zortman, who had joined them. "And I've been approached on the street twice," she added. Ruth filled the men in on the rest of the story, taking ten minutes, and then had little else to say. Ruth and Ed had lived alone since their boys had left home and, as far as Ruth knew, she had no enemies. The Finleys thanked the two detectives for their time and left the room.

Drowatzky and Zortman discussed the situation. Despite similarly ungrammatical letters Ruth's harasser didn't resemble BTK enough to worry them. They were now receiving thirty BTK tips a week in addition to their regular work, which meant they didn't have the time to follow up a minor complaint. Ruth's was what Zortman called a "ho-hum" affair, something to ignore when no one was around to remind you about it. Drowatzky had more important cases on his mind, and Zortman, a sixteen-year veteran police officer, was already looking forward to his retirement day, which he had circled on a large calendar: October 1, 1981.

3

Ruth: How would you like to put about $100 in a tablet under the seat in yor husb. p.u. I used all the other tab up & the notebook you can save you alot of truble if you will. I no how to get you truble. Don't tell no one you can get that much without yur husb to no it. I can find that Lt name on yur car . . . Don't tell him neither. I will call you and tell you when I will get it. I can tell if anybody is watch me. Dont be a dum bitch agin & blow this. I will have to see you soon if you do Dont think yur fucking frends at that tele ofs can get away with any stuff they shudnt I can tell if have them try & I will see you for it. I will try to be yur frend but when you are a dum bitch I dont like you I have some dum things you wold not like just keep yor smart ass mouth shut & have the $100 in the tablet under the seat and you wont have to take a ride & you no I can do that & I will not let a dum smart

19

ass bitch let my buddy laff at me. This time you talk
to me when I call you soon. I may have to tell some
people that yo see yur brand how wuld you like
that.

> Where ever you go on water or land
> You still got to pay or I tell about yur brand
> I am smart & no things to do
> You talk to people I dispise
> Like police Lt & tele spies.

Ruth called Drowatzky and read the letter to him,
guessing at the abbreviations: "p.u.," she assumed,
referred to Ed's Ford pickup. But Drowatzky wanted
to see the letter, so from then on, as more letters arrived, Ed took them unopened to the station. The police, in turn, gave the letters to the laboratory for
fingerprints and returned a copy to Ruth. But the writing was becoming increasingly illegible, scribbled and
erratic, filled with blotches and misspellings, at times
upside-down or circling in corners; even Drowatzky
admitted he had trouble deciphering the mess. So,
since Ruth had been searching for some means to
show her appreciation for his interest in her case, she
decided to type up neat copies. And as the letters often
contained complex words such as "prolegomenous,"
"sulcus," or "jactitation," Ruth looked up anything
she felt the police wouldn't know and added the defi-
nitions to her copies' margins. As she had hoped, Drowatzky was grateful.

The phone calls continued throughout the summer
and fall. Ed usually answered and after saying hello he
often heard only a dial tone. If the man did speak, he
simply said, "Ruth?" and hung up. But one Saturday
the phone rang while Ed and Ruth were eating their
lunch, and this time, when Ed picked it up and no one

answered, he felt like staying on the line. He waited several minutes. Then suddenly he heard a whistle. A few moments later someone started talking into the receiver. "Who is this?" Ed demanded.

"This is the damnedest thing," the voice said. "I was walking by this phone here at the post office downtown, and it's just hanging here off the hook. Who are you?"

The man didn't approach Ruth on the street again. By October the calls ceased, and Ed wondered if perhaps the man had grown tired of his game. Within a short time Ruth too thought it was over—until the cold, overcast afternoon of November 21. Ruth had just bought a birthday card for a friend while on her lunch break when she crossed Market Street and felt an odd sensation, as though perhaps she was being followed. She took a few more steps and turned around quickly. She saw nothing. Then, just as she started to walk again, an old Chevrolet Bel Air pulled up to the curb and a man jumped out. "Have you got my money?" he asked.

Ruth stared: it was the same man who had assaulted her in the alley a few months earlier. "Get in!" the man yelled. "You have to get in." But Ruth was too scared to move, so the man pushed her into the back seat, sat down next to her, and slammed the door shut. Another man was driving while drinking from a bottle wrapped in a plain brown bag. After a few moments he offered the bottle to the man in the back seat, who took a deep swig. The two men started talking incessantly, but Ruth could hear only fragments of their conversation because the man next to her was leaning into the front of the car. She did hear the driver's name, however: "Buddy."

The car's back seat was filled with all kinds of junk

—stones and rags and other things that looked to Ruth as if they came from a farm—and the door handle on Ruth's side was broken. Ruth started to plan an escape. Could she jump out? The men were caught up in their conversation and paid little attention to her. She wasn't bound. But if she did leap out, would she hurt herself?

"Give me your purse," the man suddenly said.

"Okay," Ruth said. He looked through it until he found Drowatzky's business card, which he showed to Buddy. "Shit!" Buddy said. He then turned around and struck Ruth on the side of her face with a small chunk of concrete. Ruth slumped backward, and Buddy tossed her purse on her lap.

He turned the car around in a parking lot and took off in the direction of Twin Lakes Shopping Center. All the while the two men continued their nonstop banter, which sounded to Ruth more like babbling than talking. She sat quietly, looking at the damaged handle and thinking about jumping. In her purse she kept a small can of Mace, which the men either hadn't seen or hadn't recognized, but she was afraid to take it out.

"Wait until dark," Ruth overheard Buddy say. The phrase sounded menacing and she wished she could hear more. Meanwhile the sun was going down, the temperature was dropping, and the men kept driving. It seemed to Ruth a purposeless kind of journey— empty, joyless, flat. "I have to pee," she said at last. It was the truth.

Buddy looked around and mumbled something about going home. "I have to pee now," Ruth repeated, and she wondered whose home he meant.

"Okay, okay," Buddy said, turning the car into a small park near the Arkansas River. To prevent her from escaping he ordered Ruth to take off her sweater and shoes, but as soon as she got out of the back seat, she ran barefoot until she spotted a bush and ducked behind it. She thought one of the men was close by, but she wasn't sure, so she kept still for several minutes. Finally, crouching, she worked her way up to the top of a slope, from where she could see that the car was gone. She then sprinted across the street and into a liquor store.

The store's owner was sitting in a chair as Ruth rushed past and into a back room. An old man, he got up slowly and walked through the door to see where Ruth had gone. "Someone's after me," she told him. She was panting and sweating; still barefoot, her feet hurt from running over the cold, wet ground.

"Should I call the police?" the man asked.

"Yes," Ruth said. The man did, and said the police promised to come immediately.

"Please," Ruth asked, "can you call my husband too?" The man agreed, and Ruth gave him her phone number.

"Is this Ed Finley?" he asked Ed. "I have your wife here."

Ed assumed he was talking to Ruth's kidnapper. "Let me speak to her," he said sharply.

The man shrugged and handed the phone over to Ruth, who assured Ed that she was okay, that the man was the store's owner and that he was helping her. Ed wasn't convinced, however, so after hanging up the phone, he asked the others sitting with him—Ruth's sister, Jean, and her husband, Bill—to accompany him to the liquor store.

That afternoon Ruth's boss had called Jean, who also worked at the phone company, and asked if she had eaten lunch with her sister. Jean, puzzled by the question, said no. Forty-five minutes later he phoned again, asking if Jean had heard from Ruth since his last call. Again Jean said no, but before she could ask why, he hung up. So at five o'clock Jean walked over to her sister's office, where one of Ruth's friends told her that Ruth had disappeared and that the police were calling her a missing person. But another woman in the department told Jean this couldn't be correct; only a few hours had passed since the first report, and a person had to be gone for several days to be declared missing. Yet the police were actively involved. What, the woman wondered, did it all mean?

Jean immediately called Ed, who had also been informed that Ruth was missing, and he told Jean for the first time about the harassing phone calls, letters, and encounters. Jean was deeply concerned, and as soon as her husband came home, they drove to East Indianapolis to wait for more news.

Jean had always adored her sister. One of her earliest memories was of a summer's day almost forty years before. She was in the front yard with Ruth and their brother, Carl, and the two older kids told Jean they were going to play a game in which she had to be blindfolded. Jean protested, but they told her to trust them. Then, giggling, they walked her into a tree. Jean's nose was bloodied but what bothered her more than the injury was the thought that Ruth would want to hurt her. Ruth was a model sister, the perfect teenager, and therefore, Jean felt, their mother's favorite. Growing up, Jean knew she could never be as smart or as well-behaved as Ruth, although she tried. When she was sixteen she took a job as a telephone operator, as Ruth had done. In 1956, after marrying Wilbur "Bill" Jones, a technical writer at Lear Jet, she left the phone company to raise their three children; again like Ruth, she returned to the phone company when the kids were older.

The sisters were close but didn't speak to each other every day. When they did talk, they seldom shared secrets. For also like Ruth, Jean had been taught by her mother to bury her emotions. Faye Smock's frequently repeated motto was "Life goes on." Why discuss something that belonged to the past?

Half an hour after Ruth's call, Ed, Jean, and Bill arrived at the liquor store, where they were told that officers had already taken Ruth to the police station. They got back in the car and drove downtown, where they found Ruth in a corner, hunched over on a small metal chair. They could see that she had been crying —the tears had left slight shadows on her cheeks— but in public Ruth always maintained a steady, placid demeanor. Her mother had also taught her never to cry; tears didn't do anyone any good either.

Ruth smiled and said she was okay, but Ed, who was watching his wife closely as she waited for the police to finish their report, noticed that the arteries on the side of her head were throbbing and that she was clutching the can of Mace.

"I think you can put the can away," Ed said gently. "These people at the station aren't going to hurt you."

Ed suspected the police hadn't paid much attention to Ruth's original complaint, but now Drowatzky sat down with Ed and went over what he knew about the kidnapping: the men had pocketed Ruth's $315 payroll check, a $100 United States savings bond, a book of phone company matches, some company logo pins, and some stationery that eventually returned to Ruth in the form of letters from the kidnapper. Drowatzky didn't want to scare Ed, so he omitted the fact that the police were wondering if Ruth's assailant might indeed be BTK; a few words in one of Ruth's recent letters could have referred to BTK's murder of Nancy Jo Fox.

The following day Richard Zortman went to the park where Ruth had fled from her kidnapper and wandered down by the embankment. Ruth's shoes and sweater were still lying on the ground. He found nothing else but her footprints. The only lead was Ruth's description of the car's make, so he and Drowatzky ran a computer check on every Chevy model that corresponded to Ruth's recollection and tracked down each possibility one by one. None of the cars, however, led to a suspect.

Drowatzky and Zortman also set up an intermittent surveillance on Ruth as she window-shopped during her lunch break, and Zortman's partner drove the Finleys to Fort Scott, where he coordinated a background investigation of the assault on Ruth when she was a teenager. Nothing turned up from these efforts either.

Employees at the phone company took their morning and afternoon breaks in the eighth-floor snack room, which was stocked with vending machines, hot beverages, and a microwave. A week after the kidnapping Jean and two friends were there drinking coffee and talking when another woman entered and said to Jean, "Hi, Ruth." For years people had made that same mistake. The sisters looked somewhat similar, but they presented themselves differently; Ruth was introspective and prone to jittery mannerisms, such as picking at her sleeves while talking or laughing impetuously. Jean was more gregarious and self-assured.

"Hi there," Jean replied. Then, when Ruth walked in a few moments later, the woman realized her mistake. "I'm so sorry," she told Jean. "I didn't mean to call you Ruth."

Two days later Ruth received a rambling letter in which, among many other charges, the man accused her of deliberately trying to confuse him, adding that he knew damn well which sister was which. That evening Jean ate dinner at Ruth's house. When Ruth showed her the letter, Jean admitted she was scared. "He doesn't want you," Ruth told her firmly. "He wants me. Everything's going to be fine." But after dinner Ruth was forced to go to bed. She had headaches every day now, and she was also suffering from frequent stomach cramps. The only cure was sleep; the cramps went away when she lay down. Ruth wondered if all these aches were psychosomatic, but whether that was true or not, she felt she should handle the situation herself rather than consult a doctor. She thought that a request for assistance was tantamount to an admission of weakness—another lesson from her childhood.

Ruth also believed that a proper life meant never becoming an object of gossip, and she worried as much that her friends would hear about her situation as that she might be hurt. So she was greatly embarrassed when letters from her tormentor began to appear throughout Wichita. Initially they were addressed to the police; on December 13 Drowatzky received his first note, which accused him of protecting a whore from death. He was furious. He had grown fond of Ruth and admired her good will and patience.

Drowatzky hadn't always been as taken with Ed. Experience had taught him that situations such as Ruth's—threats and persecution—generally originated in domestic arguments. But Ruth loved her husband, and the police could see that. So after they

27

decided there was no chance she was covering for him, they deputized Ed. They showed him how to clear a house properly and taught him to shoot from the police stance. (Aim for the stomach, they said, because if you shoot a man in the stomach, he'll bend over, and if he manages to get off a shot, a bullet in the foot is the worst you'll get.) One of the men winked at Ed. "If the guy shows up at the house," he said, "you'll be the first one to get your hands on him. And I promise you, we'll be a little slow getting there." Despite the situation's gravity Ed, who liked to watch television police programs, was excited: this was the closest to being a cop he could ever get.

Ed and Ruth soon developed a new nighttime routine. Instead of spending evenings together in the basement, Ruth now stayed inside alone while Ed took a pack of licorice, a twelve-gauge shotgun, and a revolver to the back yard, where he lay down behind the bushes and waited. (The licorice was to keep him from smoking.) Ed replayed the same scenario in his mind every night: the guy showed up, Ed fired bird shot into the apple tree, the shot dispersed, the guy froze, and then all their problems were over.

4

SPRINGTIME IN WICHITA IS A VIOLENT SEASON. SUM-
mers are fiery and winters frigid, but spring means
weather that shifts in minutes from calm skies to the
powerful thunderstorms that foreshadow tornadoes.
Storm watches are frequent, and when twisters are
spotted, the city sounds its high-pitched sirens, remi-
niscent of World War II, that send everyone directly
to their basements. But the spring of 1979 also brought
the reappearance of the BTK Strangler, who on April
8 broke into a house owned by sixty-three-year-old
Anna Williams. Williams never came home that night,
however; she was sleeping over at her daughter's. The
chance circumstance saved her life. When she returned home the following morning, she found a pile
of BTK's belongings by her bed; she called the police,
and the BTK task force was reactivated.

The next day Ruth went to the mall with Joyce Middleton, a close friend, and Joyce talked on and on
about BTK until she realized that Ruth was indifferent, which mystified her. Normally the two women,

from similar backgrounds, shared identical interests and opinions. Born two years apart, both had grown up on small farms and had taken jobs at the phone company in their teens. Joyce met her husband, David, when she was a secretary in his department; they married in 1948 and had three children about the same age as Ruth's. Joyce and Ruth had been Cub Scout den mothers and founding members of Faith Presbyterian Church, although both families had left that church after the arrival of a new minister who was, they felt, a hippie, and who had railed against the middle class and the scouts. The Finleys had joined another church nearby.

BTK frightened Joyce, but Ruth seemed to have other concerns on her mind, as Joyce discovered when Ruth now told her about the man who was threatening her. In the weeks that followed, Joyce, unlike others who had heard of Ruth's predicament, remained a loyal friend; just as Ruth had feared, the situation was too unconventional for a circle whose lives were so resolutely stable. Joyce, however, felt bad for Ruth: this wasn't her doing and she wasn't to blame. Now and then the Finleys invited the Middletons over for dinner, and after dessert Ruth, realizing she had a sympathetic audience, read some of the letters from her tormentor out loud: "You know in your fucked up mind you are going to die," she recited. "You don't know when but you do know why." Joyce listened to letter after letter, fascinated and horrified.

And during this period the Finleys made at least two new friends: Bernie Drowatzky and his wife Dora Ann. The Drowatzkys and the Finleys had met for dinner in the late spring so they could talk in a more informal environment than the station, and they enjoyed their time together so much that the two couples soon began to meet regularly. The Drowatzkys both thought Ed and Ruth were "super" people. The couples had a similar sense of humor and similar political views, and the Drowatzkys also attended the Finleys' new church. For Ruth this was the one aspect of her predicament that proved clouds do occasionally have silver linings. She and Ed rarely trusted strangers.

More letters arrived during that spring and early summer. They appeared sporadically, two at a time or none at all for a week. Whenever Ed said, "Maybe that's the end of our guy," a letter would show up shortly thereafter. Then in July the letters stopped and Ed thought that, with a little luck, maybe this time the man had really gone. At the least they decided to lead their lives as if he had.

On August 13, after arriving home from work, Ruth and Ed were preparing for their annual trip to Harmels, a resort in western Colorado where they fished, swam, and met old friends. Ed was mowing the grass in the back yard, because he wanted the lawn and house to look tidy while they were gone, while Ruth was taking inventory of last year's vacation gear. When she decided that what she needed most was a new pair of jeans, she called out the window to Ed. "I have to go to the store. Do you need anything?"

"Is that a good idea?" Ed asked, wondering if she should go alone. Over the last few months Ed had tried to accompany Ruth whenever she went shopping.

"I think so," she said.

"Okay," Ed said. "But don't be long."

Ruth got in the Oldsmobile and drove to the Towne East mall. After buying a pair of jeans, she returned to the car but then hesitated, thinking she might buy some hard candy for the long trip. So she dropped the jeans in the back seat and returned to the mall for about twenty minutes. By the time she came out again, the sun had almost set, creating a somber twilight. She shivered; was somebody following her? She turned around but saw no one. Still she approached the car cautiously. Then, from behind, a gloved hand clamped down on her wrist. Ruth looked up: it was the man who had kidnapped her the year before.

"Get in," he demanded. Ruth was terrified. But Towne East was part of a series of long, flat commercial structures facing the east side's main thoroughfares, and most of the buildings were fronted by huge lots that stretched hundreds of yards from the stores. They were deserted now; no one was nearby to help.

"You have to do it," the man said. Ruth had no intention of doing anything he asked. Instead she pushed him away and tried to run. But after throwing a brown paper bag into the car's rear seat, the man grabbed her, took a boning knife from his pocket, and stabbed her three times in the back. Still Ruth broke free again. She jumped into the car and rolled up the window, trapping the man's right-hand glove as he tried to stop her. Finally she started the engine and drove out of the parking lot with the glove dangling from the window and the knife sticking in her side.

The traffic was light but steady, forcing Ruth to pay attention when all she really wanted to do was swerve the car to the side of the road and crash. Then as she waited impatiently for a red light to change, her back exploded in throbbing, furious pain. She was afraid she couldn't make it home, but she knew she couldn't stop because the man might be coming after her. Blood from her wounds was seeping down her side and staining the car seat crimson. Crying and frantic,

Ruth wondered what she should do and where she should go when she spotted a gas station with a drive-up phone about thirty feet ahead, and with a burst of desperate energy she pulled the car across three lanes, lurched to a halt at the telephone, and dialed the police.

Drowatzky was off duty; the man who answered identified himself as Al Thimmesch, Drowatzky's captain.

"You don't know me, Captain Thimmesch," Ruth said. "I'm Ruth Finley . . ."

"I know who you are," Thimmesch said. "What's going on?"

"I've been stabbed."

"Are you all right?" Thimmesch's voice grew sharper. He told Ruth to stay put so he could send an officer. Ruth refused; she was much too scared. "I want to go home," she said. "Now." She hung up the phone and started the car. She had no intention of waiting there in plain sight, and the gas station was only five minutes from East Indianapolis.

Thimmesch immediately called Ed to tell him that Ruth had been stabbed and that he should bring her to St. Joseph's emergency room the moment she arrived home. "Sure," Ed said. Then, in a panic, he ran out into the street and waited anxiously for the Oldsmobile to turn the corner. Meanwhile Ruth, determined to get home, was driving erratically, alternately peering around for her assailant and staring straight ahead. Every car on the road seemed to be headed directly into hers, and every male driver at the wheel resembled a murderer. The pain in her back steadily increased. She turned too early and went down the wrong street, looking for her house, confused: where was it? Realizing her mistake, she then backtracked until she finally pulled into East Indianapolis and swung the car to the curb. Ed ran to her.

"Are you okay?" he asked.

Ruth started to pass out. "Don't fall asleep," Ed said. Then he saw the bloodstained seat and the knife protruding from her side. "Take it out," Ruth said, but Ed remembered reading that a penetrating object should be left in place, although he didn't recall why. He asked Ruth to be patient—the hospital was only four miles down the road—and carefully helped her move over the gearshift lever so he could sit behind the wheel.

Ruth, no longer paying attention, slumped down on the seat while Ed drove as fast as the law allowed. When he arrived at the hospital, he was so nervous he steered the car up onto the curb, and the jolt startled Ruth. "God, Ed's tense," she thought before passing out momentarily. A minute later she was inside the emergency room.

Bernie Drowatzky was home watching television when they called him about Ruth. He sped right over to St. Joseph's, where he found her on a bed in the emergency room. "What happened?" he asked.

"He stabbed me," Ruth said calmly. Her self-possession startled Drowatzky, but it was, as usual, a facade. Ruth was genuinely frightened, although she didn't want Drowatzky to know. Instead she moved slightly so he could see the knife, which was still embedded in her side. Drowatzky whistled at the knife's size.

As Drowatzky spoke with the attending physician, they were interrupted by a loud clank: the knife had fallen out of Ruth's body and onto the floor. "Let me have that,'' Drowatzky said to a nurse who had bent down to retrieve it.

"No," the doctor said. "I need it to see how deep the wound is." So the nurse held the knife while Drowatzky and the doctor argued and Ruth lay wondering quietly how long they would bicker. A few minutes later the doctor won the argument and cleansed Ruth's wounds. Two attendants then wheeled her to surgery, where the surgeon told her that one of the cuts had come within a fraction of an inch of puncturing her kidney; if it had been deeper, she would have died. But the operation was successful and the wound was sutured. Afterward the doctors requested that Ruth stay in the hospital to rest for six more days. Drowatzky asked for a room close to the nurses' station to ensure that someone would be nearby at all times, and the staff consented. In the room at last, Ruth was thankful for the chance to lie in peace, but she had become deeply depressed. "What's the use?" she thought. "He's going to get me anyway."

That night Ruth was the lead story on every local newscast. The following evening, she was a banner headline in the *Eagle-Beacon:* "Woman Stabbed Resisting Abduction." More news items followed: artists' renderings of the assailant, a three-thousand-dollar reward posted by Ed's boss, and a report on the previous year's kidnapping. The following week the paper caught up with the rest of the story: "Victim Received Threats in Mail before Stabbing." Ruth was now the city's predominant news event.

Because Ruth's physical condition was essentially good, she recovered sooner than the doctors had predicted. And since no further attempts were made on her life, the police let her return home Sunday morning. Still Drowatzky followed Ed in an unmarked car and, once on East Indianapolis, he checked out the yard, the street, and the house—even examining the get-well chicken dinner sent by Ed's boss—before leaving.

A few moments later Drowatzky returned, breathless. "I got a call," he said. "You've got to get out of here." A man had been asking for Ruth at St. Joseph's, and a nurse had told him that Ruth had already left. Afterward the nurse decided that the man resembled an artist's rendering of Ruth's assailant and called the police. Drowatzky wanted Ruth and Ed out of the house immediately so he could set a trap. Carl, Ruth's older brother, put his car in the Finleys' garage and closed the door. Then, to make sure no one could see Ruth leaving the house, he and Ed covered her with a blanket and drove her over to Jean and Bill's. Ed joined her for dinner there, and then Ruth went to bed while Ed drove back home.

Drowatzky waited on East Indianapolis for two days, but the man never showed up. And although the police recovered the brown paper bag that the man had thrown inside the car—it contained rope, adhesive tape, cloth, a newspaper clipping about Drowatzky, and a bottle of cheap wine—there were no usable fingerprints on any of the items or on the man's glove, which the police retrieved from the Oldsmobile's side window.

At the end of August Ruth and Ed went off on their Colorado vacation as planned. Harmels was isolated, and Drowatzky was confident no one could hurt Ruth there. In the meantime Ruth's brother, Carl, left his car in the Finleys' driveway to make it appear that someone was home night and day.

Until the stabbing Ruth hadn't mentioned her assailant to her brother. Like Ruth and Jean, the two spoke only occasionally, yet they had always been fond of each other. Carl, barely a year older than Ruth, didn't resemble his sisters physically—he was darker and very slender—but although less educated, he was similarly intelligent. During World War II their hometown high school employed only three teachers, all of whom had previously retired, so Carl decided to drop out and leave home because, as he told his parents, he already knew more than all three teachers put together. He was surprised, however, when his parents agreed; he figured they must have thought anything was better than life in rural Richards.

Carl's first stop was the Texas wheat fields, after which he drove trucks, tractors, and combines, served as a master sergeant in the infantry in Korea, and worked at an automobile assembly plant before eventually drifting into a career as an aircraft worker. Arriving in Wichita in 1955, he lived in Ruth and Ed's basement for two years until he married.

Ruth's silence hurt Carl, but he knew she had learned from their mother not to bother others with problems. Anyway, if the situation had been reversed, he guessed he wouldn't have told her either.

A month or so after Ruth and Ed returned from their vacation, Ed had an idea: perhaps he could draw Ruth's assailant out by leaving messages in the *Eagle-Beacon*'s classified section. The police didn't approve of Ed's plan, but they didn't stop him either, so he placed an ad that read, "Poet: Tell me what I owe you," and signed it "R.S.F." He used the name "Poet" because the man's letters were often written in the form of rhymed couplets, and the man himself had recently stated in one of them that he was "a Poet though people didn't know it." A few days later an *Eagle-Beacon* reporter appropriated the nickname for an article on Ruth, and from that point on Ruth's assailant was known throughout Wichita as the Poet. The man himself endorsed the new name; he now wrote Ruth primarily in rhymes, and he also began a correspondence with Ed through the classifieds, never revealing any useful information but always signing his responses, "The Poet."

On October 24 the *Eagle-Beacon* ran an article under the headline, "E-B Gets Letter Believed from Suspect in Stabbing," revealing for the first time that the paper had received previous letters, including a sealed envelope, six months earlier, attached to a note asking the paper to give the envelope to the policeman with the "long name." The paper assumed this meant Drowatzky, which was correct. The *Eagle-Beacon* also published another composite picture of Ruth's assailant, and by the next day twenty-five people had called the police station with information. Soon tips about the Poet outnumbered those for BTK. In response the police intensified their efforts: names of suspects with records of similar offenses were run through computers and their photographs shown to Ruth; detectives went back to Fort Scott to look for clues concerning Ruth's assault thirty-three years earlier; eight officers were dispatched to Towne East to keep Ruth under surveillance while she shopped, and to guarantee Ruth's safety, the police wired her for sound while she walked in high-risk areas. But none of these efforts led to a suspect.

During much of this time Ruth was seeing a doctor for her wounds, and once Zortman rode in the car with her, curled up out of sight and holding a shotgun, while

Ruth watched to see if anyone was following her. But no one was. In the meantime the Finleys were hearing strange sounds by their garage at night, and one morning a letter from the Poet was found wedged between the front porch slats, the first physical evidence of the Poet's presence on East Indianapolis. Then on Christmas Eve, while the family was eating dinner, the phone lines in the back yard were cut.

The police decided to try still another strategy. Over the last few years they had occasionally used, with some success, hypnosis, so they set up an appointment for Ruth with Dr. Donald Schrag (which he pronounced to rhyme with "fog"), a local psychologist who had worked with the police on several cases, including the BTK Strangler. Ruth agreed to go along, and she enjoyed the experience thoroughly. Schrag's office was comfortable, and the doctor himself—a handsome, powerfully built man in his mid-forties who moonlighted as the overseer of his family's cattle ranch—was a reassuring presence. Ruth fell into a hypnotic trance with no resistance—in fact she felt calmer than she could ever remember—and she didn't want to wake up. She did talk at length about the kidnapping and the stabbing, and her fright was apparent, but she was unable to add any significant details to her story.

Four days later she tried again, and this time she added one new detail: a bridge, over a river, somewhere nearby, although she couldn't explain what it meant. Zortman and his partner drove around the countryside until they parked near a bridge similar to the one Ruth had described, but they couldn't connect it in any way to the case, and so they left.

5

IN EARLY 1980 BERNIE DROWATZKY WAS PROMOTED to the vice and organized crime unit, and Captain Mike Hill took over the direct supervision of Ruth's case. Hill, six feet two inches tall, 230 pounds, had closely cropped dark hair and a rugged appearance. When he was fifteen his father, Elmer, had run away from their Wichita home; Hill next saw him sixteen years later, when he went to view Elmer in his casket in Los Angeles. By that time—1974—Hill was a cop. Four years later he was made a captain, and a year later he took charge of the police's Special Investigations Section, which was overseeing Ruth's case.

Before Hill conferred with Drowatzky, he read the Poet's case files from cover to cover and ran every possible suspect through his mind, including even the Finleys themselves. But he had to reject that last hypothesis, since the medical report established that Ruth couldn't possibly have stabbed herself and both Zortman and Drowatzky assured him that Ed would never hurt his wife. Still Hill made it clear that his primary responsibility was to solve the case, not to become friends with the Finleys. Drowatzky had shared everything he knew with Ruth and Ed, but one week into the case Hill informed Ed that he and his wife were no longer part of the loop. Ed complained about this to Drowatzky, who just shrugged and said Hill was avoiding him too. Hill and Drowatzky didn't get along.

So Ed drove downtown to lodge a protest with Richard LaMunyon, the chief of police. LaMunyon listened for a few minutes, shook his head, and told Ed that Hill was in charge and whatever he said was final. LaMunyon later reported the conversation to Hill, and relations between Hill and the Finleys soured.

As if to celebrate his entry into the case, within a few days Hill received a letter from the Poet, who, until the time of the stabbing, had mailed only about two dozen letters; he now sent out many more, including the following:

> You'll not go directly to your tomb
> Your mind must give thought there will be gloom
> Your face no more will anyone meet
> At home, day or night, or in the street
> Your mind is beaten dark forever more hid
> All because of what you did
> This game is fun to plan and plot
> But can you stop me?
> No you cannot

The Poet's covert activities also surged. In January the Finleys' phone lines were cut for the second time. With police help Southwestern Bell reinstalled the Finleys' service by burying the new lines leading to the rear of the house and laying dummy lines where

41

the original phone wire had been mounted to avoid detection of the new ones. The Finleys also placed an electric alarm system on the back yard gate. Hill went a step further; he installed a surveillance camera in the yard, and three detectives were brought in to sit at Ed's heirloom dining table and stare at the monitor in eight-hour shifts. They soon became friendly with Ed and Ruth, who often read the Poet's letters to the most amiable of the three, Mark Hephner, a young man with thinning brown hair and glasses. Hephner was never sure how to react but he always thanked her. And he noticed that often, while they were talking, Ruth would come down with a headache and have to lie down. Or sometimes she went into the bathroom to wash her hair, which struck him as odd.

Ruth felt sorry for Hephner, although he assured her he was well paid for the overtime work. She already thought her life was dull but imagine watching it on TV! So she decided to feed him, giving him homemade chili, cookies, and pies, and he ate it all gladly, as did the other two men on the watch. Ruth was delighted that she could make their time pass more easily, and the men grew fond of her and her kindnesses.

But the Poet found new ways to interrupt Ruth's life. On January 25 Ruth received a call at work from within the phone company. "I have a surprise for you in the lobby, Ruth," the man said, and then hung up. Ruth immediately called Zortman, who in turn called the lab in case the surprise turned out to be a bomb. Instead it was a twelve-inch butcher knife wrapped in a red bandana. Two witnesses saw a man at the phone booth who resembled the police's composite description, but the man had disappeared.

Two days later a poem showed up in Ruth's mail: "There was a female named Ruth/Who thought nothing of calling a sleuth/I have no doubt/My call was checked out/I didn't tell you your present was in a booth.''

In the third week of January a psychic called the police promising that in just one private session she could break the case. Hill was skeptical, but he decided to give it a try. As with the hypnosis, there was nothing to lose.

The meeting took place in a back room of the First Methodist Church, where the psychic, an attractive middle-aged woman, asked Ruth dozens of questions. While the two were talking, the psychic wrinkled her brow, closed her eyes, held her index fingers to her temple, and grimaced wildly. Then she bent her head forward and remained silent for three minutes. "Gosh, honey," she said, "I'm just not picking up any vibes from you."

The letters continued. On February 19 Ruth received a Valentine's Day note: "Here's to you a tender valentine/Red with blood and tied with twine/ Nothing too much for a valentine/Gone from here by whim of mind." A swatch of a red bandana tied with a piece of torn twine had been inserted in the envelope.

Every morning Ed and Ruth woke up and wondered about what might have happened the previous night. It was a routine: dress, check the front porch, check the back yard, check the phone wires. Look in the mailbox, inspect the garbage, go to work. Come home, cook dinner, talk to the surveillance cops, type up the latest letter for the police, watch television, go to sleep.

The Poet stalked the rest of the city as well. On February 28 he sent the Twin Lakes florist shop a five-dollar bill and a note: "Wud you send one black flower with this note. If this is not enuf for a delivered one call [Ruth's number] & tell her to come & get it." On March 5 KAKE-TV received its first Poet letter, filled with threats against Hill and Drowatzky. The same day a man called KARD-TV and asked if it was true that the police were willing to make a deal with "Buddy," the man who had accompanied Ruth's abductor. The caller identified himself as this same Buddy and said he knew who the Poet was. Ten minutes later the man called KAKE-TV too, claiming to be Buddy and promising to phone the next day with more information. Two policemen spent a couple of hours at the television station waiting for the call, but it never came.

The next incident, in March, was a sliced garden hose; the Poet had spent part of the previous night in the front yard. As likely as not, on any given night, Ed lay wide awake for hours, jumping out of bed and grabbing a gun whenever the house creaked.

When Mike Hill called a press conference in early April, a rumor quickly swept through the media that the police had caught the Poet. But on the morning of April 4 Hill went on the air only with Dr. Schrag, the hypnotherapist, and a new composite picture of Ruth's assailant. Schrag gave his own profile of the Poet's personality, describing a man who "probably has been in a mental hospital or may have been treated by someone. . . . He is likely to be withdrawn and seclusive, secretive, suspicious."

The conference received major coverage; the local newspapers were following the case on a day-to-day basis, as were state newspapers. Now the national wire services jumped on it too, and that spring Bruce

Finley, Ruth and Ed's younger son, learned for the first time of the 1946 Fort Scott assault when a fellow employee at a Colorado computer company, where Bruce was a vice president of marketing, showed him a *Denver Post* article about his mother.

Bruce, who had been told little about his mother's situation, called home the next day, concerned. But Ruth assured him there was no reason to worry, and she later sent him one of the Poet's letters with a note attached: "Hi . . . Got eggs thrown on the house last Thursday night. Some were wrapped in red bandana and had a piece of Jan. 7, 1976 Chicago Tribune— Eggs were on the sliding glass door. Only 2 to 4 and they weren't rotten. Getting new carpeting Friday— Been tearing up the old squares—House a mess. Lots of hail Sunday. Big hail! How are you? We are fine. Take care, Mom."

Because Ruth insisted on keeping her fear private, many of her friends assumed they were more scared than Ruth herself. In February Joyce and Dave Middleton had met the Finleys for dinner at the Amarillo Grill, and they talked about the Poet, but they talked about other things too: the church, their kids, their jobs. Joyce forgot about the Poet until, as Ed stood up, his coat got caught on his chair. Joyce noticed a gun stuck in his belt. The moment impressed her, for she had forgotten that Ruth was under such pressure. She took Ed aside. "I'm glad you're carrying a gun," she said. Ed nodded silently.

On July 4, 1980, Ruth's story appeared in the *National Enquirer* under the headline, "She's Living a Nightmare: The Victim of a Crazed Tormentor." The article went on to describe the case thoroughly, without any exaggeration, which meant, Ruth thought, that her life had grown so peculiar it needed no embellishment to compete with space aliens for notice.

The letters continued. The Telephone Credit Union received one suggesting it transfer all of Ruth's money to another bank. The Kansas State Department of Motor Vehicles was asked to confiscate Ruth's license because of her unsatisfactory driving habits. Twin Lakes Keys received a request for a new set of keys for Ruth's front door. A letter to Leach Construction demanded that a load of dirt be left in the Finley driveway. The *Eagle-Beacon* printed it a few days later: "Send someone to my place at . . . to break out the driveway—just the driveway & I will haul it off & you can send me the bill at the same place." The health department was notified that Ruth was spreading venereal disease ("This is an anonymous tip. There is a female spreading V.D. . . ."). The Cochran Mortuary was ordered to contact Ruth about its services which, the letter indicated, she would soon be needing. Other letters asked that the electric and gas service at the Finley home be terminated, and a motor vehicle repair firm was instructed to take the Finleys' pickup into its shop to replace the engine. Between December 16, 1979, and May 20, 1980, the Poet had mailed more than fifty letters, including this one to Mike Hill:

> Captain O Captain is iron man
> Lt. helps bitches weak & wan
> Into the bush & from my past
> Ugly mad bears from me will last
> Living in a hollow cave
> Lust of man will cause a rave . . .
> A tidal wave of demons in my soul
> Misery causes words to roll . . .

In response the police strained for new ideas. Zortman came up with a still camera camouflaged in a birdhouse in the Finleys' back yard, its lens focused on the dummy phone lines, and its shutter rigged to trip if someone tampered with the wires. No one did. Hill's idea was to assign vice and narcotics officers to look through other envelopes received by the Kansas Gas and Electric Company for handwriting similar to the Poet's. They found none. The Poet's letters were sent to a consultant who had gained national prominence in New York's Son of Sam case; after examining the documents, he sent back a psychological profile. The Poet, he said, was severely psychotic, schizophrenic, pathologically paranoid, a loner with a deep feeling of persecution, but this was nothing the police hadn't already guessed.

The letters were also given to the Wichita Criminalistics Laboratory for a handwriting analysis, but the results were inconclusive, while an FBI examination to match the Poet's handwriting with Ed's was negative. The Kansas Bureau of Investigation tried administering a chemical test for saliva on the envelopes to look for a blood type, but that too was unproductive. And a police chaplain undertook an exhaustive study of all the words and phrases in the Poet's letters, where he found 107 terms unusual or lacking in an average vocabulary. These words were broken down into the following categories: sixty-five were literary, twenty-three were psychological, eleven were philosophical, five were theological, and three archaic. None of this analysis, however, led to a suspect.

On June 3 Ruth received a letter from the Poet with an Oklahoma City postmark, the first to arrive from outside Wichita. Two days later Hill himself drove to Oklahoma City, where police had received an anonymous tip about a Wichita man whom Hill eventually tracked down in the Washita National Wildlife Refuge. The suspect was taken into custody and placed in a lineup back in Wichita for Ruth to identify. She stared at the man for a full minute before shaking her head. "He looks a little like the Poet," she said. "[But] still different."

A month and a half later at six thirty in the morning, while Ed was asleep, Ruth got out of bed and checked the house. It was clear. She then went to the front porch, where she saw a glass bottle filled with yellow liquid. Ruth picked it up and sniffed. The bottle contained urine.

More incidents occurred: a lock broken, a suspicious van sighted, a Molotov cocktail discovered, a potential suspect cleared. Then on December 21, as Ed and Ruth were watching television in the basement, they heard a loud crash. Ed ran upstairs in time to see the family Christmas wreath in flames; the noise had come from the picture window cracking from the heat. "That goddamned son of a bitch!" Ed cried. "I'm going to kill him!" First he knocked the wreath down and stamped out the fire, then he grabbed a handle from a pair of garden shears and sprinted out into the freezing night, clad only in shirt and pants, yelling, "Come back here! Damn it! Come back!" He ran up and down the street until Ruth persuaded him to come back inside.

Still more poems arrived, which Ruth patiently deciphered, typed, and gave to the police:

> Once upon the night so dreary
> Premonitions of disaster keep you weary
> The whore bore her guilt in her bed of slime
> From selling her ass & not charging a dime

Slept with strangers in evil bed
Enraged demon hunters saw blood was red
All bitchs shuld keep there names & faces secret
Defenseless instincts released with demonic sluts
   threats
Blurred vision & suffering in accusers cage
Umbilical cord connected by seed in a rage . . .

In February Ruth found a rock wrapped in the
Poet's favorite red bandana cloth in her back yard. In
April it was a pair of wire cutters and more bandana
material soaked in flammable chemicals—a Molotov
cocktail without the bottle. A poem was attached:

> Hickory dickory dock
> Yur face mounted on my clock
> Eyes at 10 & 2
> Hands to knife for you
> Hickory Dick. Dock.

A few months afterward a man called the phone
company claiming to be the Poet; the operator immediately displayed the calling number of a telephone
booth in the lobby of the Kansas State Telephone
Company in Galena, 150 miles from Wichita. Within a
day the Galena police apprehended the caller, who
turned out to be a harmless patient at a local mental
institution.

In the early hours of June 5 Ed and Ruth woke up
simultaneously to the sound of a screeching whistle.
Ed jumped out of bed, already dressed—ever since
the wreath incident he slept in his clothes in case he
had to run outdoors—and grabbed his gun. He rushed
into the dining room and aimed at a moving target, but
he put the gun down when he realized he was pointing

it at a confused and whining Sherman. The dog had somehow tripped the house alarm.

One morning two months later Ed went out to see if the newspaper had arrived yet. It had, but lying right next to it was a dirty envelope. Ed bent down and touched it carefully: it was mushy. Then he picked the envelope up, sniffed, and made a face. The envelope, a gift from the Poet, was filled with feces.

On the morning of Friday, September 4, the day before the long Labor Day weekend, Drowatzky walked toward Chief LaMunyon's office. He hesitated, then knocked and entered. "Hey, Chief," he said. "There's a new development on the Poet."

LaMunyon was a delegator and an administrator— his men did the detective work, he ran the department —so he hadn't heard of Ruth Finley until the November 1978 abduction. The case had still made almost no impression on him until the media took it up. Then the *Eagle-Beacon* and the television reporters approached him continually. What are you doing about the Poet? they asked. Is the Poet the BTK Strangler? How could you allow such a crime to continue? Still LaMunyon left the case to his detectives.

"What is it?" he asked Drowatzky.

"We got another letter from the Poet."

LaMunyon raised an eyebrow.

"This time he says," Drowatzky went on, "that after he's taken care of Ruth, he's going after Sharron." Sharron was LaMunyon's wife.

LaMunyon then read the letter, in which the Poet revealed he knew several personal details about Sharron, such as the make of her car and the route she took to drive home from the city. LaMunyon decided it was time for him to get involved, and that evening he gathered all the Poet files—now fourteen large three-ring binders—put them in the trunk of his car and drove home. Throughout the weekend he read the volumes from cover to cover, studying every aspect of the case methodically, jotting down notes, making charts, imagining each incident in his mind. He had a hunch when he started, and it took stronger form as he read. By Sunday evening he had solved the case.

6

In 1956, on his sixteenth birthday, Richard La-
Munyon's father, Orveal, asked him his life's ambi-
tion. "I've decided to become a policeman,"
LaMunyon said. Orveal, a Wichita electrician,
groaned. "Oh, no," he said. "Be a fireman. Everybody loves a fireman. No one likes a cop." But La-
Munyon had made up his mind. He also knew he was
going to be the chief, for he considered himself a natural leader. A few months after starting Navy boot
camp in San Diego, he became chief petty officer; at
radar school he quickly became the recruit officer in
charge of his company. When he eventually joined the
police, he realized that a college education was a pre-
requisite for advancement, so he enrolled in Wichita
State University and ended up with three degrees.
Thirteen years later he got the top job. Although he
was Wichita's youngest chief ever, and all six of his
deputy chiefs held seniority over him, there was little
resentment, for LaMunyon was both respected and
liked. On the Monday morning after his appointment,

he assembled his deputy chiefs, looked at each one, and then said, "Okay, guys, what the hell do we do now?" They all broke up laughing.

On Tuesday, September 8, LaMunyon scheduled a meeting for that Friday for sixteen officers in the Sedgwick County Courthouse basement, the municipal equivalent of a residential Wichita cellar—a sixty-five-foot windowless room where the government could oversee the city in case of a natural disaster. Police meetings normally convened in the City Building, which housed the department and where hundreds of people came and went daily, but LaMunyon wanted this meeting kept confidential.

Just before ten on Friday morning all sixteen men were sitting on folding chairs at a long metal table, drinking coffee in Styrofoam cups and talking. A minute later LaMunyon walked in. He didn't speak, but the room fell silent. LaMunyon's physical appearance was modest—he was barely five ten, with bland, fair looks and a bulbous nose—but his presence was charismatic.

LaMunyon sat down at the head of the table. "Here it is," he said. "The Poet is Ruth Finley herself." He didn't wait for a reaction, and the men just stared as he launched into his notes. He had made a list. For one, East Indianapolis was a quiet, dead-end street. Yet no one—not a neighbor, a cop, or a Finley—had ever seen the Poet come or go, nor were there ever any footprints in the yard. Then there was the single set of footprints Zortman saw at the park near Twin Lakes Shopping Center, although Ruth had told the police that she thought one of the kidnappers had followed her. Whenever the Finleys went away on vacation, the responses to Ed's classified ads in the paper ceased immediately; when the family returned, they recommenced. Once the recording camera was placed in the birdhouse, the Poet never appeared in the back yard again, but only the police and the Finleys knew of its presence. The Poet mailed Hill a letter as soon as he took over the case, yet at the time only the Finleys were aware that Hill had replaced Drowatzky. There was never a single witness at any of the locales where the Poet had struck, from the mall to downtown streets.

"It just doesn't make sense anyone else could be doing it," LaMunyon said. "Unless it's Ed, and I don't think it is. I doubt he's even involved."

LaMunyon guessed what his men were thinking: What about the experts and the doctors? "I don't believe any of them," he said. In his experience doctors constantly underestimated the human potential for destruction, self- or otherwise. "And I don't believe anything that woman says either," he went on. He thought that Ruth hadn't been stabbed in the parking lot at all but that after calling Al Thimmesch, she had lashed at herself in the car on the way home.

LaMunyon then explained that he had invited so many men to the meeting because he planned on adding narcotics and vice detectives trained in surveillance to the case. "For the next two weeks we are going to watch the Finleys twenty-four hours a day," he said, and added a warning. "No one is to talk about this to anyone, not wives, relatives, or friends. If one word of this surveillance leaks to the media, I intend to fire every single one of you."

LaMunyon stopped abruptly and looked around the room, studying his men silently. He couldn't read Zortman's face, because Zortman had spent most of the meeting gazing at his lap, telling himself that LaMunyon was crazy. Still in a way Zortman was pleased, for LaMunyon's involvement meant the extra resources they had always needed to solve the case were now at their disposal, whether or not Ruth was guilty.

Drowatzky, LaMunyon thought, was crushed. His face remained blank throughout the meeting, but LaMunyon imagined he could see Drowatzky's spirits slump. Drowatzky himself later claimed that the news hadn't bothered him at all. He was a veteran, he said, and was prepared to expect the unexpected. LaMunyon didn't believe him.

The following Monday LaMunyon had to attend the annual chief of police convention in New Orleans, so his last act before concluding the meeting was to appoint Deputy Chief John Coonrod, who was also his closest friend, to coordinate the investigation while he was gone.

"And that, my friends, is it," LaMunyon said, and left the room. The men stayed behind a moment, and then cleared out silently. The meeting had taken thirty minutes.

LaMunyon was convinced that he, rather than his men, had solved the case because he had never met Ruth Finley. That was the key. To meet Ruth was to believe in her. Who could be more normal than a church-attending, homemaking, job-holding wife and mother? Yet LaMunyon was positive that Ruth had hoodwinked his entire department. Nonetheless, for procedure's sake, he asked Dr. Schrag once again if Ruth could have been involved in any of the Poet's activities; Schrag, however, remained insistent that Ruth and the Poet were two distinct people, so LaMunyon gave the medical reports to his own family doctor. He too said Ruth couldn't have inflicted the wounds. LaMunyon still didn't change his mind. He was an exceedingly self-confident man whose life had never given him any reason for doubt, and he believed in his own instincts more than other people's opinions, even when those opinions were based on facts. Here LaMunyon's instincts were certain: the incident at Fort Scott never happened, the kidnapping never happened, the stabbing never happened—at least not in the way Ruth had described them. Ruth Finley, said LaMunyon's instincts, was not the relentlessly normal woman she appeared. Ruth Finley was demented.

But he refused to meet her or even talk to her on the phone. She was like a mythological beast, he thought; after a person spent a few minutes alone with Ruth, the truth seemed to dissipate. His men had looked at her, and all they had seen was Ruth Finley. LaMunyon was certain that the Poet was there too.

The Finley surveillance began that night at 5:00 P.M.; the command center was a van parked at the west end of the Eastgate Shopping Center, not far from East Indianapolis. From that moment every move Ed and Ruth made outside their house—every trip to the store, every drive in the country—was monitored by at least one police car and one police helicopter.

On Monday morning Sharron and Richard LaMunyon flew to New Orleans for the convention. LaMunyon instructed Coonrod and Hill to call him regularly, but over the next few days nothing happened worth reporting.

Ruth didn't notice the surveillance, in part because she was feeling thoroughly preoccupied, although not with the Poet. It was her own mind that worried her.

She was becoming convinced that she was going crazy. Once, in the phone company snack room, she confided her fears to her sister. "I think I'm coming out of my body," she said.

"What in the world do you mean by that?" Jean asked.

"I'm not sure," Ruth replied. The best she could do was repeat herself, because she really didn't know what she meant, and she wasn't accustomed to talking with Jean, or anyone else, about her feelings. She had become desperately unhappy and afraid, and on weekends she sat staring out of the living room window for hours, looking at clouds and watching cars, without moving or eating. Her head pounded, her stomach churned, and sometimes she had to grab hold of the arm of her chair because she was sure she was about to fly up into the sky.

One night that September Ruth was standing in front of the bathroom mirror, reaching for the toothpaste, when she felt faint. The room spun and her mind went blank. A few moments later she woke up on the bathroom floor. She had passed out, not for long, but long enough to make her feel that she was slipping out of her own life.

On the morning of Thursday, September 17, the Finleys left their home and drove to the Eastgate mall. The instant they did, the surveillance team initiated its daily operation, a car trailing the Finleys as they turned off East Indianapolis onto Rock Road, a helicopter hovering above. It didn't occur to Ruth or Ed to look up.

The Finleys' Oldsmobile swung through the parking lot and stopped at a mailbox, where Ruth mailed some letters. Then the car sped off. A minute later the helicopter lost it in the sun, and at exactly the same time the tail got caught up in traffic. The last the surveillance team saw, the Oldsmobile had made a sharp right turn and disappeared. The Finleys were gone.

"They're bolting!" the tail car's driver reported.

Hill quickly called Ed's office.

"Mr. Finley won't be in today," his secretary said. "He's on a business trip to Topeka."

Ruth, it turned out, had taken a vacation day from work to keep Ed company, but neither saw any reason to tell the police. They returned home that evening.

In the meantime the police contacted a postal inspector, who met them at the mailbox a few hours later, collected the mail, and brought it to the post office. The five letters Ruth had dropped in the box were still lying on top of the bag. Two of them were addressed to business firms and contained checks for services rendered. One was private correspondence. Of the other two, one was addressed to the police reporter at KAKE-TV, the other to Ruth. The addresses on both these envelopes were in the Poet's handwriting.

The letters were allowed to continue on their way. The one to KAKE was delivered that same day and returned to Hill, who took the letter to the Wichita Police Criminalistics Laboratory, which verified that it came from the Poet.

Now the police knew that LaMunyon was correct: Ruth Finley was the Poet. Still, because four hours had passed between the mailbox drop and the interception of the letters, the surveillance continued.

The next day, Friday, the Finleys were followed as they bought a lawn mower at Sears and shopped at the mall. No one in the car mailed a letter. But on Saturday Hill received a call from John Coonrod, who asked Hill to join him at Southwestern Bell as soon as possible. The day before Ruth had left her desk at her new job in the phone company's security department, where she had recently been transferred, without emptying out her trash. There the men found a book of prose and poetry, a swatch of red bandana wrapped in a yellow tissue hidden inside a paper towel, a sheet of carbon paper with the Poet's handwriting, and a writing tablet that matched the Poet's.

The LaMunyons returned to Wichita on Monday the twenty-first. In New Orleans LaMunyon had told Sharron about Ruth. He was customarily reluctant to discuss his work with his family, but he had no other explanation for the dozen phone calls a day from Hill and Coonrod. The news infuriated Sharron, and for the first time in their twenty-year marriage the couple quarreled seriously. The issue was Sharron's sister Kathy, who was taking care of their house while the LaMunyons were gone. The sisters looked alike. What if the Poet went after Kathy, Sharron asked. LaMunyon reassured her that everything was under control and that Ruth was a danger only to herself. Still Sharron was upset.

As soon as the LaMunyons arrived back in Wichita, Sharron made a quick top-to-bottom inventory of the entire house. Things seemed to be in order. Then while LaMunyon called Coonrod, Sharron sorted through the mail. She was a member of the local school board and had recently judged a children's beauty contest, so the letters consisted mostly of thank-you notes covered with scrawled handwriting filled with misspellings: Mrs. LaMinyon, Mrs. La-Onion. Sharron opened one of them, read it, and then threw it across the room at her husband. "I think your detectives are doing a piss-poor job of surveillance," she said. The letter was from the Poet.

"I'll have to call you back," LaMunyon told Coonrod. He retrieved the letter from the floor and stared at it. How could it have been mailed? Ruth had been under surveillance for over a week. LaMunyon studied the note, looking for some clue. Then he understood. The postmark on the envelope was two Fridays previous. The surveillance had begun that evening, just as Ruth left the phone building, and she must have mailed this one last undetected letter to Sharron from the lobby. On Monday morning, when the mailman delivered it, the LaMunyons had already left for New Orleans.

By the middle of the week Ruth—suffering from severe headaches and stomach cramps, deeply depressed, and unable to talk with anyone—made an irrevocable decision. She was going to commit suicide. She wasn't sure of the reasoning that brought her to this resolution, but she knew it was an imperative that came from within, one that she understood intuitively. Slowly she started amassing small amounts of cash, pocketing quarters and dollar bills and hiding them in her purse. Ed accompanied her wherever she went, so she wasn't able to make a bank withdrawal, because she couldn't tell him why she needed the money. But the first moment no one was watching, she planned to catch a bus to Oklahoma City, the nearest large city to the south. There she would rent a bicycle, since it would be cheap and no one would ask any questions. Then she would ride the bicycle to a bridge over a river. She didn't know what bridge or river, but she trusted that somewhere in Oklahoma she would find them. Once there she would tie a rock to her legs, slit her wrists, and throw herself in the water to bleed and drown.

On Wednesday of that week LaMunyon held another meeting. Everything he had stated at his last meeting was correct, he said without boasting. The only remaining questions were whether and to what extent Ed had participated and whether, once they confronted Ruth, they would get a confession or have to take the case to court.

The lab technicians had, through fracture comparisons, successfully matched a piece of torn paper from the Finleys' trash container with the letter to Sharron LaMunyon. Stamps on letters to Amco and J. C. Penney were also similar to those found at the Finleys'. But LaMunyon wanted more evidence, and the surveillance continued.

That Friday the Finleys left home at 7:38 A.M.; twenty-two minutes later Ruth arrived at the phone company. Ed then went into the post office for two minutes; he was at work from 8:07 to 11:50 A.M., when after stops at the bank, the mall, and Long John Silver's restaurant, he went home for almost an hour to eat. He then returned to work downtown and picked Ruth up at five. The couple attended a garage sale, shopped at the Eastgate mall, and ate dinner at Mr. Steak's. They were home by 6:51. They mailed no letters that day.

Around ten o'clock that night Ruth was walking down the stairs to the basement. On the landing she passed one of Ed's bigger canvases, a dark painting of a bridge that was modeled on one near her childhood farm in Richards. Ruth had seen this picture several times a day for twenty years but had never looked at

61

it closely. Now the image stopped her as effectively as if it had called her name. Ruth was terrified. She already knew she was going to lose her life in a river under a bridge, but now, trembling, she realized that the painting depicted the precise site of her death. This was the bridge where she had to die. She burst into tears and returned upstairs.

On Saturday Ruth and Ed watched television and worked on their hobbies until 3:50 in the afternoon, when they drove to the bank and the Eastgate mall. Ed swung into the parking lot and stopped to allow Ruth to mail some letters. Just as they were moving back into the traffic, Ruth turned around and saw through the rear window a brown car with its hood up in front of the mailbox. What a strange place for a car to break down, she thought.

The instant the Finleys drove off, the police had blocked access to the mailbox with an unmarked car, its hood up to feign engine trouble. By 4:40 they were able to reach a postal inspector, who arrived ten minutes later and removed the mail. Ruth's letters were on the top of the pile. There were four. One was addressed to a utility company in Des Moines, another to a department store in Mission, and a third was private correspondence. The last, addressed to Ruth, was printed in the Poet's handwriting.

The letters were allowed to continue on to their destinations; the police then picked them up so they could claim control over a chain of evidence if the case went to trial. They had seen Ruth mail the envelopes, had watched the postman bring them to the post office, and had retrieved them from their addressees—all but the one Ruth had written to herself. The investigation was over.

7

AT 10:00 A.M. ON OCTOBER 1, WITH LAMUNYON standing by his side in his office, Mike Hill picked up his phone and called Ed. "Have you gotten your mail yet today?" he asked.

"No," Ed said, "I'm at work." He found the question odd. After four years the cops knew the Finleys' schedule as well as they did, so why ask about the mail, which didn't arrive until noon?

"Go get your letter," Hill said. "We know you have one. We received a carbon copy here."

"I'll get it at lunchtime," Ed said. A letter from the Poet wasn't an excuse to leave work early, and when Hill didn't contradict him, Ed hung up. A few hours later he went home, fixed himself a ham and cheese sandwich, took in the mail, and saw the letter. Only when he finished eating did he take it down to the station. In the Poet's note were rhymes derivative of the BTK Strangler's Shirleylocks poem: "Curly Locks Curly Locks/Food for swine. She was not a friend of mine. . . ."

Ed expected to drop the letter off and return to work, but instead Hill tossed it aside and quickly ushered him into a small, bleak interview room furnished with an old metal table and a few chairs.

Since two police officers had to be present at an interview, Hill had asked Zortman to join him, but he declined. "I know them too well," Zortman said. "Find someone else." The outcome of the case was too baffling; he had genuinely cared for Ruth and had believed that she was in peril. And this was the day Zortman had circled on his calendar, his last day on the force. The case that had taken him through the last four years was ending exactly the same day as his job. He was glad to leave.

Hill had then selected Jack Leon, a dark, good-looking lieutenant who, unlike the others on the case, came from out of town, from Southern California. Leon, a psychology buff, had been following the department's collective wisdom concerning the case. Two camps had evolved. One, led by LaMunyon and Hill, thought that Ruth was deranged but had been fully conscious of her actions throughout. The other camp, including Drowatzky and Zortman, also believed that Ruth was mentally ill, but they didn't think her actions were deliberate. They were convinced a more complicated explanation existed than Hill's assumption that Ruth had done it all for the attention.

Hill introduced Leon to Ed, who nodded, and then he began, "You have the right to remain silent." Ed was bewildered. Why was Hill reading him his rights? But he didn't ask a single question. Meanwhile in the office next door LaMunyon was listening to the interview through a wire hidden under Hill's jacket. LaMunyon didn't want Ed to know he was being taped.

Hill next asked Ed once more about every aspect of

the case from start to finish: How had Ed met Ruth? When did they marry?—on through the kidnapping and the stabbing to today's letter. Ed answered each question simply and consistently.

Finally Hill got to the point. "We know who the Poet is, Ed," he said.

Ed stared into Hill's eyes, his heart filling with exhilaration, relief, and gratitude. He had waited four years for this moment, he thought, and now it was time. He recalled his fantasy: Ed and the police tracking the man down together, catching him, and then Ed alone putting his hands around the man's neck, strangling him, watching him die . . .

"Let's go get him," Ed said. Oh God, he thought, he was so happy.

"First," Hill said, "we want you to look at some pictures."

It was an unusual request, but as always Ed was compliant, and regardless, they had their man. "Sure, Mike," he said. "Why not?" Hill brought out the photos of Ruth mailing letters at the Eastgate Shopping Center and laid them on the table. Ed looked at them without comment. Then Hill picked one up and handed it to Ed, placing it almost under his nose. "One of those letters is a Poet letter," he said.

Ed frowned. "Are you positive?" he asked. The photographer had done a good job. Ruth's face was unmistakable, and the addresses on the envelopes were almost legible.

"I can verify," Hill said, "that she has mailed five Poet letters in the last two weeks."

"You have to be kidding," Ed said.

"No, Ed, I'm not," Hill said. "I wish the hell I was. And I've recovered stuff out of her office too."

Ed didn't speak.

"The Poet is Ruth," Hill said.

Ed stared at the photo.

"Ed?" Hill asked.

"Oh, my God," Ed said. "Oh, my God."

Hill told him about the Poet's paraphernalia found in Ruth's trash at Southwestern Bell and about the results of the surveillance. Then he showed him more pictures documenting his words. Ed listened and looked quietly.

When Hill finished, he waited for Ed to speak. Ed remained silent. "I've hit you with a lot, haven't I?" Hill asked.

"You certainly have," Ed said, shaking his head.

"I have to eliminate you," Hill said, "and the only way I can do that is for you to take a polygraph. Do you mind?"

Ed nodded his consent. He thought he knew what they wanted: to discover if he had known that Ruth was the Poet. He didn't know that some of the police, more skeptical, believed that he had actively aided her. And even if he had been aware of their suspicion, he couldn't have felt more nervous than he already did, since he had heard that innocent people occasionally failed lie detector tests. But he also thought that a refusal might be considered an admission of guilt. He sat quietly, stunned, as Hill's words circled through his mind: Ruth was the Poet, the Poet was Ruth. Then he thought about the male voices on the phone, the kidnapping, the stabbing, and he wondered, even if they could prove she had written some letters, could they prove she had done everything? He wondered but he didn't ask.

Meanwhile Leon was staring at Ed, trying to understand his apparent resignation. Jesus, Leon thought, Hill could have been lying. He could have been playing a game, trying to divert him from some other piece of information. Yet Ed looked as if he believed Hill instantly, which made Leon wonder: had Ed already suspected? It didn't occur to Leon that in Ed's world, policemen never lie. Ed believed Hill because Hill said it was so.

And Hill, who had begun the interview suspicious of Ed, was thinking, this guy doesn't have a clue. Still, to make sure, he had to drive Ed to the Kansas Bureau of Investigation for the lie detector test. On the way over he suddenly remembered that Ed often carried a gun. "Do you have your piece on you, Ed?" he asked.

"No," Ed said. "I don't carry it unless I'm with Ruth." He waited for Hill's next move: would he believe him or frisk him? Hill's eyes returned to the road. When Ed saw that, he spoke again. "If this is going to be a long afternoon," he said, "I'll need a pack of cigarettes. I'm about out."

"Sure," Hill said, and he swerved into a QuickTrip parking lot. Ed got out of the car and walked inside the store. Looking back Ed noticed that Hill wasn't watching him, which he took to mean that Hill wasn't concerned he would try to escape. The knowledge relaxed him considerably.

The test took almost an hour. After a few requisite standard questions—his name, his age, his birth date—the examiner asked Ed if he had known Ruth was the Poet.

"I did not," he said.

Had he helped Ruth?

"I did not," he said.

Had he ever seen her do anything suspicious?

"I did not."

Did he stab Ruth?

"I did not."

Then it was over. There was no doubt, the examiner said, that Ed hadn't known about Ruth. In fact, Ed was still unsure of the truth and kept repeating, "Okay, maybe she sent those letters. But if she did, she was only trying to force you guys to catch the man."

Hill told Ed that they were going to search the house next. "Fine," Ed replied. "You have my permission."

"We don't need it," Hill said. "We have a warrant."

Ed shrugged and then asked if he could go with the police while they searched. When Hill consented, Ed rode over to East Indianapolis and sat in the living room with one of Hill's men while three others searched the house. Once he got up to get a drink of water, and the officer guarding him got up too. Otherwise Ed just watched as they showed him all the evidence they were finding: a book of poetry, carbon paper, bits of red bandana, writing tablets. Ruth is the Poet, Ed thought. But what kind of emotional response was appropriate? He didn't know, for his life hadn't prepared him for this kind of revelation. Instead he replayed the events of the last four years, trying to understand how and where, over all that time, he could have missed the truth. He barely said another word to the police while they were at the house, nor did they talk to him. The only consistent emotion Ed felt that afternoon was relief: if the police were right, and Ruth was the Poet, it was all over. She was safe now.

On the way back to the station, Ed spotted his Oldsmobile in the City Building lot. "The meter's run out," he said, speaking willingly for the first time in hours. "I'm going to get a ticket."

"Don't worry," one of the officers said. "We'll take care of it." But Ed turned in his seat and stared at the meter as the police car drove past.

After they parked, the officers led him up to the fifth floor. Hill was now interviewing Ruth, and they told Ed he could wait for her. But first, because the men were hungry, they asked him if he wanted a hamburger.

Of all the incidents that afternoon, this one bothered Ed the most. He had just learned that his wife had been harassing herself for four years in full view of the whole city, and now she was being questioned, alone, in another room. He hadn't any idea what to think and not a single officer had offered any help—no sympathy, no advice, not even a hand on his shoulder. Their only concern was whether he wanted a burger. "I'll have a cup of black coffee," he said, fuming. When he finished the coffee, he went through the pack of cigarettes, blowing small circles of smoke toward the ceiling and staring at them until they vanished.

8

EARLIER THAT AFTERNOON, WHILE HILL WAS INTER-
rogating Ed, Ruth had called her husband at his office
to say hello, but Maryanne, Ed's secretary, told her
he hadn't come back from lunch yet. When Ed hadn't
returned her call a few hours later, Ruth tried again.

"Do you think I should call the police?" Maryanne
suggested.

"No," Ruth said. "Ed's a big boy. He can take care
of himself."

When work ended at five, she took the elevator
down to the lobby with some coworkers and saw Drowatzky standing by the door. Hill had selected him to
bring Ruth in, and although Drowatzky had wanted to
decline, he felt obligated; he figured he should be the
one to escort Ruth on her final trip downtown. Still he
was shaken. He had solved brutal homicides; he had
smashed drug rings; he had put criminals behind bars
for life. But Ruth wasn't a killer or a criminal, and he
wondered how she could have done it all, and why.

As her friends drifted away, Ruth assumed Drowatzky was waiting for her. She said hello. He returned the greeting and then asked, "Can you come down and look at some mug shots?"

"Sure," she replied, and they went outside.

Jean, also leaving work, walked out into the street, spotted Ruth, and waved. Ruth didn't see her, however, and so Jean watched, waving absently, as Drowatzky drove her sister away.

At the police station Ruth noticed an unusual number of detectives walking around the room, including one of the men who had been watching her yard on closed-circuit television.

"How are you?" she asked.

"Not very well," he said sadly.

"Well, I'm sorry to hear that," she replied, and left it there. She then sat quietly until Hill appeared and asked her to join him in the interview room. Once again LaMunyon had wired him.

Hill asked Ruth if she wanted some coffee. "I'd like some water, please," she said, folding her hands neatly on the table and sitting up straight. She was wearing a new tan suit with a white pinstripe and a white eyelet blouse. Leon felt as if he were interrogating a friend's mother.

"I'm going to ask you some tough questions," Hill began. "I've already talked to Ed."

Ruth shrugged. "Okay," she said.

While Hill read Ruth her rights, she stared at him as uncomprehendingly as Ed had. Her rights? Panic spread through her stomach.

"A lady hates to tell me their age, but when were you born?" Hill asked.

"I'm fifty-one," Ruth replied, answering the indirect question directly. Fifty-two, fifty-three, she was thinking.

Hill then asked Ruth a few background questions; he wanted to know more about the incident at Fort Scott. Ruth recited the story by rote. Next Hill moved to Ed and the boys: Where were they now? How old were they? What were they doing? His tone was cordial; his strategy was first to establish a genial ambiance and then to attack.

"Okay," he said, "when is the first time that you again came in contact with this individual . . . bugging you now?"

"We were working on the patio," Ruth said. "Ed thought he had a heart attack, but he didn't."

Hill walked Ruth through that incident and the phone calls that followed. By prearrangement Leon remained silent while Hill continued with the kidnapping, the cut phone lines, the burning wreath, the urine, and the feces.

After Hill asked about the knifing, his tone changed. "Ruth," he said, "here are some things that have really been bothering me, and I have got to get them straight in my mind. There are several things that have happened out at your house and other places here in the city . . ."

Leon was watching Ruth as he had Ed. Under Hill's tougher questions Ruth's body changed; her shoulders sagged and her expression changed from a friendly smile to a vacant gaze. She stopped looking at Hill and now, instead, placed her hands on her lap and studied them.

"I told you I was going to ask you some tough questions," Hill said. "The rag, December seventeenth, nineteen eighty, wrapped around a piece of rock on the front porch—who found that?"

"A rock on the front porch . . . ," Ruth repeated.

The image of a terrible blue rock shot through her head. She shook it off.

"It had a bandana around it," Hill said.

She pictured a bandana in her mind and flinched again. "Was there anything in the rock?" she asked. "I don't—"

Hill didn't let her finish. "No, just a bandana around a rock."

"I don't remember anything about that," Ruth said.

Hill began to bombard Ruth with questions: "Who found the ice pick on the front porch, March twenty-first, 'eighty? . . . Eggs on the sliding door—who found that? . . . Human deposit on the front porch—who found that?" Then he suddenly asked, "Have you ever written any of those letters?"

"No, sir," Ruth said. Another vision flashed through her head. She was sitting by a washing machine with a pen in her hand. Why?

"Have you ever mailed any of those letters?"

"No, sir," she said. Letters . . .

"What if I called you a liar," Hill said, "because I have evidence that shows that you have? It is time to come straight. I have got pictures."

Ruth could barely speak. Her voice sunk down into her throat. "Mike . . . ," she managed to say.

His tone cooled. "Now do you want to keep playing your game? You got a problem, lady."

"When did I mail a letter?" Ruth asked.

Hill thrust the pictures in front of Ruth's face, and she stared at each one. "When you put them in the mailbox right there," Hill said. "Last Saturday, when you sent the Amco bill, when you sent the Penney's bill, when you sent the personal letter, you also sent a letter to yourself. Do you want me to show it to you?"

Ruth shook her head slightly. "No," she whispered. She thought, I'm the Poet?

"Do you want to tell me about it; do you deny it?"

Ruth continued to shake her head. "No . . ."

"Ruth, why . . . It's time, it's time to tell me why." Hill reached over and grabbed Ruth's hand, but she looked at her lap.

"Ruthie, look at me," he said. She didn't. He took his hand back.

"Look at me, Ruth, look at me. Now look at me." But she didn't, she wouldn't. "I am not mad at you, Ruth; I want to know why you are doing this. I found a bandana in your trash; I found carbon paper in your trash. I found torn-up paper in the trash; it matched up. Ruthie, why?"

Ruth whispered, "No . . ."

"Do you need some help?" Hill asked.

"Yes," Ruth said flatly. I'm the Poet, she thought. Had she known that?

It's over, Hill thought. She's ready to admit it all. "I need two more questions answered," he said. "Why did you make up the story about the abduction?"

"No . . . ," Ruth said.

"Sweetheart, why did you do that? Why, why, girl, why? The deal in Fort Scott, why did you make that up?"

Ruth regained some strength. "No," she said firmly. "I did not make that up."

"Okay," Hill said, "you didn't make that up."

"No, sir, I did not," Ruth agreed.

"Okay, Ruth, tell me something. On all this I have talked to you about, what you haven't done—"

"I didn't set fire to the wreath," she said.

"Okay," Hill said, "did you do everything else?"

Ruth nodded because she was afraid not to. She must have done terrible things. She wasn't sure what they were, but the men knew.

Leon stole a look at Hill. Ruth's nod wasn't good enough. The case could still go to court and speechless compliance on tape wouldn't convince a jury. Next door LaMunyon was listening through the wire, satisfied but worried, not about Ruth, but about the morale of the men and women who had cared for her.

Hill kept asking questions. "Did you cut the phone lines?" Ruth nodded. He rephrased his question to prevent a nod. "How did you do that without the neighbors seeing?"

Ruth started to speak and stopped. Hill waited until he was sure she wasn't going to answer and then continued. "Do you have a letter in your purse now that you wrote today?" he asked.

Ruth shook her head, then said, "No, I don't."

Hill fired off a few more questions and stood up. "Can I get you a cup of coffee?" he asked, his tone now gentle. Ruth shook her head. "I'll be right back," he said, leaving the room anyway to go over his notes. Leon stayed with Ruth. He had nothing to say, however, and Ruth didn't even consider looking at him. She was listening to her mind, but she couldn't make sense of her thoughts. I did these things? she wondered. The kidnapping and the stabbing—I did that? They said she had. Had she? Sometimes, when Hill asked her a specific question, she could see lucid pictures: she was sitting by the washing machine, writing letters. She guessed she had written the poems after all. But why? And fire? Phone lines? These weren't her memories.

At other times Hill's questions had been too strange, but she had nevertheless agreed because she was terrified to do otherwise. He was angry and Ruth feared anger. The only thing she knew for sure was that she was the worst person on earth—a sick, disgusting monster.

Hill was back.

"Ruth, something else is very important," he said. "I've got Ed downstairs, and I put him through the same thing I put you through today. I even put him on the polygraph. Did he have any knowledge of this at all?"

Ruth's voice grew a little stronger. "Absolutely not . . ."

"How did you keep it from him?" Hill asked. "Did you write most of those letters there at work?"

Confronted, Ruth dropped her head lower. Leon looked at Hill. They needed her to talk, but they knew not to push.

Hill's questions returned to the one possible motive. "Ruth," he asked, "how could you stab yourself? Why? . . . This all started when Ed was in the hospital; is that what triggered it? Were you and Ed having problems? Do you need that much attention? Huh? Have you had—"

Ruth had heard enough of this. "There is not a nicer person anywhere than he is," she said, now crying hard.

Hill backed off. "Okay," he said.

But Ruth continued, "Never had any problems."

"Do you ever think he has been unfaithful to you?"

"No, sir," Ruth said. The idea—Ed!

"Have you ever been unfaithful to him?"

"No," she said.

"He doesn't know anything about it?"

"No."

Hill asked more questions, but he still felt Ruth's answers were too vague. He looked over her head at Leon, who spoke for the first time. "Excuse me, Ruth," he said. "One of the problems we have is we have to know what the truth is. . . . Do you have any more of that bandana material at home? Is there any more of it down there in the spare bedroom?"

"It is all gone," Ruth said in a whisper.

Leon wasn't sure what he had heard. "It is all gone?" he repeated, and Ruth nodded.

As they continued to ask more questions, Hill thought perhaps he was being too harsh. "Ruth, there are no hard feelings between you and me. I just want to—"

"There should be," Ruth said.

Hill jumped. "There isn't. I have no animosity toward you." But Ruth didn't believe that. She thought they were treating her like a criminal.

"I want to get everything straightened out," Hill continued. "You want to get everything straightened out, do you not?" He asked more questions, and Ruth admitted to whatever he wished. Since she was crying so much, he could no longer tell whether her head was shaking in convulsions or nodding in accord.

"Can you tell us what brought this thing in Fort Scott back to start this whole charade again?" Hill asked. "Do you like publicity? Is that what you wanted?"

"No." They must be kidding, she thought. Who would want this kind of publicity?

"The kidnapping," Hill said. "How do you account for all those hours? How did you get there? Because you had to go up there and leave your sweater and shoes—"

"On the bus."

"Pardon me, I can't hear you. I'm sorry."

"I went on the bus," Ruth repeated, and thought, had she?

"You rode the bus to Twin Lakes," Hill said, "then you planted that stuff, then called us. Is that right?"

"Called Ed," Ruth said. She didn't want to talk more, because she wasn't convinced she had taken the bus. But she had no other explanation for how she had arrived at Twin Lakes, if there had been no kidnapping, as Hill said.

"How do you feel, Ruth?" Hill asked. He leaned over and held her head up with his hands so she would look at him.

Ruth still avoided his eyes. "I wish I was dead," she said.

Hill backed away, letting go of Ruth's head so quickly that it fell and hit the table. "Ruth," he said, "right now the world has come to an end, but it hasn't."

"Ruth," Leon added, "when you were doing these things . . . was there a reason ever in your mind about it?"

She didn't answer.

Hill asked about the kidnapper. "Who were you describing; who is that?"

"He looks a little like that guy that stopped me on the street," Ruth replied.

"He really looks a little bit like Dr. Schrag," Hill said. Several of the officers had noticed a similarity between Ruth's assailant and Dr. Schrag, which they assumed was due to the fact that Ruth, under hypnosis, had described the last person she had seen, who was, of course, Schrag.

"Do you recall," Hill asked, "what was going through your mind when you were writing a letter?"

Ruth shook her head. The duration of her visions had increased, and now she could conjure up images of herself in the basement, sitting by the washing machine writing letters. Ruth Finley, she thought: wife, mother, crazy person.

"Do you mind if I look through your purse?" Hill asked. "Can I look through your purse?"

Ruth wanted to say no, because she didn't want him to see the cash she had been saving for the trip to Oklahoma City. But Hill took the purse anyway and opened it.

"Did you mean to hurt yourself as bad as you did?" he asked.

"I don't know," Ruth said. It was true. She had no recollection of the stabbing incident whatsoever.

Hill followed up with more questions, and then asked, "Do you think you need to see a doctor now?"

"I am sure I do."

"Do you think you need to see one tonight?" They had already arranged for Ruth to sign herself into St. Joseph's Hospital, or they would do it for her.

Ruth nodded.

"I'll be quite frank with you," Hill said. "I have been concerned that you might hurt yourself."

Ruth shook her head.

"No," Hill said, "you are not crazy. There is help."

"I can never face Ed again," Ruth said.

"Yeah," Hill said, "you can. You've got to."

"He is the nicest person I have ever known."

"You are just ill, Ruth," Hill said. "You only have a disease, just like any other disease in the body, okay? There is a treatment for it, and people will make you well just like any other disease you might have."

"I can never face Ed again."

"You haven't done anything except be ill."

"Yes, I have," Ruth said. "I am a bad criminal."

"No, it is not the same. I guarantee you that it's not the same."

Ruth was silent.

"Do you want some water?" Hill asked.

Ruth looked up. "Can I have my purse back?" She wanted her money.

"Yeah," Hill said, "you can have your purse." He put it on the table. Then he asked a few more questions about her boss, and she repeated that no one else had helped her.

"I'm going to go talk to the doctor for a minute, okay?" Hill said. "I'll be right back."

Ruth, in tears, didn't look up.

A few moments later Hill returned with Dr. Schrag. "Hi, gal," the psychologist said. "Would you look at me?"

Ruth kept her head down.

"Okay," Schrag said, "don't feel badly. What would you like to do now?"

Ruth had a quick answer. "Go home," she said, still looking at her lap. "Just die."

"Just die?" Schrag repeated. "How can I or we best help you right now?"

She didn't respond.

"Did you ever," he continued, "in the last two or three years, wonder that maybe something was wrong—"

"Yes!" Ruth said. This was one of the few things she had heard from these men that she could agree with. Of course something was wrong! She stopped talking again and didn't resume until Schrag asked her some specific questions about Fort Scott. She began to answer, then broke off once more.

"I guess I am just crazy," she said.

Schrag told her she wasn't crazy. "Maybe part of your mind doesn't remember what the other part thinks; you know what I am saying? Did it seem like you were a different person when you went back and thought of this?"

Ruth couldn't answer anymore, but she could sense from this question, and Hill's, that the men believed that her actions as the Poet had been willful.

The room was silent for almost half a minute.

"Well," Schrag finally said, "what would you like to do now? Wouldn't you like to rest? What about going to the hospital?"

When no answer came, Schrag went on. "You don't want to just go home and just forget about the whole thing?"

"No," Ruth said. She understood what he was getting at, but she wasn't ready to admit it to herself.

"You think it would be better," Schrag asked, "if we let you go and rest and give you some medicine?"

"I don't want to," Ruth said.

"You don't want to rest?" Schrag asked. "What do you want to do?"

"I don't know."

Hill jumped in with a question he had forgotten: the letter with the Oklahoma City postmark—how did that happen?

"Just sent it to the post office," Ruth said, "and asked them to mail it."

Schrag was surprised. "Will the post office do that?" he asked Hill.

"They did," Ruth said. She collapsed again. "Oh, Jesus," she moaned.

Schrag asked Ruth a few more questions, and then the interrogation was over. Next door LaMunyon put away his tape recorder. From his office he could see Ed sitting in the waiting room, and LaMunyon watched him for signs of guilt or anger or violence, but all he recognized in Ed's face was depression.

When Hill and Leon left the interview room, the waiting room became instantly silent, which startled Ed into looking at the door. There he saw his wife. He put out his cigarette, stood up, and smiled crookedly at her. Then he walked into the interview room, and Ruth paused for only a second before rushing into his arms and bursting into loud, choking sobs. She didn't say a word, but she cried until his shirtsleeve darkened with her tears. "We'll get through this," Ed said. "I love you." He held her tightly, with dignity, as the two of them stood alone in the room and twenty cops stared through the doorway.

"Oh, Ed," Ruth said. "Oh, my God."

A few minutes later Hill took Ed aside. "There's a very strong chance that Ruth is suicidal," he said.

Ed nodded.

"We have to get her to a hospital," Hill said.

Ed nodded again.

"Look," Hill went on, "if you don't commit her, we will."

Behind Ed, a few feet away, Ruth was alone, sapped and crying, leaning against a table for support. Ed looked at her, back at Hill, and then down at the floor. He was frantic, for the situation had shocked him out of any recognition of his wife or himself. Who were they, he and Ruth, this couple the police were gawking at in a way he doubted they looked at thieves, murderers, or rapists? What was he supposed to do? He racked his brain but came up blank. "I don't know how to commit someone," he told Hill. "I've never done it." He let the police take over while he went back to hold his wife.

PART 2

The
Little Girl

1

ON THE NIGHT OF OCTOBER 1, 1981, AT EXACTLY nine o'clock, the police walked Ruth through a side corridor and out toward a squad car waiting in the City Building parking lot. Ruth was returning to St. Joseph's, this time as a mental patient. Behind her Ed followed uncertainly. Still nobody was offering him any help, and he felt lost. Then as the group approached the squad car, he suddenly asked Leon if he could come with them so that Ruth wouldn't have to ride alone. "Sure," Leon said, shrugging.

"Where do I go?" Ruth asked, but they were already pushing her into the back seat.

The car snaked down a series of concrete exit ramps, and no one said a word until they passed the Oldsmobile. Once again Ed stared at the voided meter. "I'd better move the car," he said. "I'm going to get a ticket."

"Don't worry about it," Leon said. How odd, Ruth thought, listening from the back. Then she thought, well, he's right. Life goes on, doesn't it?

They drove out of the lot and into a tranquil, warm night. Ruth looked through the window so she wouldn't have to talk, but she saw nothing of interest. The streets were empty and the stores closed, so she shut her eyes, and then suddenly the car pulled up at St. Joseph's. Ruth was surprised the ride had taken so little time. "Hold her arm," someone said, and they walked her into the hospital as if she were infirm.

Once inside, the police handed her over to an attendant while they filled out the requisite forms, occasionally glancing at her while answering the questions. Ruth sat in the corner. I'm a bad girl, she thought. She felt a strong urge to cry, but she suppressed it and instead stared at her lap, feeling naked in the bright, institutional light. Everyone in the world could see her, she thought, and she wrapped her coat tightly around her body.

"They want me to go now," Ed said. Ruth glanced up at her husband; for a brief moment she had forgotten where they were. They hugged and Ed left.

Ruth sat back down and counted the white linoleum floor tiles until an attendant said, "Let's go." Without looking she rose from the chair and followed the man to a lonely, dull room furnished with a table, a bed, and a blanket. She lay on the bed and waited for something to happen; once more she lost track of time until a nurse came in to explain the hospital's rules. "How are you feeling?" the woman asked. Ruth thought her voice was gentle.

"I'm okay," Ruth said, and she smiled. The nurse then handed Ruth a sleeping pill, said good-night, and closed the door softly behind her. Ruth immediately looked through her purse for the bus ticket money. Mike Hill had opened the purse during her confession, but he hadn't mentioned the bundle of bills. Now she took them out, counted them, and then held them tightly in her hand, wondering how she was going to get out of the hospital and over to the bus depot.

Before going to bed, Ruth went into a small private bathroom to wash her face, but instead of turning on the water, she studied her reflection in a mirror above the sink. She didn't like what she saw. Her makeup was streaked and her eyes were red, and she thought she looked worse than if she had been physically ill. She wiped an eyelash off the top of her cheek with a tissue. Oh, God, she thought, how am I ever going to commit suicide now?

Ruth took the sleeping pill out of her pocket and held it up to the light between her thumb and forefinger. She had never taken a narcotic in her life. She stared at it for a full minute before she placed it on her tongue and swallowed it with a glass of water. She then washed her face, went to bed, and a few minutes later was asleep.

After waving to Ruth on the street that afternoon, Jean had driven off unconcerned; watching Drowatzky escort her sister downtown had become a commonplace occurrence. But when she arrived home, she turned on the television in time to watch the local news anchor report a big break in the Poet case. Jean immediately called Ed. "I can't talk to you now," Ed said, and hung up without telling her that at that moment the police were searching his house.

Jean's next-door neighbor, Kerry Crisp, was a major in charge of investigations in the police department. When Jean looked out her living room window and saw his car in the driveway, she ran over to ask him about the break. "I'll check," he said, and disappeared back inside his house. He already knew about

Ruth's confession, but he wanted to call LaMunyon and ask what he was allowed to say. The two men decided that Crisp, who liked Jean and wanted to help, might as well tell her the truth. Half an hour later he walked over and rang her doorbell. "Is Bill around?" he asked.

"No," Jean said. "What did you find out?"

Crisp hesitated momentarily. "Maybe I should wait for Bill," he said. "It's a real can of worms." So Jean phoned Bill at the golf course where he had spent the afternoon and left an urgent message. Bill, who drove home the moment he received it, was still wearing his golf shoes when he arrived.

Jean then called Crisp and asked him to return. When he did, five minutes later, he brought his wife, Merci, with him, hoping her presence would soften the impact of the news. They sat in the living room. "Well?" Jean asked impatiently.

"I really don't know how to say this," Crisp said, "but it's Ruth. She's the Poet."

Jean laughed. "Oh, right," she said, "I'm sure she's stupid enough to stab herself."

"Ruth's the Poet," Crisp repeated. Then he explained what Ruth had done and where they had taken her. Jean, dazed, was silent for a moment, and then she fired off a series of quick questions: "How did she get those letters mailed from Oklahoma City?" "How did that knife get left in the lobby?" "Who stabbed her?"

Crisp couldn't answer everything, but like it or not, he said, Ruth had confessed. And Bill, like Ed, could think of no reason why the police would lie. "I think you're going to have to accept that it's Ruth," he said.

Jean shook her head. "I'm going to prove you all

wrong," she said. "Oh, no," she added. "I've got to get to Mother's before it's on TV."

"They're not going to break the story until ten," Crisp said.

Jean looked at her watch. It was just after nine.

"I still have time," she said. But first she called her brother's house and left a message for Carl to join her at their mother's. On the way to Faye's apartment, Jean rehearsed what she would say. But if there was a right way to tell her mother about Ruth, it hadn't occurred to her by the time she arrived. When Faye opened the door, Jean walked into the living room and sat down on the sofa, still thinking about what to say and also absently watching the television, which was blaring. Faye watched soap operas all day and, if she could find nighttime soaps, through the evening too, until she fell asleep.

"Mother," Jean finally said over the noise of the television. "I have some bad news."

"What's that?" Faye asked.

"Ruth's sick," Jean said, and she blurted it all out. "She's the Poet. She's the one who stabbed herself. She's the one who's been writing the letters. But they've got her in the hospital and she's going to be okay."

Jean waited for her mother to reply.

"No," Faye said. Jean started to talk again, but Faye waved her silent with an abrupt motion and turned back to the television. Jean obediently settled back on the couch; it was remarkable, she thought, how much power her eighty-six-year-old mother still held over her. Faye didn't speak again until just before ten, when Carl, out of breath and frantic, rushed into the room. He had assumed the urgency meant his mother was ill, but now he saw her rocking calmly, looking as imperturbable as ever.

"So what's up?" he asked.

"Ruth's the Poet," Jean said.

"You're shitting me," Carl said. He sat down, and Jean told him the same story she had told Faye. "No shit," he kept saying. Meanwhile Faye listened but remained silent. Jean understood her mother's reasoning: Faye didn't believe Jean because she felt no particular need to believe her. But then at ten o'clock the KAKE anchors reported the whole story, and now that it was on television, Faye no longer had a choice. She covered her face with her hands. "Oh, no," she moaned. "Oh, no, no." She was holding her head so tightly that Jean worried she was hurting herself, but for the next ten minutes Faye just sat and moaned. "Mother," Jean asked, "would you like me to stay over tonight?"

"Why?" Faye snapped. She looked up, her face so composed that Jean was rattled. But before her daughter could respond, Faye cut her off again. "It's over and done now," she said, and she turned back to the television.

Richard LaMunyon had two teenage sons; the elder, Slade, was a lineman and special teams captain for the Maize High School football team, the Eagles, who that night were playing against the Caldwell Blue Jays. LaMunyon, who had never missed a single game in which either of his sons had played, announced he wasn't going to talk to the media for several hours. Then he left for Maize, where he watched Slade help lead the Eagles to a twenty-eight-to-seven victory.

LaMunyon had already made a quiet deal with KAKE. In return for giving him, unopened, the letters the station had received from the Poet, he had guaranteed its reporter an exclusive interview for their ten o'clock report. He had also made a similar arrangement with the staff at the *Eagle-Beacon;* because they too had been handing over their letters and cooperating with the placement of Ed's personal ads, La-Munyon agreed to let their reporter listen to Ruth's confession.

Mike Hill's first move after the interview ended was a drive to Riverside, a quiet, tree-lined neighborhood where Carl Morris Smock lived. Over the last three years Ruth's brother had become openly critical of what he termed the department's ineffective investigation, and Hill wanted to tell him face-to-face about Ruth's confession. At that moment, however, Carl was on his way to Faye's, but when Hill arrived, Carl's wife asked him to have a seat anyway. Without waiting for Carl, Hill told the family about Ruth, then returned to the police station and met with the rest of the media. He was home by eleven and asleep by midnight.

Ed was also home by eleven that night. He was tired, frightened, and alone. Still he felt obligated to call his sons before they heard about their mother on the news. Both lived in other cities, and since Ruth had refused to let them know the full extent of her anxiety, neither had followed the case closely.

The older son was a successful doctor and very much his parents' child. He betrayed little emotion when Ed told him about his mother. Bruce, the younger son, was overwhelmed. "You're kidding me!" he said. "No! Are you kidding me? Oh, my God, you're kidding!"

After Ed hung up, Bruce stared at the receiver. What the hell, he thought, his mother couldn't be the Poet. Then he had a flash and called Ed back. "Come on, Dad," he said. "You can tell me. This is some kind of trap to lure the Poet out of the shadows. Right?"

Ed assured him it wasn't, however, and Bruce hung up once more, after promising to fly to Wichita the next morning. Then he understood: Ed couldn't talk to him openly, because the plan was so complicated that the police had forbidden anyone to discuss it over the phone. The Poet had access to the lines, so of course he was listening.

The next morning Jean rose slowly, showered, dressed, and considered not going to work. "Why don't you stay home?" Bill suggested. "I'm going to." But Jean had just been transferred to a new position as supervisor of the message fraud investigation center, and this was only her second day. Besides, she didn't want people to think she was ashamed. Even so, not one coworker mentioned a word about Ruth. Although, as some of them told her later, the effort required to keep silent had made that day the most difficult in their lives, they thought it was best not to meddle.

During her lunch break Jean suddenly remembered the day she had been mistaken for Ruth in the phone company snack room and how only two days later the Poet had warned Ruth not to confuse him. The more Jean remembered, the more she wondered why she hadn't thought of the possibility that Ruth was the Poet. She quickly answered her own question: because it was unthinkable.

* * *

Ruth woke up that same morning feeling clear, un-
equivocal panic. Her head ached as usual, and she
wanted to go to the bathroom, but she was too afraid
to make a move, because she feared that another
transgression of any sort, however inadvertent, would
land her in jail. In her entire life she had never even
received a traffic ticket. What had happened?

An hour later she heard footsteps at her door and
cringed, but it was only an orderly. "Breakfast," the
man said, placing a tray containing a cinnamon roll,
orange juice, and coffee on the table. After he left,
Ruth took a small bite of the roll, decided it was good,
and ate it. When she was finished, she curled up under
the covers and stared at the empty tray.

An hour after that she heard more footsteps, and
this time two male doctors opened the door. They
peered at her, then walked in and stood at the foot of
her bed. "Hello there, Ruth," the older one said.
"Why don't we have a talk?"

"Okay," Ruth answered. The older doctor, who
was smoking a pipe, sat down on the bed and crossed
his legs. Ruth felt he was watching her as if he were
studying an insect, staring impassively up and down
her body. She put her hand over her throat to shield
herself from his glare.

The man introduced himself as Ruth's psychiatrist
and talked to her for ten minutes. Then he said, "I
think we'll be able to get your erratic behavior under
control with some good strong drugs."

"Okay," Ruth said. She was horrified; she had felt
uneasy about taking the sleeping pill. After the men
left, she cried, but then the younger doctor came back
and told her in an amiable manner that he was a friend
of her older son's. Ruth smiled at him, but she held

back a sob. Oh God, she thought, what was he going to tell people?

When Ed came to visit an hour later, Ruth was still in tears. "Can I switch psychiatrists?" she asked. She told him about the doctor who wanted to give her drugs.

"I'll look into it," Ed said, and handed Ruth a suitcase with a change of clothes.

Before they could talk any further a nurse walked into the room and spotted the suitcase. "Now don't you bother to unpack that," she said. "You're leaving."

At first Ruth thought the nurse was talking to Ed, although the woman was looking right at her. "You're going to Wesley," the nurse continued, and explained that Ruth's legal commitment required a twenty-four-hour lockup. St. Joseph's lockup, the staff had just discovered, was already full, but Wesley Hospital, on Hillside, had room.

Ed offered to drive Ruth to Wesley in the Oldsmobile, but a moment later two sheriff's officers appeared and, seemingly in a great hurry, gave Ruth only a moment to grab some flowers in a vase sent by a friend and to say good-bye to Ed. Then they led her downstairs, telling her that if she promised to behave, they wouldn't use their handcuffs. Ruth agreed but wondered what they thought—that she was going to grab their guns and pistol-whip them?

The men escorted her out of the building and into the back of a van behind heavy wire. "Don't you spill any of that water back there," one of them warned. When they arrived at Wesley, the attendants had Ruth change into a green hospital gown while they searched her clothes for sharp instruments and drugs. Then an orderly escorted her to her new room and left her there alone.

When Ed came home that afternoon he thought about Ruth's request for a new doctor and realized that he didn't know if this was permissible. But since Ruth seemed so unhappy he called Dr. Schrag, who recommended two names. Neither had the time to accept Ruth as a patient, but one, a psychologist from Schrag's church group, recommended a new member of his own group practice, Andrew Trice Pickens III, a thirty-eight-year-old psychiatrist who had recently moved to town from St. Louis. Dr. Pickens agreed to see Ruth. The Finleys' family lawyer petitioned the court for the switch, and permission was granted.

Joyce and Dave Middleton invited Ed to their home for dinner that evening. They talked about the church, their kids, and eventually about Ruth too, for most of all the Middletons wanted to say they still considered the Finleys good friends. They knew some other people had dropped them, and now many more would disappear.

Ed, in turn, opened up more than was his custom, discussing lockup, Ruth's health, and her uneasiness concerning her doctor. Watching Ed pick at his food, Joyce worried about his health too. People at Pizza Hut's home office, where she now worked, had asked her how Ed could have lived with Ruth night and day and not known. Joyce knew that Ed loved his wife, and that was the good and the bad of it. Ed had believed Ruth could do no wrong, and so he had never looked for clues. And because he saw no clues, he suspected nothing. If he had, he would have ended it: Ed loved Ruth too much to let her hurt herself.

That same night Jean drove to her mother's apartment to check on her, but Faye assured her daughter she was fine and said she was turning everything over to God. Jean correctly translated the remark as a request not to discuss Ruth. Faye never mentioned the Poet again.

On Saturday the *Eagle-Beacon,* under the headline, "Officials Await Psychiatric Tests before They Decide on Charges," ran a story in which Clark Owens, the Sedgwick County district attorney, explained that his office would wait ninety days, until Ruth's psychological testing was complete, before deciding whether to prosecute. Owens added, however, that the most serious criminal charge she faced was a misdemeanor for falsely reporting a crime. When Ed read the story, he joked to Ruth that since he had reported some of the incidents himself, didn't that mean he was also guilty?

Beneath the headline was a caricature of Ruth next to a graphic the paper was using on each of its front-page stories. The graphic said, "The Strange Case of the Poet." Beneath it was a boldfaced quote: " 'Whatever, I'm going to stand by her.' —Ed Finley."

Jean didn't learn visitors were allowed in lockup until she talked to Ed, who encouraged her to call on Ruth. So Jean and Bill drove over and spent an afternoon at the hospital, where Ruth told them stories about the strange people she was now living with. By the time visiting hours ended, the staff had changed shifts. A new nurse entered the room holding Jean's purse, which Jean had been asked to check. Ruth, who saw the nurse first, rose and said to Jean, "Well, goodbye, Ruth," and reached for the purse. Jean immediately stood up and laughed. "Wait a minute," she said. "I'll do anything for you, but not this."

During their visits over the next month Jean and Ruth discussed two subjects they had always avoided: their mother and their childhood. Ruth admitted that she had wanted to talk to Jean about the incident at Fort Scott but never did because Faye had taken her aside that night and forbade her to mention it to anyone. Jean told Ruth that she had never talked about it either because Faye had given her the same warning.

On Ruth's second day at Wesley the Finleys' minister called Ed and asked if they could talk. Ed found this gesture thoughtful, but overwrought with work and worry, he asked the minister to visit Faye instead, which the man did. Later the minister told others in their congregation that he had tried to help Ed but that Ed had built a wall around himself.

The minister never offered to see Ruth. Once Ruth saw the associate minister walking into the main lockup entrance, and she rushed back to her room to comb her hair and put on her lipstick. But the man never showed up at her door.

Bruce Finley drove to the hospital as soon as he landed in Wichita. He was still convinced he was walking into an elaborate plot until he saw his mother sitting calmly on her bed, and even then he was too confused to be confident of the truth. Ruth's equanimity startled Bruce. She talked casually about the other patients in lockup, whose stories she was learning, and her tales were very entertaining. She didn't seem unhappy and reacted sharply only when Bruce mentioned that some of his friends found it funny that she had fooled the police for such a long time. "It wasn't funny at all," Ruth snapped.

Bruce felt reassured to see his mother looking well, and Ruth was equally relieved when he left. As always she had decided that no one was going to see her pain. Whenever she received visitors at Wesley, she put on her best personality and her most charming manners, and when they left she collapsed, exhausted.

Not long after Ruth's confession the Wichita police department concluded a study summing up the various expenditures connected to the Poet investigation. The final tally was $258,892.26 in regular pay for the police personnel involved, which included one deputy chief, four captains, seventeen lieutenants, two police examiners, thirty-three detectives, seven investigators, three mpo-1s, and seventy-four police officers. Overtime for these men and women came to an additional $61,344.70, and along with other costs such as donated time, services rendered by artists and aircraft, cameras and equipment, and transportation fees, the total amounted to over $370,000.

Ruth, who had always appreciated routine, now began to follow the most severe of her life. She woke at seven, took a monitored shower, ate breakfast, talked to psychiatrists, ate lunch, sat through supervised conversations with other patients, took tests, ate dinner, and went to bed at ten o'clock.

The ward's main room was long and drab; it was lined on its north and south sides by small bedrooms, every two sharing a bath, even when men and women were neighbors. The bathroom doors could be locked from the outside and the inside, but patients often forgot to unlock them when they left and Ruth was embarrassed when she had to wander through other people's rooms to use the toilet.

The bedrooms contained two single beds, and Ruth's first roommate was a nondescript housewife who barely spoke, which pleased Ruth. She had no desire to talk either. What were they supposed to say to each other, she wondered: So, how crazy are you? But her second roommate, Mary, a suicidal young mother of three girls, was pleasant, and the two women enjoyed each other's company so much that the orderlies had to force them out of their room to mingle; socializing was considered therapeutic. To her surprise Ruth liked some of the other patients too. Her favorite was a cute eight-year-old boy who, whenever his mother phoned, walked up and down the hall as far as the telephone cord reached and then told Ruth that his mother couldn't visit him because he had tried to kill her. The truth was that she had tried to kill him. He and Ruth played games and puzzles with another boy, and when the children discovered Ed was an artist, they asked him to draw them pictures whenever he visited.

The other patients included drug addicts, alcoholics, and depressives. Ruth had little in common with them, which she found a relief. Mostly she just wanted to sit quietly and embroider, but the staff wouldn't permit it because the rules forbade possession of scissors. But Mary also sewed, and the two complained until a kind orderly relented and found them a pair of blunt kindergarten scissors that barely cut thread. The women used it as a saw, hacking at the thread until it broke.

Because Mary was under a suicide watch, every night the orderlies cleaned out the room: clothes, toothbrushes, toiletries—everything that belonged to Ruth and Mary was removed. Once Ruth made a casual remark: why bother to take blue jeans? If she were planning on suicide, she said, rather than using jeans she would take a light bulb, which the orderlies left behind, break it, and slit her wrists with the glass. Her remark was immediately reported to the staff and the next day she was grilled: What did she really mean? Was it a threat? Ruth realized that the kind of offhand comments she and Ed always enjoyed making were highly suspicious in psychiatric lockup.

She landed in similar trouble during a bed check. The orderlies occasionally searched the room for drugs, always looking in the same places—under the radiator, then under the bed. One night Ruth said, "If I ever do have any drugs, I certainly know where I won't hide them." The orderly on duty reported that Ruth had mentioned hiding drugs. Once again she was interrogated: What kind of drugs do you want? Where would you hide them? What did you really mean?

The ward population was very transient, and after only a few days Ruth was a veteran. One woman appeared in the middle of the night after she had swallowed a bottle of sleeping pills; she had discovered that her husband was having an affair. After talking to the woman, Ruth thought she was normal but terribly unhappy. Another woman was crazy, Ruth decided. She told Ruth she couldn't keep a job because all of her bosses abused her verbally and her psychiatrist gave her a mirror so she could savor her loveliness.

Was Ruth as crazy? She was extremely upset that Hill and LaMunyon believed she had willingly fooled them. Why would she have done all those things on purpose? They had brought her the worst shame of her life. No one in her right mind would have done such things. But had she known what she was doing and then forgotten it all? Could she be in her right mind? Many of the other people in lockup were crazy, but not everyone. Sometimes Ruth liked the ward because she felt safe. A month ago the thought of being there would have frightened her. Now she was glad—occasionally. Other times she wondered if she would be there forever. Or until she remembered everything she did.

On the third day of lockup Ruth began a series of court-mandated psychological tests. Most of them were standard: word associations, problem-solving quizzes, Rorschach exams. But another test comprised a series of questions using such props as newspapers, and the newspaper the doctor showed Ruth was topped by a banner headline: " 'I Must Be Crazy' Says Ruth Finley." It was a recent front page of the *Eagle-Beacon*, quoting from her confession. "Here," the doctor asked. "What do you think of this?" Ruth burst into tears and the doctor sent her back to her room. The next morning she had to return to his office again, where again he showed her the paper, and again she broke down.

2

DR. ANDREW PICKENS HAD DECIDED TO BECOME A psychiatrist when he was twelve years old, influenced by an old movie he saw on television, *The Snake Pit,* in which actress Olivia de Havilland played a woman institutionalized after a nervous breakdown. The film fascinated Dr. Pickens, who had already given thought to being a doctor. He now realized for the first time that emotional problems, too, could be understood and treated and were not simply mysterious or frightening.

In high school he was short, although he grew to almost five eleven just prior to college, and the caption beneath his yearbook picture was "Little man, big brain, future psychiatrist." He then attended Washington University in St. Louis and medical school at St. Louis University, where several instructors in the psychiatry courses were psychoanalysts and taught psychiatry from that perspective. This method of treatment came closest to what Dr. Pickens considered a real understanding of mental illness. To him every patient was like a character in a mystery novel, and a good psychiatrist was like a detective who unearthed clues, unscrambled hidden meanings, and put the pieces of the puzzle together to solve the mystery, all in the context of an empathic relationship.

Dr. Pickens interned at the University of Kansas, did his formal psychiatric residency at St. Louis University, and set up a private practice in St. Louis while also working at Veterans Hospital. He then chose this time to undergo his own psychoanalysis, which went well; he considered it indispensable for his own career. But after six years he grew restless in St. Louis and wanted a new practice where he could emphasize long-term psychotherapy. He found one in Wichita, a city about which he knew little. He accepted an offer in January 1981 and moved in the late summer. By this time he and his wife Judy, his former college girlfriend, had two children, Andrew Trice IV, twelve, and Rebecca, eleven. Dr. Pickens, not familiar with current events in Wichita, was only vaguely aware of the case of the Poet.

The first time Dr. Pickens visited Ruth at Wesley, he knocked on her door, then entered, introduced himself, and asked a few questions. While he spoke, Ruth looked him over quickly, careful not to let him see her watching. She immediately liked him more than the other doctor and decided he was attractive in an academic fashion—wire-rimmed glasses, straight dark hair, serious brown eyes, and a slight build. The only discordant element, she thought, was an oversized mustache that resembled a nineteenth-century cowboy's.

"How are you doing?" Dr. Pickens asked.

Ruth said she was okay.

"And are you comfortable?" he continued.

Ruth nodded. She also liked his voice, which sounded genuinely concerned. No one else had convinced her they cared. By continuing to steal looks at him, she tried to tell if he thought she was a terrible person, but she wasn't sure what she saw. She had already heard that he had just moved to Wichita, and she wondered if maybe he simply didn't know enough about the case to understand the extent of her craziness.

It was true that Dr. Pickens knew little about Ruth, but he wasn't interested in the newspaper articles. Ruth herself was his concern, and he watched her carefully. In a first discussion with a patient he looked for nonverbal clues. Was she telling the truth? Was she holding back? Was she omitting major details? He decided that the look in Ruth's eyes, her general carriage, and the tone of her voice were all guileless. He was also impressed with her exceptional degree of emotional withdrawal and bodily tension.

Ruth acknowledged that she was afraid. As she spoke, her conversation was marked by frequent pauses and interruptions, indicating to Dr. Pickens a high degree of distress and anxiety. Ruth constantly tried to avoid eye contact, but when he did manage a fixed look into her eyes, he saw hopelessness, sadness, and fear, reminding him of a scared child or a trapped animal.

Ruth told Dr. Pickens how much she disliked the other psychiatrist. "All he wanted to do was give me drugs," she complained. She looked at Dr. Pickens for reassurance that he wouldn't do the same.

"First off, I'm not assuming you need drugs," he said. "I wouldn't automatically rule out medication, but we'd talk it over first before deciding. It's your decision as much as mine."

Ruth paused. "Am I crazy?" she finally asked. And she wondered if he would say so if she were.

"Do you think you're crazy?" he asked.

"I don't know. They say I did things, and I guess I did, but I don't remember."

"What do you remember?"

"Just some flashes of things, like mailing a letter. It makes me feel crazy."

"I understand that you are confused and afraid, but that's not the same as being crazy," he said. "If I thought you were what psychiatrists call psychotic, I would tell you. You can count on me to be honest."

When they finished talking, Dr. Pickens rose to leave. "I'll be back tomorrow," he said.

Ruth was glad to hear it.

"And maybe we can take a look at some of your test results," he added.

Ruth's mood darkened. She was convinced the tests would prove she was insane, and she didn't want Dr. Pickens to know. "Whatever you want . . . ," she said, her words trailing off.

His interpretation of her unfinished sentence was, "Whatever you want . . . just please don't hurt me." Another animal analogy flashed in his mind, this time of a deer caught in oncoming headlights. He thought Ruth's terror was primitive and real.

Dr. Pickens went back to see Ruth the next afternoon. Earlier that day Southwestern Bell had decided that it wasn't going to let her return to her old job. She was extremely upset, because she had worked for the phone company almost all her adult life. Ruth had spent the day on and off in tears, and she was still crying when Dr. Pickens entered the room.

He sat down next to the bed and watched her quietly for a few minutes. Then he broke the silence. "Can you tell me what's going on?" he asked.

Ruth hesitated before deciding to admit, for once, that she was angry. "They shouldn't have taken my job away," she said. Her growing fear was that the rest of the city, including her boss, agreed with La-Munyon and Hill that she had acted willfully, and that people wanted to punish her. But she didn't want to discuss it anymore and lapsed back into silence.

The remainder of Dr. Pickens's visit was routine; he asked Ruth to tell him about her background, from her earliest memories to the present, and he noted that her responses were straightforward when his questions were direct. But if the questions contained emotionally charged issues, particularly those concerning the Poet, Ruth became uncomfortable and allowed a long pause before answering.

"Do you remember much about being the Poet?" he asked.

"Very little," she said. "Sometimes I remember sitting by the washing machine writing. And mailing some of the letters. But I can't remember much more." She glanced quickly at his face to see if he believed her. His face revealed nothing, but she was relieved.

While they were talking, Dr. Pickens was deciding if psychoanalytic psychotherapy was the best form of treatment for Ruth. He was also trying to establish a friendly therapeutic alliance. Dr. Pickens didn't think Ruth understood yet how he could help her, but they had formed enough of a connection that she appeared willing to undertake the therapy on faith, and hope for the best. She seemed to trust him.

After the visit Ruth thought, he doesn't seem to hate me.

The next day Dr. Pickens asked Ed to join him and Ruth while he described his own particular interpretation of therapy. It consisted of two conventionally accepted approaches. One was supportive therapy, which helped a patient find the means to repress a conflict deeply enough to make it nonsymptomatic, while also helping to shore up relatively healthy defenses—unhealthy defenses being those that impair reality the most, healthy ones those that distort reality the least. An unhealthy defense could be denial—for instance, someone might undergo all the symptoms of a heart attack, yet from fear deny the attack—whereas a healthy defense might be humor. Most psychiatric and psychological therapies fell into this category of supportive therapy.

The psychoanalytic therapy Dr. Pickens recommended to Ruth was more insight-oriented. It was also less common, partly because, he explained, many psychiatrists and psychologists lacked the necessary training, and because some simply denied its usefulness.

To Ruth all these therapies sounded like something only demented, sick people were forced to endure. "What kinds of patients benefit from the kind of therapy you're recommending?" she asked, afraid of the answer.

Dr. Pickens explained that patients must meet certain criteria. They cannot be overly impaired, and yet they must need the therapy enough to justify the extensive amount of money, time, and effort required.

The therapy would take, he added, at least one year and maybe much longer. Above all, the therapist looked at each potential patient to see if he or she had the necessary ego strength. Dr. Pickens then paraphrased Freud's definition of the term: the ability to work and the ability to love. "In other words," he said, "undergoing therapy doesn't mean you're insane at all," and he told her that her successful thirty-year relationship with Ed, her two well-adjusted children, and her reasonably fulfilling career at the phone company were proof of her ego strength.

Ruth wondered, however, if he was just trying to make her feel better. She found it difficult to believe she had any strength left at all.

Dr. Pickens then told Ruth that her tests had revealed she was in a state of massive repression. He didn't mention the tester had also noted that Ruth's profile was the most repressed he had ever seen.

Although he thought Ruth was probably ready to go home, Dr. Pickens decided to keep her in the hospital a few more days. The hospital's sheltered environment was helping her regain her strength, and he guessed that she needed time before facing the world. He suspected that if she hadn't been hospitalized, the odds were even or better that she would have killed herself. But the probability of an attempt had decreased every day since her arrival in lockup, and he doubted that she was a suicide risk at all anymore.

Nor did he worry the Poet would return. The defining incident in the Poet's existence had been his exposure; once the Poet had been uncovered, he could no longer serve whatever psychological purpose had generated his creation. The Poet had allowed Ruth to express certain feelings while simultaneously hiding others from herself and the world. Now that those feelings had been exposed, the Poet was gone.

During the second week, Ruth cried. Dr. Pickens simply watched and listened during those times when, between her sobs, she sometimes spoke. "I'm humiliated," she said. "I've embarrassed everyone in my family. I can never show my face in public again."

"Why do you feel this way?" Dr. Pickens asked.

Ruth looked up, surprised. "Because I'm a bad, bad person," she said.

"Did those things really make you a bad person?" Dr. Pickens asked.

The answer was so apparent to Ruth that she didn't bother to reply. Instead she continued crying.

After a few minutes she stopped and regained some of her composure. "I'm a bad little girl for crying," she said.

"Does crying really make you bad?" he asked. He noticed that Ruth's grammar and tone had reverted to that of a young child.

"Well," Ruth explained, "my mother always told me it was bad. I was a crybaby when I was growing up, and all my mother's relatives used to feel so sorry for Mother because I cried so much."

"I don't think there's anything wrong with crying," Dr. Pickens said. "If you feel like crying, go ahead and cry. Everyone cries."

"Oh, no!" Ruth said. "I don't!" Later she thought this was funny, since she was in tears when she said it.

She also wondered about her actions as the Poet. "I can only remember a little bit of what I did," she said.

"I don't think that's most important," Dr. Pickens

said. "The idea is to understand what this has all been about."

That wasn't an option Ruth had considered. She was afraid that he was going to force her to spend all their time going over the last few years in painstaking detail, making her remember and retell each and every misdeed.

"Those memories are all somewhere inside," Dr. Pickens said, "but they may never surface unless you want them to."

Ruth shook her head, smiled at Dr. Pickens, and thought, no, thank you.

On October 12, eleven days after Ruth had entered lockup, Dr. Pickens visited her in a meeting room instead of her bedroom. "I've finished your report for the court," he said. "But I haven't been told I can give you a copy, so I won't."

He did, however, want her to look it over. First Ruth went back to her room for her glasses, trying to keep her mind blank. Then she returned to the meeting room and read while Dr. Pickens watched her.

Dr. Pickens's report, written to the Honorable Judge Willis W. Wall in response to a court order of October 5, summed up his initial diagnosis:

Mrs. Finley has utilized repression in a massive way ever since childhood to effectively bury unacceptable feelings and wishes. These unacceptable feelings and wishes relate to anger and sexuality. Such repression takes considerable psychological effort but occurs unconsciously, not through conscious intent. The price she paid was in terms of limitation of flexibility of personality. In a sense, she has been "too nice"; prone to deny her own needs in favor of doing what others seem to expect of her. Therefore, the pressure of buried feelings grew throughout her life. She was able to maintain the repression until stressed by her husband's illness about four and a half years ago. Although his condition proved not to be serious, it was originally thought that he may have had a heart attack. I believe that this stimulated fears of abandonment (should he die) in Mrs. Finley. This, in turn, caused a weakening of her repression with resulting symptoms of anxiety, followed by the "Poet's" activities. . . . What followed was a partially conscious, but largely unconscious attempt by Mrs. Finley to both gratify and defend against unacceptable sexual and aggressive wishes. Although most of the time she was fully aware of what she was doing, she was never aware of why she was doing it. When she functioned as "the Poet," she was giving partial expression to repressed aggressive and sexual feelings. Because she also has felt guilty about these feelings, she made herself the target of "the Poet," as punishment. The intensity of her guilt is reflected in the act of stabbing herself. . . .

The "Poet's" behavior was also an attempt to ward off anxiety and depression. My diagnosis is Atypical Impulse Disorder with dissociative and depressive features. . . . The essential feature is a sudden, temporary alteration in the normally integrative functions of consciousness, identity, or motor behavior. If the alteration occurs in consciousness, important personal events cannot be recalled. If it occurs in identity, either the individual's customary identity is temporarily forgotten and a new identity is assumed, or the customary feeling of one's own reality is lost and replaced by a feeling of unreality.

In summary Dr. Pickens recommended that Ruth be treated in intensive psychotherapy on a twice-a-week basis.

Ruth pretended to read the report well after she had finished because she was afraid to comment. But Dr. Pickens sensed this. "How do you feel about what's in here?" he asked.

Ruth still wouldn't look at him. "Oh, it's not as bad as I thought it might be," she said. She had been positive the report would conclude she was a dangerous monster who should be taken off the streets forever. She also feared that, no matter what assurances Dr. Pickens had given her, he would say she was crazy. Ruth was constantly terrified that she had lost her mind. That morning an attendant had escorted her to the examination room for a test, and when it was over, Ruth went to the door, glanced at the attendant, and frowned: the woman looked so different. The attendant caught Ruth's look and laughed. "No," she said. "I didn't bring you here, honey. That was another girl." Ruth had just shrugged, but relief had surged through her body.

Ruth was so relieved to discover Dr. Pickens didn't hate her that she didn't notice that the report confirmed the belief held by LaMunyon and Hill: "Although most of the time she was fully aware of what she was doing, she was never aware of why she was doing it." Soon after writing this, however, Dr. Pickens decided that Ruth hadn't been aware of her actions as the Poet and that her condition was not an impulse disorder but a dissociative disorder. He was convinced that her experience as the Poet had been completely divorced from her conscious mind.

During Ruth's third week at Wesley, Ed decided he should call Dr. Pickens. "Hello, Dr. Pickens," he said, "this is Ed Finley, Ruth's husband. I'd like to talk to you about my wife—"

"There's something you need to know," Dr. Pickens interrupted.

"Fine," Ed said.

"It's important that this kind of therapy remain confidential," Dr. Pickens said. "In the meantime you can tell me whatever you think might be helpful, but remember that I have to be free to tell your wife anything you say. Of course, if I feel that she is ever in danger, I will let you know. Is all this okay?"

"Oh, sure, I see," Ed said, and hung up the phone. Actually he wasn't sure at all what Dr. Pickens meant. He just wanted to find out what was wrong with his wife and how he could help. Later, when he mentioned the conversation to Ruth, she shook her head.

"Well, if that's what Dr. Pickens wants . . . ," she said. Apparently Ruth wasn't supposed to talk to Ed about her therapy, and neither of them found that easy to understand. It wasn't that they talked all of their problems through with each other, but the notion that one of them was talking to someone else was unsettling.

Given Ruth's continuing progress, the hospital moved her out of twenty-four-hour lockup and into a much nicer room on another floor. Her roommate was Mary, Ruth's likable friend from her first week, but then Mary was released the next day. Ruth's new roommate was a young woman who announced as she walked in the door, "I'm here to find myself, so you'll just have to put up with me."

She then unpacked a large suitcase filled with more cosmetics than Ruth had bought in years—dozens of hair sprays, lipsticks, and mascaras. When she was finished unpacking, the woman walked around the room. "See this phone?" she said. "It's mine." Ruth nodded politely. "See this radio?" the woman continued. "It's mine. The dresser? Mine." Ruth curled up in bed while the woman took possession of the rest of the room.

In another session with Dr. Pickens Ruth finally summoned up the nerve to ask him more about the Poet. She talked about some of the Poet's actions and the few actual memories she had. "But," she said, "I guess everyone knows all about that stuff."

"I don't," Dr. Pickens said.

"You don't?" Ruth was startled. She didn't believe anyone could live in Wichita and not know about the Poet. She was convinced that everyone in the city was talking about her.

Dr. Pickens asked her about the anger in the Poet's poems and the feelings it aroused in her now. Ruth wasn't sure. "But one thing," she said, "at least I know why I wanted to kill myself. I had been doing all those horrible things and I guess some part of me was beginning to figure it out."

"What do you mean?" Dr. Pickens asked.

"Well," Ruth said, "if it had been the Poet trying to kill me, it would have worked. I'd be dead. So it was me. But I guess I just couldn't figure out a way to do it."

Dr. Pickens asked Ruth what suicide meant to her. "I think it's an escape from an impossible, intolerable situation," she said. "And it's kind of a brave thing, to get yourself out of everyone's way and do it in a way that no one ever finds you." But, she added, she no longer wanted to kill herself.

Ruth then wondered if she could ask a question; she wanted him to define the word *dissociative*.

"Maybe the best way to explain dissociation," he said, "is to compare it to sleepwalking."

"I wasn't asleep," Ruth said, and felt stupid for saying so.

"It's not the same, biologically or psychologically," Dr. Pickens explained. "It's just an analogy. As in sleepwalking, someone in a dissociative state can perform a goal-oriented activity and not know he's doing it, nor can he remember the deed afterward."

"So I really didn't know what I was doing?" Ruth asked. She already knew that herself but she was thrilled to hear a person in a position of authority confirm it.

"Right," Dr. Pickens said, and Ruth felt better than at any time since her confession.

"And the stabbing? How could I have done that?"

"In a sense the doctors were correct when they said that you couldn't have inflicted those wounds, but it wasn't really you. If you were in a true dissociative state, you—Ruth—wouldn't have felt the pain."

"Is being dissociative like having a split personality?" she asked.

"No," he said. "Your degree of dissociation didn't progress to the point of a fully separate alternate personality. The Poet never directly interacted with others."

Ruth thought about that for a moment. "Will I ever remember what happened when I was the Poet?" she asked.

"As we've discussed, the memories are probably inside you, and if you wanted, with some work you might be able to retrieve them."

Ruth thought about that too. "I'm not sure," she said, "that I ever want to get them back."

"You don't have to," Dr. Pickens said.

Ruth had nothing else to say, but again her apprehension eased.

The next day Dr. Pickens walked into Ruth's room with a surprise. "I'm giving you a pass to go home this weekend," he said. "Maybe we can even discharge you next week," he added.

Ruth was startled. She still feared she would never be let out until pronounced fully cured. Dr. Pickens had assured her, however, that the regular outpatient psychotherapy he planned for her would satisfy the authorities' requirement that she seek help, and that a weekend pass wasn't against the law.

Ed picked her up at Wesley the next morning and drove her home. In the car, after inquiring after each other's health, they lapsed into silence. Ruth stared out the window, thinking how bleak fall had become since she had been committed. The foliage was gone, storm windows were up, and the sidewalks were almost empty. The cold air felt filmy.

Ed turned into the driveway of their house, and Ruth saw that the garage door was open. "Oh, Ed!" she exclaimed, touched by what she saw inside. Their garage had always been much too small for the family's needs, and for years boxes and bicycles had blocked the passenger's side of the car, forcing Ruth to slide over the driver's seat to get out. But while she was at Wesley, Ed had straightened out the cartons and hung the bicycles so that Ruth could now exit from the passenger door.

"Thanks," she said, and he smiled.

Ruth walked inside the house and sat down on the living room couch. She hadn't planned on just sitting, but once there, she felt too overwhelmed by the last three weeks to move again.

Ed watched her for a while, concerned. He then took care of a few chores and came back into the room. "Would you like something to eat?" he asked.

Ruth nodded.

"How about hamburgers?"

She nodded again.

Ed went out to buy the burgers. When he returned, Ruth was still on the couch. But now, with a reason to get up, she went into the kitchen, where they ate and talked a little about the boys and family finances. Then they went down to the basement to watch television. Ruth looked around. She glanced at the painting of the bridge and the washing machine where she had written the letters, but she felt no fear or curiosity. She was too exhausted.

Ruth considered telling Ed more about her life in the hospital but decided against it, and Ed didn't ask. Ruth guessed they were both so overwhelmed by circumstances that they had nothing sensible to say.

Before going to sleep that night, Ruth took a long bath, the first time in weeks she was able to bathe without wondering if someone was going to walk in and join her. She fell asleep quickly, happy to lie next to Ed instead of a stranger.

Ed and Ruth spent a quiet Sunday together before her return to the hospital, and on Monday, because the weekend had gone well, Dr. Pickens released Ruth from Wesley with the proviso that she schedule an appointment to see him later in the week.

The next day after breakfast Ed went off to work and Ruth sat on the couch for a while, then in the dining room, and then she lay down, trying her best not to think or worry. Late that afternoon Dr. Pickens's office phoned to say that, because of a death in his family, he had left town and Ruth's therapy couldn't begin until the following week. Ruth's first response was unadulterated relief. Then she became apprehensive. The authorities had been informed that she had left Wesley for private therapy, but now that Dr. Pickens was away, would she have to return to lockup? She waited nervously, but no one called or came to arrest her.

3

On Wednesday Ruth looked at television, slept, and washed her hair three times. As a child she had felt that her hair was always dirty, and even now she shampooed it twice a day or more, particularly when she was upset.

She also baked an apple pie, read a magazine, wandered through the house, and then went into the back yard to stare at the phone wires, the hose, and the back gate. Perhaps it was strange that no witnesses had seen the Poet, but if she had truly done all they said, why had no one ever seen her either? She wondered if by remembering just one incident, she would make all the others return, but none of them did. The hose and the gate looked exactly as they always had; she could remember nothing more about them. So she went back inside the house, washed her hair again, and watched more television. She took another nap, and she tranquilized her nerves by crying.

Late in the afternoon the minister from their church

phoned to ask if he could visit. "Of course," Ruth replied. "Whenever you wish." She was pleased he had called, and she hoped he might offer some insight into her recent history or maybe even an explanation as to why she hadn't seen him in the hospital. But when he came to the house the next day, he sat in the living room, drinking coffee and eating cookies, and chatted only about the church and the weather. Finally Ruth, exasperated, mentioned that she had spotted his associate at the hospital.

The minister looked slightly surprised, which Ruth, now embarrassed, interpreted as an indication of her own rudeness. The associate hadn't stopped in to see her either, but she offered the minister an easy exit from the conversation. "Maybe he wanted to see me, but the staff wouldn't let him come in," she said. "I guess not everyone can."

"Oh, no," the minister said. "We can see anyone we want!"

Well, Ruth thought, I'm certainly being put in my place!

When the minister rose to leave, he smiled shyly and confided that Ruth had made this visit much easier on him than he had expected. Ruth smiled back and said good-bye, but later she wondered just who had been trying to help whom. Ruth and Ed believed in God, as always, but churches, they both decided, were hypocritical. If Ruth had been stricken with cancer, the ministers certainly would have visited her, and they would have been sympathetic and caring. But a situation such as hers was too confusing for them, Ruth guessed, and she thought everyone would just as soon she stayed away from the church. She told Ed how she felt, and he was sympathetic. Without any more discussion they began spending their Sunday mornings at home.

The following week, the day before her appointment with Dr. Pickens, Ruth drove past his office building to see where she could park, but also to hunt for anything that might help her face her future with equanimity. The more she knew ahead of time, the happier she felt. She had no real conception of how a session with Dr. Pickens might work. The only scenario she could imagine was of the two of them sitting in comfortable, overstuffed armchairs, each talking for equal amounts of time. Ruth worried that she didn't possess adequate skills to maintain her side of the conversation.

The fact was she dreaded therapy. Back in Richards people had always said that just one visit to a psychiatrist doomed a person forever, because after a shrink got through with your head, you could never be the same. Ruth had no conception of what psychiatrists did to heads, since none of her family or friends had ever visited one. She had seen the process only in the movies, where psychiatry seldom looked appealing. Basically therapy was, she felt, as frightening a prospect as jail.

On the morning of her first session, Ruth and Ed ate breakfast and chatted until Ed left for work. Ruth spent the rest of the time watching television and staring out the windows until her eyes watered. Then at three o'clock, an hour before she was due at Dr. Pickens's office, she couldn't bear sitting at home any longer. She got into the Oldsmobile and drove from one shopping mall to another, staying in the car and weaving through the parking lots. She was still fifteen minutes early when she walked up to the receptionist in Dr. Pickens's office.

"I'm Ruth Finley," she said. "I'm here to see Dr. Pickens." Ruth didn't dare look the woman in the eye.

The receptionist wrote Ruth's name down in a book and then led her upstairs to a small waiting room outside Dr. Pickens's office. "Please have a seat, and Dr. Pickens will be right out," she said, and then left.

Ruth sat down and thought, here I am. Now what? She worried for the next fifteen minutes until, at exactly four o'clock, Dr. Pickens opened the door and smiled. "Come in," he said.

She entered his office and sat down in a chair. Then she glanced around the room, looked at her feet, picked at her sleeves, and thought about what to cook for dinner. She had positive feelings toward Dr. Pickens, but she had nothing to say to him. Their sessions together in the hospital had lasted no longer than twenty minutes, and even then she had found them difficult. Now she was supposed to talk for more than twice that time.

Dr. Pickens didn't speak either. He sat in a chair near his desk, looking comfortable but silent. From outside in the hall Ruth heard the same kind of easy listening music she played in her own home. It occurred to her that Dr. Pickens wasn't going to open his mouth. What was going to happen? Could she endure fifty minutes of silence? Would he care? Her mind flooded with questions, none of which she dared ask aloud.

Finally Ruth couldn't tolerate the silence any longer. "What in the world do people talk about in here?" she asked abruptly.

"You can discuss anything that's on your mind," he said.

After thinking a few moments about what that might be, and feeling relieved that the man had actually spoken, she said, "Well, I'm worried that the police are still going to charge me with something." She talked about Mike Hill and Richard LaMunyon, neither of whom Dr. Pickens knew, and then she stopped. When Dr. Pickens didn't comment, she changed the subject and told him how much the publicity had upset her. "I'm a bad person who's done all this horrible stuff," she said, "and I don't even know why. The police think I did it on purpose. Can you imagine someone actually wanting to do that stuff? No one believes me. I think everyone just wants to squash me."

"What was so bad about what you did?" Dr. Pickens asked. "Did you hurt anyone?" These were the same questions he had asked at the hospital—questions that she would never ask herself. But her answers made it clear that she knew she hadn't hurt anyone else.

She didn't want to pursue this subject either. "I also feel bad about losing my job," she said, and they talked more about the phone company. Ruth wanted to know if Dr. Pickens thought she would be ready to work again soon. He nodded and said that his official recommendation to the judge would probably include a request for her reentry into society. His sense was that she could perform any job as long as her notoriety didn't conflict with her work. She couldn't be a receptionist, for example, which was fine with Ruth, who disliked high visibility anyway.

But then Ruth felt she had nothing more to say. Since they had already talked about her family in the hospital, Ruth guessed that Dr. Pickens would want her to discuss her upbringing. "I had a perfect childhood . . . ," she said. "We didn't have much money, but the family was very loving. We all got along well and we never fought. Let's see now. . . . Well, we played with toy cars, and I had dolls too. We didn't have many neighbors, so we spent a lot of time together. I was the most obedient and never got into any trouble. Now my brother Carl, or Morris—we used to call him that because my dad was named Carl too, but he had a different middle name—he never cared if Mother yelled at him. But I did everything I was told. . . .

"We lived in different houses until my grandfather died and we moved into the main farmhouse. It didn't have electricity, but it did have a better outhouse, a two-and-a-half holer. The half was for us kids. . . .

"We never traveled, except to Fort Scott or Nevada, Missouri, which was also close. When I was a kid, I thought Fort Scott was the biggest city in the world until I saw Nevada, which had this big courthouse on a square. . . ."

She waited for Dr. Pickens to say something. He didn't, so she continued. "It really was a wonderful childhood. We were poor, but we had everything we needed and we were healthy. I don't remember anything being wrong. Oh, I do know one thing we did that was bad. We were real ornery to our cousins from the city. Grandma Duncan had neighbors who raised these Shetland ponies that were cute but real mean. So we'd tell our cousins to play with them, and we'd help them through the fence and leave them with these horses. Well, of course they never got hurt or anything. I think that's probably as bad as we got. . . .

"My mother was very religious, and she used to read the Bible late into the night and sometimes she even fell asleep holding it in her hands. She sent all of us to Sunday school every week, although my dad wasn't as anxious to go as she was. She was a Methodist, but when her church got struck by lightning, they combined it with the Presbyterian church.''

Ruth told Dr. Pickens more stories about her early years, all of which alluded to a happy childhood. ''Everything was that good?'' Dr. Pickens asked.

Ruth thought it over. ''Well,'' she said, ''the only negative thing I can remember is that my parents told me when they had me, they had wanted a boy instead of a girl. Otherwise we had plenty to eat. It was a bad time, but our parents gave us everything we needed.''

Dr. Pickens made a mental note to be alert for other evidence of the Smocks' desire for a boy. He wondered if this hint might be the tip of some emotional iceberg.

While Ruth talked, she avoided Dr. Pickens's eyes, gazing instead at the floor. Dr. Pickens sensed that she felt the rules of therapy weren't sufficiently structured; she was finding it too easy to do or say something inadvertently that could lead to embarrassment or criticism. Clear instructions soothed Ruth, and she would have preferred more structure than less. She was also thinking, what in the world am I doing here?

Before the first session ended, Dr. Pickens told Ruth about his conversation with Ed. ''Again, it would be best for you to avoid talking about your therapy except in very general terms,'' he said. ''If you do, it might inhibit your openness here.''

''Not even with Ed?'' Ruth asked.

''Right.''

''What if he asks me?''

''As I said, it would be best not to talk about any specifics.''

How odd this was, to be forbidden to talk to one's own husband. Ruth didn't know how Ed would cope.

Would he understand, or would he protest? She contemplated the possibilities until Dr. Pickens spoke again, startling her.

"It's time to stop for today," he said, and she smiled slightly, trying not to give away how surprised she had been to hear his voice.

Dr. Pickens rose, walked to the door, and opened it for Ruth, who had a difficult time making eye contact as she left. "Bye," she murmured, and she slipped past him and down the hall.

On the outside of his office door Dr. Pickens kept a metal clip under which the receptionist placed messages that had come in while he was in session. He now took his messages, snapping the clip loudly. It was the last sound Ruth heard as she walked quickly down the stairs and out of the building. Once in the parking lot she almost ran to her car. She wondered if she had any energy left to drive. Thank goodness that's over, she thought.

When she arrived home, Ruth went to bed and lay under the covers, trying to sort out what had happened in that office. No matter, she thought. She had to return in two days and then had to go back again and again. She had barely enough to say today; she was convinced that Thursday would be worse. What about the rest of the fall and the months that followed? For all she knew, she could be sitting there silently, forever.

Ed came home from work an hour later. "How did it go?" he asked. "What happened?"

"I'm not supposed to talk about it, remember?" Ruth said.

Ed frowned. He wasn't adjusting easily to the idea

of Ruth talking to a stranger rather than to
least tell me how you are," he said.

"I'm okay," Ruth said. That night she made spa-
ghetti and garlic bread for dinner, then watched television for the rest of the evening. Feeling weary and
disconcerted, she went to bed early.

4

Dr. Pickens's associates called their building
the Wichita Psychiatric Center; located in a charm-
less, semi-industrialized neighborhood, it was an inex-
pensive relic of the 1950s: unattractive, covered in
rectangular wood paneling, and surrounded by flat as-
phalt parking lots on its north and south sides. At any
given time approximately ten people worked inside the
building, among them transcriptionists, nurses, two
receptionists, three full-time psychologists, and five
psychiatrists. (To avoid what they felt was the local
social stigma connoted by the word *psychiatric,* the
doctors later shortened the name to "The Center."
Ruth told Dr. Pickens the new name made it sound
like a gym.)

Dr. Pickens's office was on the second floor, and
like the building, the room was paneled in wood. It
was windowless and contained four chairs—but no
couch—and a small desk. On one wall he had hung
two nondescript pictures. He kept no photographs or
personal belongings in the room in order to prevent his

patients from learning any details about his private life. This impersonality baffled Ruth, and when she later mentioned it, Dr. Pickens explained that the patient's lack of personal knowledge helped promote therapeutic transference, the psychoanalytic process in which the patient unknowingly focuses feelings on the therapist, or has expectations of the therapist, that are actually directed toward an emotionally important person in the patient's childhood, such as a mother or father.

Transference, Dr. Pickens told Ruth, occurs in all our lives: everyone projects feelings from childhood into day-to-day relationships, in both positive and negative ways. Psychoanalytic therapy is structured to foster that transference. To achieve success, the psychotherapist must be empathic, but he must also avoid direct expressions of his own emotion or opinions so that the patient can project personal feelings and expectations onto the therapist, who thus experiences that patient's emotional conflicts in the context of therapy, rather than hearing them secondhand. The therapist then points out these feelings, helping the patient work through distortions in her view of herself and others.

Ruth understood Dr. Pickens intellectually, but her first reaction, which she kept to herself, was, hogwash!

The office's clock also annoyed Ruth. Dr. Pickens had placed it where he could see the clock's face by moving his eyes slightly, but the patient could not. Ruth thought that the clock should be situated so that either she couldn't see him looking or it was visible to everyone.

* * *

Ruth arrived ten minutes early for her second session on Thursday. She was too apprehensive simply to arrive and commence a session, so she sat in the waiting room and stared at the closed door, hoping whoever was inside would talk past the hour. Oh please, please, be late, she thought. But once again Dr. Pickens opened the door at exactly four o'clock, and Ruth realized that if another patient had been inside his office before her, he or she had already left.

Ruth walked in quickly and sat down, but she couldn't talk. Her mind wandered, although her primary preoccupation was her inability to speak. Finally, almost forcibly opening her mouth, she picked up where the first session had left off, discussing her mother and the farm and her relatives. "I just have so many nice memories," she said. "Let's see now. Well, in the winter our bedroom got so cold, Mother would give us a feather bed. And when it was time to go to sleep, first I'd throw my sister on the bed, and then I'd jump in and we'd nestle down in the feathers. If it was really cold, they'd let us heat an iron and wrap it in newspapers and take it to bed with us. . . ." Ruth stopped talking. Dr. Pickens waited for her to resume.

"I guess I really am such a bad person," Ruth said.

"You hurt yourself far more than you hurt anyone else," Dr. Pickens repeated.

"Maybe." Ruth stopped. "How could I have done all that stuff?" she suddenly asked. "I don't remember it. And what about the calls Ed heard, and the newspaper clipping, and the man on the phone? I know that a man came up to me on the street. I remember that. I think."

She stopped speaking again, and then, deciding not to continue her questions, she said, "I'm upset about not being able to work.'' She talked about the phone company for a few minutes, and when she was through discussing her job, she admitted feeling some resentment toward Ed. He had been talking to one of their neighbors, who had accused Ed of knowing Ruth was the Poet all along. It was impossible, the neighbor said, for anyone living with Ruth not to have guessed.

Ed had repeated the conversation word for word to her. ''You see what I'm having to take?'' Ed had asked angrily. Ruth wanted to remind him—but didn't —that she was the one who had suffered the humiliation, not him.

''Did Ed know what you were doing?'' Dr. Pickens asked.

''Of course not,'' Ruth said. ''I wish he had. Then he would have stopped it.''

Dr. Pickens suspected Ed wasn't fully supportive of Ruth's therapy, but he didn't want to pursue the subject. He thought Ruth would address it when she was ready, and since he doubted that that would happen for some time, when she let the subject drop, so did he.

Ruth felt she had nothing left to say and spent the remainder of her session explaining where she had gone to grade school and why, when she was sixteen, her parents had sent her to live in Fort Scott: she was the only girl left in her high school class, and they thought she would get a better education elsewhere. As long as she was in a larger city, she could also get a job and save a little money. But that memory made her think about her recent trouble at the phone company, and she stopped talking.

At home Ruth and Ed dutifully obeyed Dr. Pickens's request to avoid any discussion of therapy. Both of them knew, however, that even if they had been given permission, they still would have refrained from any exchange. They also never brought up the Poet, because, Ruth thought, they had nothing intelligent to say. Instead they talked as they always had, about work and family, and often about the television producers who continued to call and ask Ruth for the rights to her story.

One producer phoned during the first week of therapy. "May I speak with Ruth Finley?" asked a woman with a British accent.

"This is Ruth."

"Are you in for Jack Sartin?" Ruth didn't have a chance to say yes or no, or to ask who Jack Sartin was, because the woman put her on hold. Ruth waited impatiently, but she didn't hang up. She felt guilty because she could tell the man was calling long-distance.

"Hello, Ruth?" a man's voice asked.

"Yes," Ruth said.

"Jack Sartin. I'm going to do your story, Ruth," the man said. "I love women's pictures. I've produced three movies this decade."

Ed watched from across the room as Ruth listened. He was used to it. Ruth always let these people talk and talk because she didn't want to hurt their feelings. "They don't have feelings," Ed said. "They just want to make money off you."

Ruth agreed with him, but whenever Mr. Sartin called, she listened politely to his pitch. Several other people phoned or wrote letters about collaborating on books and articles, and Ruth always had a difficult time saying no. She didn't want anyone to dislike her, but she wished they would leave her alone, and so eventually she turned everyone down by never saying yes. Both Ed and Ruth were convinced a book or a movie would just produce more negative publicity. I'm a bad person, Ruth thought. Just look at all these people coming out of the woodwork to prove it.

When Ruth was in her second week of therapy, she received a call from the head of her department at Southwestern Bell. The man insisted on talking to both Ed and Ruth, and they decided he must have thought Ruth was too deranged to talk on the phone by herself. The man told them that executives at the phone company had discussed Ruth's "problem" further and had decided that they were concerned about her "health." Ruth felt that the man referred to her "condition" so gingerly that his words sounded like euphemisms in quotes. Finally he suggested that she consult a company doctor. Ed put the receiver aside and told Ruth, who shrugged. "Okay," she said.

"Okay," Ed said.

When Ruth saw the doctor at his office a week later, she realized then that when the man had said "doctor," he had meant "psychiatrist." The psychiatrist spent most of the session asking Ruth about her background and the Poet, questions to which she had grown accustomed, but Ruth thought he seemed unable to sort out the facts. He kept repeating himself and then became muddled, referring to Ruth's sons as daughters and calling the Poet a "he," a "she," and once an "it." Ruth thought that the doctor was either weird or unprepared or that perhaps this was his own special methodology. She remembered from Wesley lockup that some of the psychiatrists there had odd ideas, such as the one who in the name of treatment had forced her friend Mary to scrub the bathroom repeatedly.

The doctor summarized the visit by telling Ruth that she was very confused. Ruth wanted to say, "No kidding, doc," but she had also learned from lockup to watch her words. The doctor then added that perhaps Ruth could return to work in the future, but if so, she would be situated in a different department. Ruth figured that he was telling her she couldn't return to her old job but wasn't going to do so in plain English. She also guessed that the phone company wanted a letter in her file with his recommendation.

Ruth left his office and didn't think much about their discussion until she received a bill in the mail. She and Ed had assumed the phone company, which had made the appointment, was covering the cost, and they were both angry. "He was a jerk," Ruth told Dr. Pickens during her next session. "And now they want me to pay him? I'd really like to write a letter and complain."

"Why don't you?" Dr. Pickens asked.

The idea floored Ruth. She hadn't considered that such an option existed; instead her fantasy was that Dr. Pickens would take care of it for her. She even had it in her mind what he would say: "That big old meanie. I'll write to the medical board of whatever and tell them this guy hasn't done my good patient Ruth Finley right." When Dr. Pickens didn't offer to do that, she was disappointed but resigned. And she was suddenly very curious about him, wanting to ask questions, although she remained quiet.

Most of Ruth's therapy that fall consisted of either long silences or her memories of what she considered an exemplary childhood. "It was real difficult for my folks to keep everything going," she said. "They were good parents, but it was a tough time. That's why we were encouraged to survive, not to succeed. I think that's also why we all left home so early. Not because, you know, we didn't like our parents or anything. We really loved our parents."

Ruth talked less about her father than her mother, whom she praised vigorously. "She was very strong," she said. "She didn't want us to be bragged on by anyone. She wanted us to be like her. If someone said anything complimentary to me, she'd find a flaw in it because she didn't want us to become conceited. I guess maybe that's why none of us ever had a lot of self-confidence."

Sometimes Ruth felt that Dr. Pickens was challenging her on these memories.

"You feel that your mother was flawless?" he asked.

Ruth bristled. "Yes, she was," she said.

She realized later that all he had done was repeat her words, but she questioned his tone. Yet when he did talk, his voice was kind. Still, she thought, there was something unnerving in all this, but she couldn't identify it.

Ruth continued to describe various incidents from her childhood. "There was this railroad bridge nearby where we lived," she said, "with water way down underneath. What we used to do was, we'd wait till the train got almost on us, and then we'd jump off the bridge into the water."

Dr. Pickens noted that Ruth's childhood appeared to be composed of normal experiences; she didn't seem to have had major inhibitions or compulsions, and her peer relationships had been sound.

Occasionally Ruth talked about Ed and their sons. Ed had been adopted, she told Dr. Pickens, but his parents, Elmer and Josephine, had never told him. He found out only accidentally, through a friend, and when he asked Josephine to confirm the story, she became enraged and refused to discuss the subject again. He was sixteen at the time. So he dropped it, nor did he ever try to learn the identity of his biological parents. Yet Ruth said Ed's childhood was as exemplary as hers, and he loved his family very much.

Ruth told Dr. Pickens that Elmer had owned and operated a drugstore but Ed had wanted to be an artist. For as long as he could remember, he had painted or drawn, and he had genuine talent. His college advisers made it clear, however, that artists don't earn a decent living, and they strongly recommended that Ed take up something more serious, such as accounting. That became his career, although he still painted whenever he could.

Ed and Ruth had met while living in the same apartment house in Fort Scott. Ruth thought Ed had nice eyes and charming manners, and soon he was the first man who made her nervous. She hadn't dated much and suspected that this might be love. Ed too was in love, and a year later, while they were holding hands in a parked car near Rock Creek Lake, he asked her to marry him. Before agreeing, Ruth asked if he knew about her assault three years earlier. Ed shrugged and said he had heard about it from a friend, and anyway, he added, it didn't matter.

They were married in a Fort Scott Presbyterian church. Ruth's brother, Carl, was the best man. Ed was twenty-two, Ruth twenty. For their honeymoon, they borrowed Elmer Finley's car and drove around Kansas and Missouri for a week.

Regarding her own children, Ruth thought that both had turned out well. The older son, who resembled his parents in looks and spirit, studied conscientiously and was well-mannered. After graduating from Wichita State, he went on to do graduate work in engineering and chemistry before eventually attending medical school; he was now a doctor. Bruce, however, the younger son, was more a product of the 1960s; he continually hassled with the police and argued with Ed until one day, when he was eighteen, he walked out the door and didn't return for two years, at which time he called from a nearby pay phone. Ed invited him over for dinner—it was Christmas—and Bruce accepted. No one discussed his absence.

Bruce never graduated from college. Instead he moved to Colorado and tried out a few different careers before settling into a computer-related job in Denver, where many of his high school friends had moved. From what Ruth said, Dr. Pickens surmised that the relationship between both sons and their parents was amicable and dutiful, though not particularly intimate.

"Do you have any children?" Ruth asked Dr. Pickens.

"Why do you ask?"

"Well, I just want to know."

Dr. Pickens explained to Ruth that in order to facilitate the therapeutic transference they had discussed previously, he generally wouldn't answer personal questions, just as he kept no clues in the office to his private life. "But you can gain insight into yourself if you ask these questions and guess at some answers," he said. "We can then explore your answers together."

Ruth felt bad. Had she violated one of his special rules? She stopped talking and stared at the floor. Thoughts darted through her head, but she edited them carefully, because she felt too insecure to speak.

When Ruth didn't talk, and was trying not to think about her problems, she counted the pencils on Dr. Pickens's desk, the books on his shelves, or anything else in her mind. When she had nothing concrete to count, she just counted numbers, going from one to a hundred, stopping, and starting again at one. The counting bothered her. She realized that all through her life, whenever she was under stress or unhappy, she had counted, and yet she had never mentioned it to anyone. Now she took a gamble. "I count a lot," she said sheepishly.

Dr. Pickens nodded and asked her why she had mentioned it. "I just do it so much," Ruth said, and then she explained how much, and when, and why it seemed strange.

"Perhaps when you're counting," Dr. Pickens said, "what you're doing is channeling your mind so you can avoid thinking about other things."

"I see," Ruth said. His comment made her wonder what it could be that she wasn't thinking about. She shivered, and this in turn started her counting again.

After another long silence Dr. Pickens said, "It's time to stop for the day."

Ruth looked up from the floor. Once again she was surprised that Dr. Pickens would just ask her to leave when she had been in the middle of a thought and was perhaps even ready to talk. This was one of several aspects of therapy that bothered her. She looked at the floor so much she seldom saw his face. If she was talking when her time was almost up, Dr. Pickens would simply say so. She considered that rude behavior, but she kept her opinion to herself.

By the first week of November 1981 the county had made a decision. "No Charges to Be Filed against

Poet" ran the headline in the *Eagle-Beacon*. The article quoted District Attorney Clark Owens: "I've now had a chance to review [Finley's] psychiatric report . . . I have reached the decision that there is no reason to pursue any criminal prosecution." He agreed with Dr. Pickens's conclusion that there was no evidence to indicate that Ruth had intended any malicious action.

The article ended with Owens's comment that Ruth had escaped detection as the Poet "because her actions appeared normal to people around her." At home on East Indianapolis, Ruth read his words in the paper and tried to remember how it felt to be perceived as normal; she wondered if it was something she could recapture. Still she was pleased to know she wouldn't go to jail.

The *Eagle-Beacon* had also published a lengthy three-part series on the Poet that Ed had clipped and saved, but Ruth had never been able to read any of it. When she mentioned the clippings to Dr. Pickens, he said, "Perhaps you could bring them in and we can read them here." Ruth agreed, but back home when she saw the papers, she could barely touch them. They felt tainted and foul. She threw them in a bag and tossed it in the car.

At her next session she took the bag into Dr. Pickens's office and handed him the articles. He glanced at them and then gave them back to her. "Do you think you could read them out loud?" he asked.

Ruth was distressed; she hadn't expected this. But she didn't dare disagree, so she paused for a moment, trying to gain some strength, and started to read. " 'She was climbing the basement stairs when the phone rang. It was ten thirty P.M., and her husband, Ed, was in the hospital. A night in early June nineteen seventy-seven. Ruth Finley said she thought the caller was an old friend. "He asked if I used to be Ruth Smock. I was so nice to him—" ' "

Ruth burst into tears. Because she couldn't go on, Dr. Pickens told her that she could read the articles at home instead. She nodded, but she knew she wouldn't.

Dr. Pickens never asked Ruth direct questions about the Poet, allowing her to discuss the subject only when she wished. He did ask, however, about the incident at Fort Scott.

Ruth shrugged. "There isn't that much to say."

Dr. Pickens didn't reply, so Ruth began to tell him about the incident's aftermath. She had passed out just before the man branded her with the iron, she said. Later, after she came to, she waited silently in the dark in case the man was still in the room. Only when she was sure she was alone did she get up from the floor and call her parents, who showed up shortly thereafter, along with a doctor and the police. Ruth said the police had questioned her at length: Did you know the man? Could you identify him? What did he look like? Where did he go? Where did he touch you? Ruth remembered answering as best she could, but she felt the police were brusque and angry because she couldn't give them a better description.

That night she went back to Richards with her parents, but a few days later they told her it was time she returned to Fort Scott. Ruth consented, but when she got to the apartment house she became so sick with fear that she vomited every night and Faye had to find her another place to live.

Dr. Pickens listened carefully as Ruth told him the story. Over the past month he had been giving it a great deal of consideration, wondering if the assault could be the primary cause of Ruth's repression. His hunch was that the incident hadn't been sufficiently powerful to create the Poet. He suspected that the event was a screen memory—a memory from later in life that retained some aspects of an earlier, more severe trauma. There was also the possibility, Dr. Pickens realized, that the Fort Scott assault had never occurred at all. He didn't mention this to Ruth, but the entire incident, like the kidnapping and the stabbing, could have been a consequence of dissociation. Dr. Pickens believed that something had happened to Ruth in her room, for he had learned that she didn't fabricate without a trigger. It wasn't critical, however, to determine if the attack had taken place as Ruth described it. Besides the practical point that there were no witnesses, and therefore no one could ever know for certain, Ruth herself believed the incident was real, and its emotional impact on her life was lingering and substantive.

"What are your thoughts and feelings about me?" Dr. Pickens asked Ruth. It was the late fall, Kansas-cold outside. The session had only just begun, and Ruth wasn't through warming herself.

The question surprised her. The subject had arisen before, but he had never asked her outright for an opinion. Ruth wasn't sure how she was supposed to respond; it was such an odd question. Oh, shut up, Dr. Pickens! she thought. I don't have any feelings for you, you old bat! But she realized it was best not to say this out loud, and regardless, since they never discussed him, she knew her reply would become the focus of a discussion about her instead.

"I don't know," she said, and then glanced at his face to gauge his response. But there he was, looking at her without any visible expression. Just once she wanted him to stick out his tongue or make a face or show some emotion, but he never did. She felt perturbed, and she was sure he was feeling superior to her. How mortifying, she thought. Here she was, talking to him about things she had never even told Ed, and there he was, looking at her as if he were God.

After returning home Ruth sometimes jotted entries about her session in a notebook. "Why do I do this?" she wrote one evening. "Come in, sit down and start babbling how everything is fine. I know it's not and you certainly know it isn't. I'm very down on everything. I'm afraid. I'm sorry for all I did—the humiliation I've brought on myself and my family. I have always denied to myself I have feelings. If something makes me aware of having feelings, I can stop—sort of freeze myself and repeat over and over—I don't care, I don't care. Soon I don't—why can't I tell you this? Part of me thinks you might toss me out on my ear. I know you won't."

She wrote the notes for only a few months, and she addressed them all to Dr. Pickens, but she never showed them to a soul.

5

BY LATE 1981 THE BTK STRANGLER SEEMED TO HAVE
vanished from Wichita. Not only had he stopped killing, he had also stopped writing letters to the police
and the media. But updates on the Poet continued to
appear on television and in the newspapers: accounts
of Ruth's institutionalization, the decisions being
made in the district attorney's office, the cost of the
police investigation. Whenever Ruth heard or read
these reports, she felt humiliated. Now everyone in
town knew just how crazy she was, she thought, and
exactly how much time and money Wichita had
wasted on her.

One day Ed came home from work and found Ruth
sitting at the dining room table, looking at the newspaper and crying. All she could say was, "I wish they
would all go take a flying fuck." Ed put his hand over
hers, patted it, and said that he wished they would
take one too.

Ruth spent much of that fall in tears, although she
tried to look composed when others were nearby. She

kept thinking what a horrible person she was, what terrible things she had done, and she couldn't understand why, which confused and scared her. When the Poet was loose, she had felt both protected and constricted. Now she was free to travel wherever she chose, but her preference was to stay home. When she had to go out, as much as she disliked asking for help, she often called Jean or Carl to drive her around. She refused to visit many of the stores where she used to shop, because she thought people were looking at her strangely. At home she saw few friends. Occasionally Joyce Middleton dropped in for coffee, and the two carried on as before, laughing and gossiping, but they never mentioned the Poet. A few other people came by too, including the church organist, Helen Blakemore, and her husband, Glenn, and Ray Weller, a financial adviser who was helping Ed and Ruth budget their money to cover Dr. Pickens's psychiatric bills.

That Christmas Ed gave Ruth her present a little early. It came in a large box, which Ed recommended that Ruth open at once. Before Ruth could take off the bow, the box began opening itself and an English bulldog puppy poked his head out. (Sherman had died a few months earlier.) Ruth named the new puppy Gingersnap.

But Ruth's primary thought over the holiday was, thank God, I won't have to see Dr. Pickens. He'll be away!

Although he didn't tell her, Dr. Pickens was pleased with Ruth's progress. Above all he felt that they had already formed a strong therapeutic alliance—so much so that even if Ruth weren't obliged to see him, he was confident she would come voluntarily. Still Ruth was vulnerable to shame, and her self-image highly impaired. Furthermore the continual descriptions of her perfect childhood concerned Dr. Pickens. No family was flawless, but he knew Ruth wasn't consciously lying. Rather he suspected that her mind was filled with other perceptions, which she was hiding from both herself and him. As yet he didn't know what these perceptions were, however, or why she was repressing them.

Therapy could make Ruth so despondent that on many days she could barely breathe. Once, in a session just after the holidays, when she thought she was going to pass out, she surprised herself by voicing her feelings. "I wish I could get out of here," she said.

"There's the door," Dr. Pickens said calmly. "You're always free to leave if you wish. But we can't deal with your problems if you're not here."

Ruth was shocked. Yeah, she thought, that's what he'd like, to get rid of me. But I'm sticking it out and he's going to have to put up with me until my time is up. She didn't dare say this out loud; she was afraid that if she did, Dr. Pickens would indeed throw her out of his office and tell her never to return. She suspected that he didn't really want her to leave anyway and was only reminding her that he couldn't force her participation.

The long stretches of quiet during her sessions still left her feeling uncomfortable. At home she was accustomed to filling such silences, but here she had no clue about what she was supposed to say; there were no conversational niceties. She sat in the chair, and Dr. Pickens waited for her to talk. She wished they could have had just a little small talk first, to warm up her tongue, but she knew that she couldn't ask for that because he would want to know her thoughts.

For the most part Ruth continued to discuss her childhood. "There weren't many people around, so we spent a lot of time alone," she said one day. "The closest house belonged to a farmer and his wife. The man was nice to me, and he used to tell me what a pretty girl I was and what pretty hair I had.

"Let's see . . . ," she continued, and she suddenly felt a blast of emotions that made her think of a tornado. "Once we were over at Grandma Duncan's canning beans when this storm came up. My Uncle Ross, he was our bachelor uncle, he tied a rope from a porch post to the cellar, and we helped each other all get down there. When the storm finally blew away, we went back upstairs and the roof had moved several inches."

Ruth also talked about farm life during the Depression. "One of the worst things we had to do was clean all the crap out of the chicken house, because we'd get chicken lice in our hair and Mother would have to wash it to kill the lice. We had a lot of chickens. I remember that whenever we were going to have one for dinner, my dad would just grab it and wring its neck. But when Mother killed it, she'd chop off its head and it'd flop around for a while. I always remember Mother chopping the heads off those chickens."

Ruth smiled rigidly, thinking she was recalling a pleasant memory. But Dr. Pickens saw her entire body tense, and he wondered if she was revealing that she feared her mother, who, if Ruth weren't careful, would chop off her head too.

In a subsequent session Ruth remembered another incident concerning her mother and chickens. "My mother used to paint their legs with poison to keep them from getting mites," she said. "And she kept the brush behind this buffet we had on the back porch.

Once I climbed up there and found the brush, and of course I started playing with it. Then, being the little thumb sucker I was, I put my thumb in my mouth. Then I got sick and ran inside, and I was foaming at the mouth. My mother was scared to death. She ran back outside and flagged down a neighbor who was driving by and told him what was going on. When he asked what she was going to do, she said that she was just going to wait until my dad came in from the fields. But the neighbor said they had to do something, so they came back inside, and my mother shook me and got me to tell her what I had eaten. I guess I said it was that old brush or something, so then she knew what it was. They made me vomit. But it bothered me later that she wanted to wait for my dad to come back from the fields. I probably would have been dead by then.''

Ruth stopped for a moment, listening to what she had just said. ''No, I wouldn't have,'' she said. ''It was hard, raising kids on a place like that.''

After that session Ruth wrote in her notebook: ''It is a heavy load when you know not a single person cares. I deeply wish someone did. After what I have done, why should they? Why can't I go in your office and tell you this? Maybe I am afraid you might care and there's no way I could stand that.''

As Ruth began to speak more freely, Dr. Pickens asked her specific questions about her family. Did her parents express physical affection or verbal affection? Who in the family was responsible for discipline? Was one sibling favored over another? The questions about siblings were easier for Ruth to answer than those about her parents.

''Well,'' Ruth said, ''I always thought Mother liked

Jean better than me. She was always saying that Jean had prettier hair, and she was nicer to Jean than to me. But of course Jean was more attractive than I was."

Dr. Pickens took note of the issue of sibling rivalry and how Ruth used it to feed her negative self-image: her parents preferred boys to girls; her sister was prettier than she was. There was something wrong with her; Ruth was convinced of this because she was sure her mother felt that way too.

Ruth stopped talking, then resumed. "Of course," she said, "by the time Jean came along the family was doing much better. And it wasn't so tough for my mother anymore."

During the next session, after Ruth had apologized for giving voice to an unfavorable memory about her mother, she added more to the story about the poison. She remembered that her mother later told her that if she hadn't been such a terrible thumb sucker, she wouldn't have become so ill. Her words scared Ruth into thinking that she was going to die from sucking her thumb, and Faye had to sew little cotton mittens to slip over Ruth's thumbs at night. "Yet I took the blame for all this," Ruth said. "I think that was a big load for a child to bear." Then she shook her head. "No," she added quickly. "It was just right."

When Ruth was a child, the Smocks never discussed sex. Ruth said this struck her as odd because, growing up on a farm, she often saw animals mating. "Once we had a dog who was in heat," Ruth recalled, "and one day when we let her out, a male dog ran up to the porch, and the two of them were, you know, getting it on, and my brother and I watched. Then my dad yelled at us. 'Get back here in the house!' he said. 'We're not running a three-ring circus around here!' "

Another time Ruth asked her mother why cows and horses had just one baby, but cats and dogs had many. Faye said she didn't know, but Ruth asked again and again. Finally her mother said, "Ruth, why do you have to talk this filth?"

When Dr. Pickens asked her how she felt about her mother's reaction, Ruth immediately felt angry and flushed. "Well, she was right not to answer me, of course," she said, and she returned to more pleasant childhood reminiscences.

One day Ruth began to recall a strange, obscure memory. "I'm sitting on someone's lap," she told Dr. Pickens, "and I'm naked, and it's not my mother's lap." Her body tightened as she talked.

She stopped, and after she had remained silent for a while, Dr. Pickens spoke. "What are you feeling?" he asked.

"Oh, nothing," Ruth said, but that wasn't true. She felt terrible. "I think it's my neighbor or his wife," she said. "Yes, it's his wife, and she's wiping something off me." Ruth shivered. "I don't want to talk about it," she said.

"That's okay," Dr. Pickens said.

"I don't," Ruth protested, as if he had told her she had to talk.

"Fine," he said.

Ruth pushed the memory aside. Suddenly she started to cry, and Dr. Pickens asked again what she was feeling.

Ruth decided that her present-day experiences must be causing her tears. "It's so difficult to go any-where," she said. "It's hard for someone to have to shop and do things and have people stare." She continued to cry but then said, "And anyway, it's not right to cry."

"Why shouldn't you cry?" Dr. Pickens asked. "You've been through a lot of painful experiences."

"Right," Ruth said sarcastically. "I suppose that means someone could cry in front of other people whenever they wanted to!"

That night Ruth made another entry in her notebook: "Maybe I think if I try hard enough, you will believe I have no feelings and mark on my sheet: 'This person has no feelings—never has had and never will. She doesn't care. She is tough.' "

Now that's the mark of a strong person, Ruth thought, someone who isn't influenced by her own emotions.

By January, two months into therapy, Ruth had allowed a few more negative memories of her childhood to slip out, usually when Dr. Pickens asked her direct questions. Once Ruth talked about how often her mother had called her a crybaby. Then she stopped talking.

"Can you tell me more about your mother and crying?" Dr. Pickens asked.

"Well," Ruth said, "as a kid I wouldn't let my mother out of my sight. I'd always cry when she wasn't around. It was very embarrassing for her, and a lot of her relatives were upset that she had this crybaby daughter. They'd try to help her by taking me away, just to get me on my own.

"When it was time to go to school, everyone knew it would be real hard on me. So one day before school started, Mother fixed me a little lunch and had me visit school with a teacher friend of hers for the whole day, so I could spend it away from home. Well, it was one of the worst days of my life. I cried and cried.''

Ruth's report of her clinging behavior indicated to Dr. Pickens one of two instigating factors—an over-protective mother or a rejecting mother. In Ruth's case he now knew enough about Faye to assume she had been the latter.

''Another time my parents took me to Fort Scott,'' Ruth said, ''because they had come up with a plan to help me. There was this Penney's in town with both a main and a side entrance. So my mother took me to the main entrance, and the idea was that I was to walk all by myself to the side entrance, where my dad was waiting. If I couldn't do it, I could turn back to my mother.''

Ruth stopped talking.

''So what did you do?'' Dr. Pickens asked.

''Oh,'' Ruth said, ''I just stood in the middle of the store and cried. No wonder my mother was so upset.''

''How do you feel about that?'' Dr. Pickens asked.

''My mother worked very hard,'' Ruth said quickly. ''It was a tough life. I was a difficult child.''

She paused. ''I probably did cry too much too,'' she said. Then she thought for a moment and added, ''You know, there was one nice thing about crying. My mother used to tell me how ugly it made me. So whenever we were going someplace, she'd take me aside and powder my nose, and that smelled nice.''

On January 8 Ruth came into Dr. Pickens's office feeling dizzy. Her recent dreams had been unpleasant, and although she didn't remember them well, they had reminded her somehow of an incident from her past that she hadn't yet mentioned. Now for some reason she brought it up. ''Once I went over to this neighbor's house with my folks. It was that man I've mentioned, the one who lived close to us. He was maybe a few years older than my father, and he was a farmer too. Most everyone nearby was.''

Ruth stopped speaking. Dr. Pickens waited while she looked at the floor and smoothed her skirt.

A minute later Ruth started again. She was breathing heavily. "No one had electricity then, so when it got dark outside, it got dark inside too. I remember someone lit a kerosene lamp.''

She stopped talking again, and Dr. Pickens could see that she looked pained, as if she were physically ill; her forehead was creased and her posture sagged.

"Anyway,'' Ruth resumed, "the man took me inside. I guess my folks were talking to his wife. He led me to the living room, then into the bedroom.''

Ruth stopped and started several more times as she told the story. "It was dark and the man had this rope and he tied me to the end of the bed and left me there. He didn't do anything, but he just left me there and I started to cry. They could hear me in the kitchen, and I guess the man heard me too, since he came back in and untied me. Then Dad came in and asked the man what was going on. The man said we'd been playing a game, and then I started to cry again.

"Well, since Mother thought I was a crybaby, it upset her that I was crying again. But I was really scared, and I was crying one of those cries where you choke back your sobs because you're too afraid. So the man's wife gave me a cookie, and they told me to eat it so I would stop. But I couldn't stop, and we had to go home.''

It took Ruth much of the session to tell the story, and then she fell completely silent. Dr. Pickens waited until he thought she was ready to talk again before he asked her how she felt about the incident.

Ruth was adamant. "I don't have any feelings about it," she insisted. "I don't care. It's over and done with." That was how she should feel, she thought. It was simply a bad moment from her past. But she changed her mind and considered telling Dr. Pickens that she thought her parents should have been more concerned. Then, surprising herself even more, she told him. "I can't believe that they weren't more caring. They must have known something was going on. Dad probably saw the rope the man used. Why didn't they say anything?"

"Why do you think they didn't?" Dr. Pickens asked.

Ruth shrugged. "I don't know."

"How does that make you feel?"

"I guess it makes me a little angry."

"How do you feel now?"

Ruth thought about it. "I guess I am angry. The poor little girl. Why didn't her mother and father do something about her?"

Dr. Pickens wondered where this story was leading. It wasn't sufficiently traumatic in itself to have caused Ruth's repression, but he knew Ruth wouldn't be able to tell him any more until she was ready.

That night Ruth jotted down in her notebook: "Today I told you about being tied up. You would not just listen, you asked me how that made me feel and I told you. I can't believe I told you that and that I didn't like it that my mom and dad had taken it so lightly. I felt rather bad all evening that I did that. I will never do it again. I will have to be more on guard."

* * *

"I'd like to talk more about that incident," Ruth said during their next session. She had been thinking about the story all week.

"Go ahead," Dr. Pickens said.

"I've decided that my parents were right," she said.

"You have?"

"Yes. I shouldn't have cried. I was a bad girl, and my parents did the best they could."

Ruth spoke this last sentence in an ambivalent manner, and Dr. Pickens was suddenly reminded of Chinese Communist prison camps, where prisoners were forced to confess to sins they had not committed and were then rewarded. Ruth seemed to be expecting him to confirm that her confession was correct—that she was a bad girl—and yet at the same time he heard a glimmer of hope in her voice that perhaps he might not think she was such a bad person after all.

"Is that how you feel?" he asked her.

"Yes," Ruth said. "It was all my fault."

"Maybe you had a right to feel angry. Have you considered that?" Dr. Pickens asked.

But Ruth didn't want to consider that possibility; she found it frightening. "I mustn't blame them for small things," she said, and changed the subject.

Ruth started the next session with more memories of her mother. "She was always worried about what her friends thought of me. Mostly she was afraid they'd see how much I always wanted to be with her, and this was of course wrong. So if I spent too much time with her, she'd push me away."

"How do you feel about that?" Dr. Pickens asked.

"She worked hard," Ruth said promptly. "I wasn't a good child."

Once more Dr. Pickens asked how she felt.

"You have to understand, it was very different back then, and she had a tough time," Ruth said, and she thought, he keeps asking me this question. Why do I defend her every time? The more I talk about her, the more things I think of that make me unhappy. But Ruth wasn't one of those people like Christina Crawford, whose *Mommie Dearest* she had read. It wasn't fair to make mean-spirited comments about mothers who weren't present to defend themselves. Anyway, Faye Smock was hardly Joan Crawford.

"It's hard to criticize your mother," Dr. Pickens said. "I understand that. But sometimes, even though you say she did her best, it sounds as though you felt hurt."

"Maybe," Ruth admitted. "I don't know. She had such a hard life."

Ruth brought another memory about her mother to the following session. "My aunts used to tell me this story," she said, "about how I made my mother have such a terrible childbirth. There was blood everywhere and it was horrible. Apparently Mother had had a bad time with my brother, and I guess she'd decided not to have another baby and then there I was, thirteen months later. I just caused her all kinds of blood and pain. She had almost no energy left after I was born. . . .

"Also, Mother was a real teetotaler. But she was so sick after my birth, the doctor told her to take a little wine in the afternoon, so she did. And then the minister showed up, and Mother just knew he smelled the wine on her breath. What did the minister think of her! And she told me this was all my fault."

Ruth stopped to consider her words. As with most of her recollections, she had never repeated this story aloud before.

"The way you tell the story of your birth," Dr. Pickens said, "it sounds somewhat like the movie *Alien*. Have you seen the movie?"

Ruth nodded.

"You remember when the creature comes out of the people's stomachs, and it causes them to die in pools of blood . . . ?"

"Yes!" Ruth said. "That's just what they told me my birth was like!"

Throughout the rest of January, Ruth was almost completely silent. When she did talk, her conversation was composed primarily of complaints—about Wichita, the weather, her boredom, and also her fear of going out in public. She told Dr. Pickens that one night she and Ed were eating in a restaurant next to a couple and their young daughter when the woman must have mentioned Ruth, because the child suddenly stood on her chair, pointed at Ruth, and said, "Which one is she, Mom? Is that her? Is that the one?"

"Shut up!" the mother whispered loudly.

After Ruth told the story to Dr. Pickens, she laughed. "I thought it would have embarrassed me. Actually it was kind of funny."

Still, the complaining continued for the rest of the month because Ruth suspected stronger emotions were fighting their way to the surface and she didn't want to deal with them. At the same time her headaches and stomachaches were worse than ever, but she decided it was best not to mention any of this to Dr. Pickens.

"I do remember one time," Ruth said during one session, "when my mother did something I didn't like." She stopped as soon as the words were out. She wished she knew how to take them back.

"What was that?" Dr. Pickens asked.

Ruth sighed but decided to go ahead. "Well, every night I used to ask her the same questions over and over."

She stopped.

"What were they?" Dr. Pickens asked.

"I wanted to know if we'd all be there in the morning, and if mean things would get me at night. My mother answered, but she got really disgusted with me for asking again and again and said so. I guess maybe that bothered me, that she was so disgusted."

Ruth stopped again. Dr. Pickens heard in this story a reflection of Ruth's childhood insecurity. Apparently she needed to ask the same questions repeatedly because she didn't believe her mother's responses. Since Faye constantly undermined Ruth's security, her replies could never reassure Ruth. But Ruth had to pretend it wasn't her mother she feared.

Dr. Pickens mentioned this interpretation to Ruth.

"Oh, that doesn't sound right," she said. "I mean, I don't blame her for being so disgusted with me. If you think about it rationally, how could she have ever answered those questions?" Ruth nodded, as if there was no doubt in her mind that this was the proper way to think, and she brought up other, more enjoyable recollections.

The following week Ruth came up with a memory long buried in her past. "This is one of my earliest memories," she told Dr. Pickens. "I must have been about three and a half or so when my Aunt Isabel gave me this book with a thick cloth cover. In the center of the cover was a picture of a little girl who had a curl right in the middle of her forehead, and the girl was

blond, just like I was back then. The book was filled
with children's poems. It was wonderful.

"My aunt and I went outside on the porch to read
it, and I remember she told me the little girl on the
cover looked just like me, and that made me very
happy because the girl was so pretty. Then we read
out loud. I only remember some of them, 'Hickory
Dickory Dock' and 'Mary Had a Little Lamb' and
'Jack and Jill,' stuff like that. I was really proud of
that book and I carried it with me everywhere."

Ruth paused and frowned. "Then one day I had it
out in the yard," she said, "and I looked at the poems,
and well, all the poems had turned bad. They weren't
about Jack and Jill and Little Red Riding Hood anymore. They were all about me and what a bad little girl
I was. So I got really scared, and I knew I had to hide
the book from everyone or I'd die, because if anyone
saw how horrible I was, they'd have to kill me. But I
didn't know what to do, so I ran over to this post pile
that my granddad had, where he had tied all these
fence posts together, and I hid the book inside the pile
and I never saw it again. If whoever owns that farm
has that pile, the book's probably there."

Listening to the story, Dr. Pickens began to understand why poetry was so important to Ruth and how,
when she was an adult and her self-hatred and fear
joined to create a dissociative personality, she had remembered those verses that confirmed her wickedness
as a child and, as the Poet, had recreated them.

Meanwhile Ruth changed the subject to something
more pleasant. She related a story about how much
she had enjoyed high school and what a good student
she had been. Then she paused for a moment and the
image of a silver house key flickered in her memory.

She felt a chill. "I have to leave," she said. "Right now." She started to tremble.

"You're perfectly safe here," Dr. Pickens said. "Tell me more about what you're feeling."

"I can't," Ruth said. She looked at him, helpless, now feeling even worse because she had failed him. But she refused to say more.

"It's up to you," Dr. Pickens said, and Ruth was grateful that he wasn't angry. But she felt desperate, as if she were dying, not of a physical illness but of terror. Why was a key so frightening? She didn't say another word for the rest of the session.

At home that night she made a final entry in her notebook: "I know this is not a feeling I should have so I can't tell you. I am walking down the street and get this feeling I am going to be devoured by people. They are closing in on me."

Aspects of Ruth's emotions regarding Dr. Pickens were touched on in many sessions, sometimes briefly, occasionally at some length. "What are your feelings toward me?" he might ask. The question, which at one time had only startled Ruth, now alarmed her. Over the last few months she had grown to revere him, and she wanted him to be her parent. But she was afraid to say so. What if this angered him? What if it was the wrong way to think, or what if it meant that she didn't understand how therapy was supposed to work? Ruth thought and thought until she finally decided to tell the truth. "I wish you had been my parent," she said one day, and cringed a little.

"That's understandable," Dr. Pickens said. He had already guessed Ruth's feelings. "In some ways you probably feel more comfortable with me than you did with your parents as a child."

Ruth was more than relieved that he neither disapproved nor rejected her. Looking at Dr. Pickens, she decided he was the most perfect person God had ever made. She wondered if he really did have a life without her, or did he just sit in his office all the time waiting for patients to arrive? Then she started fretting about the day he might go off on a vacation. But she kept that to herself and instead said that she was worried something might happen to her outside of therapy. How would she reach him? What if she called his service and nobody answered, or nobody could find him? What would she do?

"Let me give you my home phone number," Dr. Pickens said. "If you need to call me, feel free to do so." He wrote it on a slip of paper and handed it to her.

The thought that she had his phone number in her purse thrilled her, and she kept it with her wherever she went.

Ruth spoke about her father considerably less than she did her mother. But when she did mention Carl, she sounded relaxed and spirited, recalling memories of the farm, where her father had encouraged her to spend time with him. He enjoyed her company and frequently told her so. He even made such comments as, "What a pretty dress you have on," which thrilled Ruth. But essentially Carl had left the parenting to Faye.

Ruth felt that the world revolved around her mother. She told Dr. Pickens that, according to family lore, every time Faye took out her ironing board, little Ruth immediately showed up with her high chair, sensing that this was the one time she had a captive audience. She then sat down and talked nonstop about everything she could think of—her chores, the weather, the animals—while her mother ironed and listened to what Ruth assumed her mother felt was a stream of babbling.

Ruth remembered that her family kept an old wooden picture box in a kitchen cupboard, and among the many pictures in the box was one of an unhappy little girl, screaming, her mouth wide open. This was Ruth, Faye often told her when she was a child. What a big crybaby she was! Much later Ruth took a closer look at the picture. "It wasn't a photograph at all," she said. "It was a magazine clipping, and the little girl wasn't me. This really bothered me."

In their next session Ruth apologized for having mentioned negative thoughts about the picture. Dr. Pickens had already noticed that whenever Ruth criticized her mother, she changed her mind in the following visit. But despite her denials Dr. Pickens could see that Ruth was slowly creating a new conscious image of her mother, who was not as flawless as Ruth had originally claimed.

One quiet Wednesday afternoon Ruth put on her coat, got into the Oldsmobile, and drove to Eastgate Shopping Center. She was nervous and scared, but for the last several weeks she had been forcing herself to appear in public alone, because she was pragmatic enough to know that someday her life would have to return to normal. While at the mall she ate a sandwich, looked at a few store windows, bought a magazine, and then headed back home, thoroughly relieved that no one had seemed to recognize her or had made a rude remark.

When Ruth made a right-hand turn off Kellogg, going south, she noticed a car coming toward her. The driver was staying in his lane, and the car was quite ordinary, but Ruth felt a surge of alarm. Fixing her eyes on the windshield, trying to look past the sun's glare at the driver, she saw he was wearing a red bandana, and the sight of it caused her to tremble with anger. She was furious. She wanted to jerk the bandana off the man's neck; she wanted the man dead.

Then the moment passed and she thought, oh boy, I'd better tell Dr. Pickens about this one. She didn't want her anger to get stuck inside her head again and force her to write poems. She was still convinced that one more impropriety would land her in jail forever.

"You've brought up a bandana several times before," Dr. Pickens said after she told him about the incident during their next session. "And you've mentioned one along with the Poet activity. Is it related to that?"

Ruth considered his question. "Maybe," she said. "Maybe it's just a reminder about what a bad person I was to have done all those things."

A dark memory lingered inside Ruth's mind, but she shook her head to push it away and then glanced at Dr. Pickens, who, she thought, was looking at her as if thinking, what is this woman, nuts or something? Well, of course she was nuts, she answered herself, or she wouldn't be here.

Dr. Pickens waited, but Ruth couldn't speak.

"Do you want to talk about it?" Dr. Pickens asked.

"I don't," she said, and she never meant it more.

A few days later Ruth was mopping the kitchen floor. Outside the temperature was unaccountably balmy, and Ruth was feeling peaceful, humming along to her easy listening station. Then she opened a kitchen drawer. There, lying on a towel, was a skeleton key. She became instantly angry and agitated, although she had seen the key many times before, and slammed the drawer shut.

At her next session Ruth mentioned the key to Dr. Pickens. "I have no idea what this means," she said. "All I know is looking at the key made me feel terrible. Why?"

"What do you think?" he asked.

She shook her head sadly. "I don't know."

Ruth continued to arrive fifteen minutes before each appointment because she wanted the time to adjust from her home life to the world of therapy. Since she was so early, she noticed that whenever Dr. Pickens saw a patient before her, he invariably closed his office door after that patient left.

Dr. Pickens functioned on two levels during therapy. On one he tried to identify closely with his patients, empathizing with their feelings and experiences —a process, he felt, similar to becoming emotionally connected to the protagonist in a good novel. On the other level he was an observer—analyzing, integrating, and attempting to understand and eventually explain the links between past experience and current symptoms. Between any two sessions it was possible to suppress, but not forget, the experiences of the prior session while preparing for the next patient. Rarely did feelings from one patient intrude upon another, but he did like to take some time alone to ready himself for his next appointment.

One afternoon that winter, while Ruth was sitting in the waiting room, Dr. Pickens's door accidentally slipped open, and Ruth did her inconspicuous best to eavesdrop. For a moment there was only silence. Then she heard him dial the telephone. She leaned forward as far as she could, but she couldn't hear what he was saying until he raised his voice. "That's unacceptable behavior toward your mother!" he said, then hung up the phone. Ruth wondered who was on the other end. She also thought, right on! You can get mad too!

When Dr. Pickens came to the door and opened it, Ruth quickly leaned back as if she hadn't nearly fallen off her chair listening. She wanted to ask him why he had lost his temper and who the object of his anger was, but she was afraid he would become angry and make her leave. She kept her thoughts to herself.

It was actually one of his own children on the other end of the phone, although he wouldn't have said so to Ruth. Instead he would have encouraged her to explore her own feelings about the conversation. He still hadn't told Ruth that he had any children, and he never intended to.

Ruth was having nightmares. She mentioned this to Dr. Pickens during a session in late January, and then asked if he wanted to hear them.

Dr. Pickens always told his patients that exploring dreams could be helpful, but he avoided overemphasizing them in order to prevent patients from using them defensively—talking about one dream after another to avoid discussions of major issues. He did say, however, that if a patient ever felt a need to talk about a dream, he would certainly allow it, because the process could be helpful.

Ruth brought in fewer dreams than most patients, which Dr. Pickens assumed was partly due to his lack of encouragement: he knew Ruth tried to please him. But it also seemed to be a by-product of her actions as the Poet, which were themselves a kind of representation of subconscious impulses. Dr. Pickens guessed that Ruth, having already acted out her dreams, found them overly threatening.

Ruth described a particularly vivid nightmare in which she had been walking through a parking lot when a car suddenly spun around and hit her, killing her instantly. She was carrying no identification, and while she lay on the ground dead, strangers milled around above her, but no one knew who she was. Moreover, no one cared.

"What do you think that means?" she asked.

Dr. Pickens usually tried to collaborate with the patient as much as possible when discussing a dream rather than making outright interpretations. "What do you think?" he asked.

"I got killed, so I guess I died," Ruth said, and stopped.

Dr. Pickens then asked if she wanted to discuss the dream in more depth, but she remained silent. Actually, at that moment she had become utterly consumed by him and his own life. Most of all she wanted to know if he had a daughter. Her fantasy was that he did and that this little girl was the luckiest girl in the world. Ruth continued to daydream about what her own life might have been like if she had been his daughter. She barely spoke at all for the rest of the session, instead losing herself in a rich fantasy of how much better her life could have been with Dr. Pickens as her parent.

The images of a bandana and a key continued to flicker in Ruth's mind, and although Dr. Pickens repeatedly asked her about their significance, Ruth couldn't respond. During one session she became so agitated over the images that, unable to utter a single word, she stood up, walked over to Dr. Pickens's desk, and started to cry.

After a few minutes had passed, Dr. Pickens asked her what she was feeling.

"I have to get out of here," Ruth said.

"Well, you can, of course," he said. "But do you really have to?"

Ruth didn't reply.

"Why don't you come back to the chair?" he asked. "It can help to put your feelings into words instead of trying to run away from them physically." He wanted Ruth to know he was asking her to sit down again for her sake, not for his.

But she had been hoping he would say, "Shut up and get out." That would really put her in her place! She was momentarily filled with self-loathing, and she hated him for not hating her. Instead of storming out of the room, however, she sat down as he suggested and tried to understand her feelings. She was still uncontrollably disturbed, but the worse she felt, the gentler she found Dr. Pickens's voice. Sometimes she hated it that he was nice to her.

Dr. Pickens couldn't recall one patient in his practice who had ever stood up and walked around the room. Ruth's movement indicated, he felt, that she was on the verge of being overwhelmed by terrifying memories; it was equivalent to the actions of an upset child too young to deal with feelings consciously and verbally, who therefore acts them out, often indirectly. Adult patients, however, due to the intensity and occasional irrationality of their feelings, tend to restrain their actions in order to create a sense of control. Ruth had passed that state; some memory inside was too close, and too menacing.

*   *   *

In the next session Ruth repeated a similar procession of thoughts and actions: the bandana, the key, the anger, the tears. So she talked about everything else: her dog, the weather, her family. When the session ended, she was able to numb her mind, for which she was grateful, and drive home. That night she chatted with Ed, played with Ginger, and watched television. For the first time since she had started therapy, she couldn't stop thinking about herself, but exactly what she was thinking remained unclear.

A few days later Ruth dredged up a nice memory of her mother for Dr. Pickens. When Ruth was twelve, she had developed a full-fledged case of acne, and her mother took her to a doctor in Fort Scott whose treatment was to burn Ruth's face with ultraviolet light. The acne got worse. "Then one day my mother and I were walking in town and we saw this elderly doctor," Ruth said. "He had been my grandparents' doctor for years. He looked at my face, and he said, 'My God, what is going on?' My mother told him, and he said, 'I don't like to do this, but she's going to have a horribly pitted face if you don't get this cured right. Burning it is just going to get it in deeper.'

"He said he had something in his office that would cure it if Mother would give him a chance. Well, she agreed, so we went up these creaky old stairs to his office and he gave Mother a great big pill with a skull and crossbones on it and some gauze and told her to dissolve this pill in water and soak the gauze and wet my face with it.

" 'You'll have to spend a lot of time doing this,' he said. 'It won't be easy, but it will work.'

"So Mother did it, and even though it hurt, I knew

it was nice of her. I would cry, though, and she would just agree with me and say, 'Yup, I'm really rotten for making you hurt like this.' She did it for three full days.

"And then, sure enough, all the acne went away and I didn't have any scars at all. I have no scars."

6

IT WAS LIKE A ROUND BALL IN A SWIMMING POOL, Ruth had told Dr. Pickens. Ruth rarely used metaphors in her conversation; both she and Ed preferred plain talk to showy phrases. But now, because she was trying to express an emotion her vocabulary couldn't describe, she reached for an image. That image was of herself standing in a swimming pool, holding on to a ball that was beneath the water but pushing its way toward the surface. The ball stood for her memory. As long as Ruth kept it under water, she was safe. But the moment she let go, the ball would surge out of the water and into the air. Were memories like that too? she asked. If she let them out, would she lose control?

Ruth thought this image was hers alone, but actually Dr. Pickens had used it in Wesley lockup when he was explaining the principles of psychotherapy. At the time Ruth hadn't seemed to hear, but now Dr. Pickens guessed that, not being ready to understand, she had buried the words in her subconscious. They were there when she needed them, although she had forgotten their origin.

On February 1 Ruth appeared at her session unusually nervous. When she sat down, she fidgeted, and for a few moments she didn't even consider talking. Words formed inside her head but then evaporated; she mentioned the swimming pool again and shuddered. Then inexplicably Ruth felt as if the ball had sprung free. It didn't happen as she had feared. She didn't lose control, nor did she grasp for help. Her discipline surprised her. Another repressed memory from her childhood had emerged, and although she spoke slowly and haltingly, sometimes pausing for several minutes at a time, she was able to talk about it articulately.

"It was a nice, cool day, and I was about three years old," she began in such a faint tone that Dr. Pickens could barely hear her. "It had been raining just before, but now there was a lot of sun and clean white clouds. My dad was driving us somewhere in our Model A. I don't really know where we were going, but we stopped at our neighbor's house. He was outside, and my father left the car and talked with him for a while. I stayed inside the car, watching them."

Ruth stopped talking. A minute later Dr. Pickens spoke. "What happened next?" he asked.

Ruth smiled slightly. She didn't look at Dr. Pickens but after clearing her throat, spoke again. "My dad was going somewhere," she said, "and for some reason he didn't think I should come along. The man suggested I stay with him instead, so my dad wouldn't have to worry. Well, I didn't want to do this, but my dad agreed, and so I stood there and watched him drive away.

"The man took me inside his house. His wife wasn't around and we were alone, and then he asked me if I wanted to play a game. Well, I didn't, but he was so much bigger than me, I didn't know what to say. I remembered that rope he had tied me up with, and I was really scared."

Ruth stopped, then started again. "The man said he was glad the little girl wanted to play with him and he had this nice game they could do together. The little girl didn't say anything because maybe she was thinking that if the game involved hiding, she could hide from him. So when he said the game he most wanted to play was hide-and-go-seek, that seemed okay. But still she was scared.

"Then the man went to a drawer and took out a skeleton key"—Ruth sucked in her breath when she said the words—"and he said they were going to play with the key. He said they weren't going to hide from each other but that they'd both hide the key, and then they could both find it. The man started the game by putting the key in the pocket of the little girl's coveralls. Then he found it."

Once more Ruth paused. When she talked now, it was for only a few minutes at a time.

"What are you feeling?" Dr. Pickens asked quietly. He noted that Ruth had switched to the third person when the memory overwhelmed her, but he knew this wasn't the appropriate time to discuss it.

"I guess I'm okay. I don't really want to think about this," Ruth said.

But a moment later she continued, and Dr. Pickens noticed that she was talking as if she were a little girl. Her diction changed, her voice was higher-pitched, and her sentences had the lilting rhythm of a child's.

"This wasn't much of a game," Ruth said. "The

man got to hide the key, and all the little girl did was stand around while the man searched her. Then he put the key in another one of her pockets. 'Now where's the key?' the man asked. The little girl was wearing coveralls with lots of pockets in them, and soon he was dropping the key in all of them and reaching in and finding it. Then the man dropped the key right down the little girl's pants, and he put his hand against her skin, near her neck, and then he started to reach down inside her clothes. But he said that he could never find the key now that it was hidden so far inside her coveralls.

"Then he said if he was going to ever find that key, he'd just have to take the little girl's pants off. So he did. At this point the little girl decided she didn't like this game anymore, and she began to cry and said she didn't want to play. Well, the man didn't seem to be playing a game now. He was real serious, and he took her arm and jerked it really hard. The little girl was trying to hang on to this chair near her, but the man just ripped the little girl off it. By now the little girl was kicking and screaming, but the man tucked her under his arm, like he was holding a chicken or something, and then he just threw her on the bed. He kept telling her to be quiet, and every time he did, she just screamed louder, yelling for her daddy, asking where her daddy was."

Ruth started to cry. "Whenever the little girl screamed, the man got angrier," she said. "But she kept fighting him off because she was so afraid of him, and that really made him mad. So he reached in his pocket and took out this dirty red bandana and put it in her mouth, but she kept kicking and hitting.

"Then maybe he changed his mind or something,

because he took it out of her mouth, and instead he tied it around her wrists and put a pillow on top of her head.''

Ruth couldn't continue. She looked down at the floor. After a few minutes she still hadn't spoken.

"Our time is almost over," Dr. Pickens said finally. His voice was soft, and Ruth found herself oddly attracted to it. But she kept silent.

"What are you feeling?" he asked.

"I'm okay," Ruth said. She had stopped crying.

"That was an extremely painful situation," Dr. Pickens said.

Ruth nodded her head.

"It's time to go now," Dr. Pickens said, keeping his tone firm but also hoping to convey concern and reassurance.

"Okay," Ruth said. "That's okay." She waited a few moments, regained her composure, and looked at the door, which Dr. Pickens was now holding open. Then she rose and left, hurrying down the steps, past the receptionist, and outside into the cold air. The bright sun pierced her eyes, which were sore from crying, and when she got in the car, she had to wipe them with a tissue.

At home she played with Ginger until it was time to cook dinner—meat loaf and rolls—and then she and Ed watched television. She was afraid to speculate on the memory she had talked about that afternoon because she didn't want to know where the story was heading. She just wanted to curl up and sleep for the rest of her life.

On the following Thursday Ruth spent the first ten minutes starting and stopping. "It was . . . ," she said. "I was back . . . The little girl . . ." She also tried talking about the weather and Ed, but after another long silence she picked up the story where she had left off.

"So now the man's in the bed with the little girl, and it's terrible," she said. "It's really terrible. The little girl wanted to leave, but she couldn't. She was so frightened. Then it got worse. It's like, well, he's poking her with a stick. The little girl didn't think much about what the stick was because at that point something else happened. You see, the little girl now knew that she was going to die. She was crying, and the man was all over her, poking her and putting it in her mouth. She was feeling really sick, and she just knew she was going to die.

"But all of a sudden there was this other little girl who was floating right above her, as though maybe some part of her really did die. The other little girl was in a pretty blue sky with all these white clouds around her, and she started floating in the white clouds in this clean white dress. It made her look like a little angel. She was so happy up there, she felt like she was in heaven and everything was wonderful.

"Now the little girl in the sky could look down at the little girl in the bed. But she didn't want to, because it was so awful. And the little girl in the bed could see the little girl in the sky, and she longed so much to be up there with her."

Ruth stopped. She looked around the room and felt trapped; she wanted to walk through the wall and never return. Dr. Pickens could see the agitation in her face and body: her shoulders were taut and her back stiff. "I have to go," she said. "I have to get out of here now." Tears rolled down her cheeks. "My God."

Dr. Pickens's expression didn't change. He looked at Ruth and chose his words carefully. "Of course you can always leave," he said, as he had told her before. "But I want you to know this is a safe place and we can deal with anything that comes up."

Ruth thought about this for a moment and decided not to go, at least not quite yet. "Then the man took the pillow off the little girl's face," she said, "and she could never figure out exactly what he did, but her teeth hurt. He must have not wanted her to bite him, so he did something to them. Then the man tried to put, you know, something in her mouth again, and somehow he injured her, because now she was bleeding, and she had to eat her own blood. Oh God, she was bleeding and had to swallow it. And then he peed into the little girl's mouth. And after he did this, she threw up."

Ruth was wringing her hands, winding them around each other, staring at them, Dr. Pickens thought, as if they were all she could see at that moment.

"Well, this infuriated the man even more," Ruth said. "He couldn't believe she would do such a thing to him. But even worse, now that it was all over, the little girl up in the sky had to come back, and she didn't want to. But she did, and she was very ashamed of herself, because she knew that if she hadn't left the little girl on the bed, she might have helped her. Maybe she could have kept her from being hurt. She said she was very sorry, that she felt terrible she had left, and now the two little girls were holding each other tight and sobbing."

Ruth stopped talking.

"Flying into the sky was your way of coping," Dr. Pickens said. "It was all you could think of to do to deal with the overwhelming fear and pain."

Ruth nodded. "I guess the man's wife came home about then," she continued, "because at some point she was cleaning the little girl. Or maybe she was there all the time and the little girl just didn't know it because the wife always did whatever her husband told her to do. The girl was really sobbing at this point, just sobbing and sobbing, and she couldn't stop."

Ruth paused again. Dr. Pickens waited until he thought she wasn't going to speak. "This is a very sad story," he said. "Go ahead whenever you feel comfortable."

To Ruth, who was listening to the sounds of her memories, his words seemed distant. "Then the wife," she said, "tried to stop the girl from crying so much. She went into the living room and sat down in the rocking chair with the little girl on her lap, and they started rocking back and forth and back and forth, and the wife kept saying to the girl that nothing had happened and that everything was fine, and she kept rocking and rocking. The woman had a pan of water, and she was cleaning the little girl's hair with a washcloth. Meanwhile the woman and the man were yelling at each other, and the little girl knew that something was wrong, you know, when big people yell at each other. But the little girl just kept feeling sicker and sicker, and so the wife asked her if she wanted a nice cookie. The little girl didn't say anything, because she didn't want a cookie at all, she just wanted to be with her daddy, but the wife gave her a cookie anyway. The little girl always remembered that room, with this clock in the middle of it, and the lace curtains on the windows that were sort of pretty, except you really couldn't see out of them.

"That was when the little girl's daddy showed up, and he was very upset because she was crying so much. 'What a little baby you are,' he said. He took the girl and went home.''

Ruth stood up and, for the second time during her therapy, walked over by Dr. Pickens's desk and sat down on a chair. She couldn't look at his face. Instead she placed her head on the desk and hid it beneath her arms.

After a moment Dr. Pickens asked her what she was feeling.

"I'm okay," she said. She raised her head and wiped her tears.

"Do you feel able to come back to your chair?"

"Yes," she said, but she didn't tell Dr. Pickens that she wanted him to hug the little girl that minute; she wanted him to pick her up and make her feel better. She wasn't sure why she couldn't tell him this, but she thought maybe the little girl was too revolting for Dr. Pickens to touch and that she, the adult Ruth, was also foul. Then again, maybe he would hug the little girl. She was confused. If I had to tell the whole story over again, she thought, I think he'd listen. That made her feel calmer and less dirty.

"We only have a few minutes left," Dr. Pickens said. "Let's take some time to help you prepare for leaving."

Ruth had hoped that when it was time to go, Dr. Pickens would snap his fingers and she would be ready, as after a hypnosis session with Dr. Schrag. It didn't work like that here, she was disappointed to realize, and she thought she was going to be sick.

"You've experienced a lot of pain," he said.

"Yes," she admitted. "I'm sorry."

"Why should you apologize?" Dr. Pickens asked. "This is very painful stuff. It's as if these terrible memories have been frozen and buried out of your awareness since the time these events happened. Now, in a way, you're remembering them for the first time, and perhaps that makes it feel as intense and real as it did when it all happened.''

"Yes," Ruth said, for that sounded true.

"But it's different now."

"How?" she asked.

"When it happened," Dr. Pickens explained, "you were totally alone, and you weren't safe. Now you're an adult. You have me. Also, you are no longer physically a little girl."

Ruth nodded, feeling torn between her enormous shame for the child and her thankfulness to Dr. Pickens.

"It's time to stop," he said. "Are you ready to leave?"

Ruth smiled shyly. "Okay," she said.

"How do you feel?"

"Okay," she repeated, and then stood up and smoothed her skirt. She wasn't telling the truth and they both knew it, but she didn't care. As always, Dr. Pickens opened the door for Ruth, who gratefully left the room.

When he had closed the door behind Ruth, Dr. Pickens sat at his desk and wiped his eyes with a tissue. While Ruth was telling her story, he had cried, but not in a way that she could notice. He didn't want her to worry about his feelings. He compared their situation to that of a child watching a parent cry over the child's hurt: the child doesn't realize that the parent is empathizing with her; she only sees that the parent is upset and therefore not available as a source of essential security.

Dr. Pickens had felt Ruth's sorrow and had identified with her pain, but the story hadn't surprised him. He had assumed that she was repressing disturbing memories, and incidents of sexual abuse were as likely as not. Nor did he think this particular incident was the only one in Ruth's childhood. He was correct, for within a week Ruth started recalling another.

Once again she entered the office shyly, averting her eyes from Dr. Pickens's and unable to talk. When she did speak, she mentioned insignificant matters, changing the subject frequently and sometimes losing her train of thought. Only after fifteen minutes of rambling could she begin her story. "There was another time," she said, "when the little girl was in her granddad's barn and all the men were working there with him. Then the neighbor told the others that he needed to get something, and he left the barn. The little girl didn't see where he went.

"A while later she was outside playing in the yard when the man grabbed her and told her to come with him. This time he threw her in some hay, and he put it into her mouth and started hurting her."

Ruth stopped talking. This was as much of the story as she could recall or wished to.

"You," Dr. Pickens said, speaking as gently as he could. "The little girl was you. Can you tell me the story using the words *I* and *me?*"

Ruth glanced over at him, then away. She knew what he was asking for and why, but she didn't want to do it.

"While the man was hurting her," she said, "the little girl floated to heaven. Once again it was very pretty up there, with all the nice white clouds, and the girl was wearing that same white dress. Then she watched from above as the other girl stayed with the man while he did all that stuff to her.''

Dr. Pickens felt that he had already made his point that Ruth was the little girl. By doing so, he was trying to help her make an emotional link between past and present. He still didn't feel that this was the appropriate time to push the matter, however, so he let her continue.

"I guess she felt very sick again and she had to throw up," Ruth said. "So she went down to the horse trough, and she pumped herself some water.''

Ruth sighed heavily. "My granddad saw me at the trough," she said, "and he told me to get away from the water right that minute or the livestock wouldn't drink it.''

Absorbed in her past, Ruth waited some time before talking again. Then suddenly she smiled. "You know," she said, "I remember something else. Once we were out in the barn lot with our dog, Stubby, and the man walked by and tried to put me on a wagon, but Stubby ran over and got between me and the man and barked and barked. Dad had to come over and make the dog leave, and I remember the man said, 'That's a good dog; he really guards those kids.' ''

Stubby was half German shepherd and half collie, Ruth told Dr. Pickens; he had a shaggy multicolored coat and large, wet brown eyes. He belonged to the entire family, but he preferred Ruth and she adored him. One Christmas Faye showed Ruth and Jean a photograph of the dog and a print of a guardian angel and asked Ruth which she wanted to place at the head of her bed. Ruth grabbed the picture of Stubby, and Jean, to her displeasure, was left with the angel.

One day a few years later, Ruth told Dr. Pickens, she went out to call the dog. " 'Hey, Stub!' I yelled.

'Hey, dog!' But he didn't come, and that was strange because Stubby always came when I called. So I looked and looked, but I couldn't find him, and so I was really upset and crying, like always, until my dad came outside and saw I was in tears. He tried to calm me down, although at first he didn't say much. Then he said, 'Ruth, Stubby's gone.'

"I looked at him and he looked away. There was this rabid dog that had come through the area and was biting everything in its path. So now Dad said that he'd had to take Stubby round back and shoot him. After he told me, I ran in the house and cried forever."

Ruth was crying by the time she finished telling the story. "You must think I'm such a wimp to act like this," she said. The truth, however, was quite different. Dr. Pickens was a dog lover, and he was strongly affected by Ruth's remembrance that she had formed as close a bond with Stubby as she had with anyone else in her family. He recalled the sadness he had felt over the death of his own dog a few years earlier. His wife discovered the dog had died while he was at work, but their children refrained from tears until he came home. Once they saw him crying, however, his children began to cry too.

"Why would I think you were weak because you were crying over your dog?" Dr. Pickens asked, remembering the tears he had shed himself. But he didn't want Ruth to feel that the only memories with which he could truly empathize were those he had somehow shared, so he said nothing more.

"Don't you?" she asked.

"Do you have any reason at all," he asked, "for believing that I think you're weak?"

She thought about it, still crying silently. "No," she said.

"Who do you think you might be confusing me with when you feel I dislike you because you're crying?"

"I don't know," Ruth said, but she thought, he means my mother.

After the session Ruth walked outside into the clear, cool afternoon. She saw children bicycling across the parking lot and a busload of students going home; overhead she watched two B52s from McConnell Air Force Base soar out of sight. She thought, everything here is going on just as it was when I went in. But something has happened to me at least. And I want everyone else to understand. Then she thought, but they can't. Still she wanted to walk up to someone on the street, anyone at all, and say, "Don't you know what has happened to the poor little girl? Don't any of you care?"

At another session Ruth remembered more. "Once my dad and my granddad were talking to the man in the front yard. Then I came by, and as soon as I saw him, I started to run away. But my granddad caught me and told me I shouldn't ever run away from anyone. Then the man picked me up and held me over his head with his thumb right there on my pelvic bone, and he hurt me. When he let me down, I ran away."

"How do you feel about that?" Dr. Pickens asked her.

Ruth looked at the floor to avoid eye contact. She couldn't talk.

"Maybe you're not looking me in the eye because you're afraid of what you might see there," he said.

Ruth didn't comment.

"Look at me," he said softly, and his voice scared her. She did look at him, though, directly into his eyes, and she thought they were the kindest she had ever seen. And she felt better; she could tell he didn't hate her for what had happened to the little girl. But Ruth herself refused to offer any sympathy. "The girl was okay this time. She got away this time, didn't she?"

"She got away?"

"I got away," Ruth said. She thought, I wish I hadn't started this. "I don't want to say *me*. I can't do it."

"It's very painful to accept that these things happened to you," Dr. Pickens said.

Ruth didn't speak. She knew she was the little girl, but she still couldn't say it out loud, because she wanted so much to believe it wasn't the truth. She felt tears forming. "You must think I'm really out of it," she said. "I can't do what you want me to do."

"It isn't a matter of what I want you to do," Dr. Pickens said. "I realize this is difficult, but in the long run it will be helpful to get these things out. In the meantime, have I done anything to make you feel ashamed?"

"Oh, no," Ruth said.

"Perhaps you're expecting me to act like someone from your past."

Ruth nodded slightly.

"Since you felt your mother didn't like you when you cried, maybe you're assuming that I won't like you either."

"Well, maybe," Ruth said, as if agreeing with him. But she wasn't sure what she believed.

7

As always, Ruth and Ed avoided any discussion of her therapy. Their life together, Ruth now realized, was invariable to a degree she had never before taken the time to notice. But she found genuine solace in this consistency and also in her husband. She had wondered while she was in the hospital if Ed would leave her, but now she knew he would stay. Since she had also feared he might blame her for having brought shame to the family, Ed's silence, combined with the familiarity of their daily life, seemed kind.

But she was bored. Not since the boys were children had she spent so much time away from work, and her only hope for any respite came from some gossip Jean brought back from the phone company. Apparently, the rumor went, the marketing department was considering giving Ruth work as a reports clerk. It wasn't a taxing position, but it was something she could do to occupy her day, and it was in a department where Ruth knew and liked several people. When Jean's information proved accurate and the phone company made its offer in mid-March, Ruth accepted. Ed wasn't convinced she was ready, however, and told her so, but she reminded him that the phone company wouldn't pay her disability forever, and the Finleys needed the money for the therapy, which was costing seventy-five dollars an hour.

On the morning of her first day back at the phone company, Ruth woke feeling queasy. She knew, however, that it was the right thing to do, to get on with her life, so she got up, dressed, and drove downtown with Ed, as they had always done in the past. Once she had met with her new boss, she sat down unobtrusively at her desk and started typing some letters. A few minutes later several acquaintances from her old department walked by. "Hey there," they all said. "Hi," Ruth responded, and she smiled, but she wondered what they must have been thinking. Although no one asked her a question or even looked at her oddly, she felt as vulnerable as if she had been sitting at her desk naked.

"I don't want to go back there," Ruth told Dr. Pickens the next day. "I was afraid the whole time, and I still am."

She waited for him to tell her that this was an unreasonable attitude, but he didn't. She found that remarkable in itself, and she wondered if feeling afraid was really as shameful as she had always thought. She wasn't sure, but nonetheless within a few days she was able to go to work without dread.

"I remember something really bad," Ruth told Dr. Pickens a few weeks later. She could barely speak; the session was already half over when she started her story.

"It was Easter," she said, "and I was wearing this

special dress Mother had made. She'd let me pick out the material, and it was very pretty, with a real difficult sleeve to it. I even got to pick which buttons I wanted on the dress. I was very proud of it.

"When we came home from church, the man stopped by for a visit, but as soon as I saw him, I hid behind my mother. The man went on and on about how cute I was and how he wanted to take me back to his house to show his wife, because I was the cutest little girl he had ever seen."

Ruth stopped.

"Tell me more about what he did," Dr. Pickens said, when he realized Ruth didn't want to continue the story. "I know it hurts to talk, but in the long run you'll feel better if you share it with me."

Ruth looked at him and saw concern in his eyes. She thought, he seems to care. The notion that somebody wanted to know what had happened to her struck her as odd. What if he heard the stories and didn't like her? Then again, he was the first person she had ever been able to talk to this way. Still undecided as to what to think, she was surprised when she heard herself speak. "My parents were pleased the neighbor thought I was so pretty," she said, "but I didn't want to go with the man, and so I started to cry. Well, Mother had had just about enough of this crying of mine, so she smacked me on my legs—and Mother never, ever hit me—and she told me to go show off the pretty dress she had made. Mother was very proud of the dress too.

" 'You won't be gone long,' she said. But the little girl wouldn't go, so the man had to carry her, and the girl kept crying. When she got into the car, she tried to scurry across the seat so she could get in the back and run away. But the man grabbed her feet and pulled off her shoes so all she was wearing were her little white anklets. And then she rode around in this junky back seat with all this horrible stuff all over it, bits of rags and stones and other things from the farm.

"When they got to the man's place, the man parked by the barn, and the little girl tried to escape again. But she wasn't wearing shoes, and the little girl's feet got stickers all over them. Her feet hurt from running over the wet ground, and she couldn't run anymore. Then the man just walked over and picked her up and carried her into the barn."

Dr. Pickens was struck by the visual clarity of Ruth's words; it was as if, in each memory, she was reliving the child's trauma rather than recounting the incident from the perspective of an adult.

"She kept trying to escape," Ruth said. "Well, this made the man angrier, so he threw her on the floor where some scratchy stuff was lying all over, and this time he didn't take the girl's dress off, he just started hurting her.

"He used to try to have . . ." Ruth found it hard to continue. Then she said, "Well, he was trying to, you know, rape her, but this never worked, but still he would try it for a while.

"The little girl floated off to the top of the barn again, right up into the white clouds. She was wearing that pretty white dress, and it was all clean and beautiful. Her hair was real clean too, and it sparkled in the sun, and she was very glad to be up there, except something in her knew she should be helping the little girl below. Then the man did what he always did, you know, he tried to poke her all over, and when that didn't work, he did something to the little girl's teeth and then there was stuff in her mouth, like he peed."

189

"What you are really saying is that he ejaculated in your mouth," Dr. Pickens said.

Ruth frowned and nodded. "When he left, she threw up," she said. She made a face. "The little girl from above floated back down, and the girl in the barn got up and cleaned herself off. Then she left the barn."

Ruth paused. "Oh, God," she said. "This is the worst." She waited a full minute before she continued, breathing irregularly. "In the middle of the barn was a hall," she said, "and now the man was sitting in the hall on a stool, and his body was all bent over, and he was holding his head. It looked to the little girl as though he was crying. Well, she was crying too, but she thought, what have I done to make this man cry like this? Because men aren't supposed to cry, so I must really be bad."

Ruth's identification with the man who had just raped her startled Dr. Pickens. The child had found someone who shared her secret shame, another crybaby with whom she could sympathize.

"The little girl went to the man," Ruth said, "and patted him on the back to make him feel better. Well, I guess it was a trick because then he grabbed the little girl by the arm and went back to the stall and did the whole thing all over, and the little girl escaped into the clouds again. At this point she could probably do it just at the sight of him."

Ruth burst into tears. "Oh, she was so stupid to want to help him. But he was crying, and she had to help him, and then he did it to her again. Oh, no!"

When she resumed talking, she couldn't complete a sentence. "Once again he hurt the little girl's teeth . . . and she was crying . . . and he hated it when she cried. . . . It was like he didn't know what to do with all the tears and everything, so he took the little girl out of the barn when he was done . . .''

Ruth started to sniff, and then she reacted as if to a terrible odor. ''There's a dead animal on the ground near the barn, and now he's taking the girl . . .'' She made another face; the smell was getting worse. ''And he's holding her upside down and, oh, God, now he's putting her head over the animal like he's going to drop her . . . !''

Breathing very heavily, Ruth stopped talking.

Dr. Pickens waited.

''I'm going to throw up,'' she said. ''Oh, God.'' But instead she closed her eyes and cradled her stomach with her arms. A minute later she was calm enough to continue. ''The little girl knew he was saying he would hurt her if she ever told anyone about it,'' she said.

Ruth immediately became agitated again. Dr. Pickens was watching her carefully. Her eyes were darting, her body was shaking, and she had extended her arms slightly, as if to ward off being pushed into the animal carcass.

''The little girl couldn't even remember how she got home that day,'' Ruth said. ''The man was crying, wasn't he? The poor little girl . . . it was so wrong . . . I was so stupid. . . . Oh, God!''

She slumped forward in her chair, sobbing convulsively.

During her next session Ruth felt no desire to talk. Her sorrow was too great, and she wondered if, by keeping silent, she could make it all go away.

''I know this hurts very much,'' Dr. Pickens said softly. ''But in the past you've gotten through these kinds of things, and you've felt better for having talked about them.''

Ruth thought about his words but remained silent.

"Can you tell me what's in your way?" Dr. Pickens asked.

Some days, Ruth thought, she simply couldn't talk. "You must think I'm pretty dumb," she finally said, "not to be able to tell you what's going on."

"Have I done something to make you feel dumb?" he asked.

She shook her head.

"Has anyone else?"

Ruth shook her head, but she thought, he's probably talking about my mother, but I'm not going to give him the satisfaction of saying so.

Dr. Pickens asked her how she felt about her memories.

"I don't know," Ruth said. "If it had been someone else besides me, I guess I would feel real bad. I guess I could have given the little girl more sympathy. But since it was only me, I needed to accept what happened and go on."

"But why can't you feel for yourself?" he asked.

"I'm not supposed to," Ruth said, and Dr. Pickens believed this was an accurate statement of Ruth's personal belief, learned a half-century earlier as a child.

After giving her words more thought, Ruth told Dr. Pickens that she had learned to fear the memories because they hurt.

"But no matter how traumatic they might eventually become," Dr. Pickens said, "they're beneficial for you to explore. And they won't damage you." Ruth hoped this was true.

Dr. Pickens also told her that unfortunately, remembering these incidents wasn't all the work they had to do. Just as important, they had to discover the impact the sexual assaults had on Ruth's life and explore the full emotional and familial context in which they had taken place. Ruth nodded, but she felt almost as uncomfortable discussing these issues as she did talking about the incidents themselves.

Over the next several sessions Ruth resurrected more memories of her childhood. "I remember something else the man told the little girl," she said one day.

"Yes?" Dr. Pickens asked.

"He said that if she didn't shut up, he'd put her in a sack and throw her over that bridge near the farm into the river. The little girl was sure he meant it. She kept thinking that if someone was going to kill you, you had to make yourself small and crawl inside yourself so that no one could see you, and then you could make yourself dead, and then finally you were glad."

Ruth stopped. "I don't really know what all that means," she said. But at last she understood why Ed's painting on the basement landing, the one of the bridge, had scared her so.

She didn't speak for several minutes. When she did, she asked Dr. Pickens why she had such ambivalent feelings about death.

"Perhaps it comes from your view as a child," he said. "In part you thought death was bad, for it meant leaving your family. But at the same time it was a means of escape from the neighbor, and from your mother too, when you didn't like her."

Ruth nodded. As always, she knew she would have to give this more thought before she could agree aloud.

Ruth took two more sessions to tell all the details of the next memory. She started slowly and interrupted herself several times, but finally she began. "Another time the man and his wife were keeping me at their house for some reason. Of course I didn't want to be there, but no one listened to me. I mean crying didn't do me any good. And Mother was glad they thought I was so cute."

She waited some time before continuing.

"The man never bothered the little girl when her mother was around, but this time he grabbed her after her mother left and threw her into the storm cellar and did it again. The one girl floated off to heaven while the other stayed there and took it all. Then the man left and shut the door. It was pitch-black down there, and the little girl floating in the clouds knew that she had to go back and help the other girl. So she did, and the two girls together had to push the cellar door open."

"That sounds very frightening," Dr. Pickens said.

"I guess so," Ruth said. She looked away.

"I know this is very upsetting," he said, "to accept that this actually happened to you and that you were unable to escape. You had to pretend then, and a part of you still wants to pretend."

"Right," Ruth said flatly. She knew that.

Dr. Pickens continued. "But we are both going to have to understand that this really was you, and eventually we are going to have to deal with that reality."

Ruth nodded. She wasn't ready to talk about it further. She wanted so much for the little girl to be someone else.

When Ruth left that day, Dr. Pickens followed her out of the room, said good-bye, and took his messages off the clip on his door, snapping it loudly. Ruth heard the noise and thought, he's mad at me. I bet he made that noise because he's angry. She considered asking him about it later but decided against it in case she

was correct. She wasn't sure why he would be angry
—unless it was because she had been such a bad girl.

"Once the little girl won," Ruth said in a session a
week later. This time she wasn't crying. "The man
came over to our house, but my mother was home, so
he couldn't do anything, but I ran away anyway. I
didn't know if he was coming after me or not, but I
didn't see any reason to take a chance, so I ran under
the chicken coop and hid."

Ruth made a face. "Oh, it was awful in there, all
smelly and filled with chicken droppings. And it was
real wet too, since the light never got inside."

Ruth was squirming, dodging the man in her past.
"Maybe her mother left or something, because now
the man is outside the coop, and he's trying to get the
girl, he's reaching in after her, and she can see his
arms and his hands. But it's too small where she's
hiding, and he can't get in." Ruth shifted her weight.
"Now she's all right. The man is leaving."

Ruth sighed. "For a few minutes the little girl lay
under the coop, making no noise at all. She was waiting to see if the man was around, but she wasn't sure
where he was, so for a while she kept still. Then she
thought she heard her mother call and she slowly
crawled out."

Dr. Pickens was struck by the similarities between
this memory and Ruth's accounts of her kidnapping
and the incident at Fort Scott. In all three instances
she had waited after having been attacked, hiding and
hoping that her assailant had left before she made a
move.

Ruth was silent.

"What are you thinking about?" Dr. Pickens asked.

"These memories," Ruth said. She didn't take it any further.

"What about the memories?" Dr. Pickens finally asked.

"Well," she said, "back then, I didn't know what I was doing with them. I mean, they weren't there sometimes. I don't recall thinking about them much, and maybe I tried not to. But I do remember something weird. Sometimes I thought I was two people. I'd be playing under the porch with my dolls, and it was like there were two of us there, me and the other little girl, except I was the only one. Once the two of us talked about what the man was doing, and the girl that flew away said she was sorry and she promised the other girl she wouldn't fly away again, because they both thought that maybe if she stayed, no one would get hurt. But she did fly away, every time."

She paused. "That girl seemed so real," Ruth said. "More real than I was."

"The girl who flew into the sky was a forerunner of the Poet," Dr. Pickens said. "Do you see that?"

"The Poet was a lot worse," Ruth said. She laughed self-consciously.

"It's not exactly the same thing," he said, "but it's similar. The assaults were too painful for you to bear, so you simply left the pain and became someone else, flying up into the clouds where it was safe."

Ruth thought about it. "Maybe that wasn't a good thing to do," she said.

"And," Dr. Pickens continued, "when you were an adult and Ed went into the hospital and the BTK Strangler was on the loose, you were frightened, just as you were as a child, and you unconsciously remembered from your childhood how to dissociate."

Ruth nodded. There was too much to think about.

The BTK Strangler? But she didn't say a word. She had considerable difficulty talking to Dr. Pickens once she finished recalling the past. She felt she had nothing else to say about her life. Even when he asked her outright about her feelings, she either denied having any or simply said that she was sad. Their sessions, when they weren't filled with Ruth's recollections, were generally silent.

8

ONE NIGHT THAT SPRING RUTH WAS DOWN IN THE basement at her ceramics table, lost in concentration while working on a complicated ginger jar based on a model from a book. In the background her easy listening music was playing on the radio at a low volume.

"Tears and years."

Ruth looked around. She thought someone had spoken, but she was alone, so she dismissed the sound and returned to her jar.

"Worse. Hearse."

Ruth put down her work. Ed was upstairs, and no one else was near. She shook her head sharply.

"Right and night."

Oh, dear God, no, she thought. Horrible scenes from the last few months shot through her head: the confession, the lockup and therapy. It was starting all over again, she thought; she was hearing words, and they were coming from somewhere inside. Worse, they were rhymes, just like the Poet's. She had thought it was all over; Dr. Pickens had assured her the Poet was gone, and for months she had felt calm. What was happening? She tried not to listen. Everything was all right, she told herself; she was fine.

"It's not all right. Under the pillow it's dark as night."

Oh, God. What do I do? Ruth wondered as the rhymes kept coming. She got up and walked around the room. Maybe if she put the words down on paper they might stop, she thought, so she found a notebook and a pencil and wrote automatically, without thinking or looking at what she was writing. Her hunch was correct: once they were written down on the paper, the rhymes ceased in her mind. Then she cried. She could see she had written a poem three pages long, but she refused to read it for she suspected something was very wrong.

"I'm cracking up," Ruth said.

She laughed nervously and glanced at Dr. Pickens's face for clues to his reaction. It was May, a month after she had written the first of several poems; it had taken her that long to tell him. In the meantime their sessions had been generally silent.

"What do you mean by 'cracking up'?" Dr. Pickens asked.

"Well," she said, "I'm hearing rhymes in my head again. And I'm writing them down."

Dr. Pickens didn't respond.

"I'm writing *poems* again," Ruth said through her teeth. Didn't he hear? Then nerves overcame her. She laughed again and waited for Dr. Pickens to tell her she was nuts. "Last time I wrote poems," she finally said, "remember how much trouble I got into?"

"Well, you're not going to mail them to anyone, are you?" he asked.

"Of course not," she said.

"Then what's the problem?"

She couldn't answer. "Well, I'm not sure I want to write poems."

"But you are."

"Yes."

"What are the poems about?" he asked.

A long silence followed. Ruth couldn't say.

"Can you share them with me?" Dr. Pickens asked. Ruth shook her head.

"Well, then," he said, "maybe you can bring one in, and we'll take a look at it."

She didn't speak.

"What are you feeling?" he asked.

Ruth's entire body quivered and her jaw tensed. "Things are fine," she said, barely allowing the words to escape. Once again Dr. Pickens could see Ruth denying her feelings as she simultaneously expressed them with her body.

Ruth didn't want Dr. Pickens to read the poems because she feared his reaction. Still, she had expected him to be scandalized by much of what she had already told him, and so far he hadn't been. He always seemed to suggest that behavior Ruth considered shameful wasn't shameful at all. He often made it a point to tell her that he didn't view the world as she did, which permitted her to wonder if her perspectives were always correct. And he reassured her that she need not worry about the freedom that new perspectives could bring. She wasn't going crazy—as she sometimes interpreted changes in her perceptions to mean—nor were these changes going to prompt a loss of control.

* * *

After spending another week fretting about whether or not to bring in a poem, Ruth walked into Dr. Pickens's office and, after a few casual comments about the weather and her job, handed him a piece of paper. "Here," she said. He glanced at it and then carefully gave it back, which frightened her.

"Why don't you try to read it out loud?" he said.

She grimaced. She thought she had brought the poem to the office so that he could read it to himself.

"It would be easier if you read it," she said.

He shook his head. "If I read it, it might distance you from your own feelings."

"Oh," she said softly. That wasn't what she wanted to hear, but Dr. Pickens sensed that she didn't really disagree. He thought of a child who knows something is good for her but doesn't want to acquiesce to a parent's wishes.

Still Ruth couldn't read the poem.

Dr. Pickens found Ruth's need to write understandable. It was, he felt, on a continuum with the many poets and writers who have suffered severe depression or personality disorders. What was more unusual was his decision to allow her to read in therapy something she had written outside the office. Normally he forbade his patients to use any props generated outside their world together. But Ruth was mired in her silence, and he believed the process of reading aloud might help her recapture and discuss some of the emotions she was trying to express in her poetry.

A few months previously Ruth had told him about the book of poems that her aunt had given her. Now Dr. Pickens realized that the book had appeared at about the same time as the abuse. Her writing in rhymes as an adult indicated to him the importance of that book in Ruth's life. It was a rare gift at a time when the Smocks were poor, and at first Ruth was able to identify with the positive emotions and images expressed in the poems. But the abuse shattered her self-image, which the poetry in the book reflected and reinforced, and writing poems as an adult became a channel through which Ruth could express her anger and self-hatred.

Ruth still refused to read the poem. She looked at it, put it on her lap, and stared at the floor.

"Take your time," Dr. Pickens said. "You can start when you want to and stop when you need to."

"I know," Ruth said. But she didn't feel as if she knew anything. She was terrified and could barely even look at the paper. The session dragged on, mostly silently, but punctuated with occasional comments by Ruth about the weather or her work. Finally, when her time was half over, Ruth forced herself to look at the poem. She cleared her throat and began to read.

Because she read very slowly, Dr. Pickens had time to listen to the content and the process of the poem, or what he thought of as the lyrics and the music. He heard the literal words and noted their factual accuracy, but he also considered their emotional context and significance.

While Ruth spoke, her voice became girlish. She sounded, Dr. Pickens thought, like the traumatized child she had once been. "A little girl alone in tears," she began. "The worst person born in years. I don't have a mother I am not born. No one upset and she's not forlorn."

These verses were, Dr. Pickens thought, an acceptance of some of Ruth's recent realizations that as a child she had felt unloved by her mother, and he was impressed by her ability to express them openly. Ruth was unveiling a significant shift in her perceptions of her childhood and her mother.

"All you think and all you say is written down even how you play. And in the book is written down. Bad things happen to little clowns."

Again Dr. Pickens heard Ruth reaffirm her parents' judgmental nature. She felt that everything she did or said had been checked off to see if it was acceptable; the little clowns were an image of herself as a silly girl who deserved to be punished.

"Please don't leave me please don't go. My daddy let me die or is it so. I'm evil and poison and no one worse. In the book I saw a hearse, carry her mother away for good."

Here Ruth was, Dr. Pickens thought, attempting to deal with ambivalence, fusing on the one hand her wish that her mother would die, because she was mean and depriving, and on the other hand her belief that if she did die, Ruth would be to blame because she was a bad girl. If she were better, her mother would love her more. But no matter how ambivalent she felt toward her mother, Ruth needed her; her words expressed the little girl's fear that her mother would die and leave her.

Ruth glanced quickly at Dr. Pickens, who saw she was looking to him for support. "I know this hurts you," he said. "You can stop if you want or go ahead."

Ruth nodded. "It's okay," she said, but she felt terrible listening to the unhappiness expressed by the child in the poem. "Carried her mother away for good," she read. "Blood on my hands and bugs on her head of wood."

Dr. Pickens thought of Ruth's *Alien*like birth, as

203

Ruth had pictured it from her family's comments, and the blood of the sexual assaults.

"I won't turn my head and look at the man. Please for my daddy I'll die if I can. No one can hear me. It's not all right. Under the pillow it's dark as night. Something is happening I'm sorry I'm bad. Now I'm dead and I am glad."

Dr. Pickens guessed the verses about her father reflected Ruth's desperate desire for her father to save her; if he couldn't, she wanted to die.

But he didn't interpret "Now I'm dead" to mean an actual death, but rather the little girl's equation of dissociation with death and a trip to heaven, where she would be safe. Ruth was writing from the point of view of a three-and-a-half-year-old child, and Dr. Pickens felt that an accurate concept of death didn't emerge until age eight. Before that, death was an irrational, incomplete, and distorted concept and could mean simply sleep or departure. For the little girl in the poem death sometimes meant just an escape from pain.

Ruth spoke even more softly and haltingly now. She was having trouble seeing the words through her tears. "She screamed and cried I am so scared. I'm falling apart and my bottom is bare. I'm going away so she won't scold. Good little girls do only what they are told. Get away get away it's not all right. Please someone help me to stop a fight."

In these verses Dr. Pickens heard Ruth express her vulnerability and terror of the assaults. Even if she was a bad little girl, she was crying out for help because she didn't deserve such punishment.

"Fall backward and watch yourself go," Ruth read. "I'll die and die but it's too slow. Teach me a lesson with a key. I'm sorry I sat on someone's knee. This is not me to make him dead. See he's dead on this same bed. Can't tell if I'm dead or asleep. Both of them in a big heap."

Here Dr. Pickens thought the little girl was expressing the fear that the man assaulting her had died since he was lying inert on top of her. And because she seemed also to be watching it from above, he noted that she had been able to achieve some distance from the scene; her dissociation as a three-year-old hadn't been constant, perhaps because the little girl who flew away felt so much guilt at leaving the little girl in the bed.

"I can't breathe or move or see. I hear a man and feel him on me. Pushing me oh please somewhere my hands. Ripped them off where did they land."

These verses were, Dr. Pickens assumed, an expression of the literal experience: the man had stuffed something in Ruth's mouth and was lying on top of her. He was also holding her hands or perhaps had tied them to the bed.

"Voices inside my head say I can't feel him anyway. Nobody can hurt me no one will kill me. A little girl I still can't see. She's bad as bad to scream and cry. Seems like someone sewed up my eye. If I could move I'd run away. Hide and seek was what I came to play. I can't stand it in the dark I can't stand it. If I could find my hands I might hit. The book with this in it is now black. God in the sky is the one who keeps track."

In these verses, as Ruth was moving back and forth between the dissociation and the pain of the actual experience, Dr. Pickens heard another expression of Ruth's belief that she was bad. The black book was the Bible; the judgment of God and the judgment of her mother were synonymous.

"The little girl is ugly and dead. See the man pat her on her head. I didn't mean to hurt my mother. Sometimes I did wish she was some other."

Apparently, Dr. Pickens realized, the man had made occasional gestures to soothe Ruth after an assault. The next lines referred to the child's explanation for the attacks; Ruth had hurt her mother by being born so violently and as a child had continued to upset her. She was being punished as well for wishing her mother dead.

"I'm lost from her and my daddy in this bed. I'll go away and soon be dead. Now I can see but I can't look. Get away fast but kill the black book. Let my head turn around. Cried and screamed and tried to get down. She's sorry she cried and now she's killed and gone. The top of my legs on fire to the bone."

At this point the poem manifested an agony so devastating that Dr. Pickens felt Ruth was horribly divided between her fear of death and her longing for it as a release. She wanted to get rid of the evidence of her badness by destroying the black book in which her actions were being judged. Ruth was also expressing her conviction that she had been killed as a punishment for crying, revealing a corollary between her mother's criticism and the actions of the man who was assaulting her. Her mother was angriest when Ruth cried. The man was also the most brutal when she cried, so her belief that tears were sinful and deserved punishment was being reinforced. The last line referred to the actual rape, as the man tried unsuccessfully to penetrate Ruth's vagina, perhaps drawing blood.

"Make his eyes go away. I'm an angel and in the sun I'll play."

Here Ruth simply dissociated.

"My legs are gone just like my hands. Everything's turning I'll die in this sand."

And now she returned to the little girl and the ferocious pain of the abuse.

"Babies will come from my ears and mouth and will be heard."

As a child on a farm, Ruth already understood to some degree that male ejaculation (in part confused with urination) produced small babies. She wasn't sophisticated enough to know more, but she feared she would have babies, which would be further proof that she was bad.

"I'll die and die and die before I say a word. My tummy is wet and cold and warm. I hate them all I am not born. The animals got out of the cage. Killed the man on every page."

The little girl hated her mother for mistreating her, she hated her father for leaving her with the man, and she hated the man also, but she was too terrified to tell anyone what he had done. The forces aligned against her were so massive that all she could do was wish she hadn't been born. Dr. Pickens had often heard children identify with animals, so he wasn't surprised that Ruth imagined that animals would carry out her revenge. She wasn't strong enough to do it herself.

"Drowned in the river in a sack."

The man had threatened to drown Ruth if she told on him. Also, Ruth had mentioned to Dr. Pickens that as a matter of course on the farm, her parents drowned unwanted animals, and she remembered her father putting a litter of kittens in a sack while she stood by and watched, panic-stricken. She immediately identified with the kittens and feared that someday when she misbehaved, she too would be stuffed in a sack and drowned.

"My daddy's gone and never looked back. Bad little girls wet the bed. Go in the air and now she's dead. Tell her over and over what to do. Kill them cause they won't find you."

Ruth's father had unknowingly left her with the man, and Ruth wasn't old enough to understand fully her father's apparent indifference to her pleading. Once again the words and the syntax of the verses reflected the confusion of a child who wished both that she were dead and that she could kill her tormentors.

Ruth stopped, thoroughly exhausted from the poem's intense emotional impact, as well as from her effort to pretend that its sorrow hadn't affected her.

"What are you feeling?" Dr. Pickens asked.

She shrugged her shoulders. "I'm okay," she said, relapsing into stoicism.

Dr. Pickens looked at the clock.

"Your time is almost up," he said quietly. "You can use the remaining minutes to gather your thoughts before you go."

"The poem isn't over," Ruth said plaintively.

"We can continue Thursday," he suggested.

Ruth nodded. Inwardly she dreaded the notion of ever continuing. "Fine," she said.

"Are you ready to leave?" Dr. Pickens asked.

"Yes," she said firmly. She got up and left.

That night she went through her usual routine—dinner, ceramics, television, bed. If only she were as normal as her life, she thought. She went to work, came home, and took care of the house with Ed. People left her alone. She didn't make any new friends, nor did she wish to. And she felt no need to tell anyone about her therapy or about the abuse. She did drop a few hints to Jean that something ugly had occurred when she was a child. Jean waited for Ruth to tell her more, but Ruth said nothing else.

Ruth brought the poem to her next session on Thursday. "I'm back," she said. Dr. Pickens smiled.

"I just bet you're glad I am," she added. She feigned indifference, sat down, and looked around the room.

"Why wouldn't I be glad to see you?" Dr. Pickens asked.

"Oh, right," Ruth said.

She heard what she had said and thought, he must think I'm such an idiot. Still she realized at some point she was going to have to continue reading the poem. She looked at it; the words were misty. Only after a considerable time could she begin to read, and again so slowly that Dr. Pickens had time to consider the verses carefully.

"Legs are straight and like a clock I see. Big hand at nine and little one on three," Ruth began.

Dr. Pickens instantly pictured the man holding Ruth in a position that would enable him to attempt penetration while Ruth was looking away from the bed, watching the face of a clock. Two forty-five was probably the actual time of the assault, and the placement of the clock's hands reminded Ruth of her own position.

Ruth had stopped reading. "This must have been horrible for you," Dr. Pickens said.

"Yeah," she said. "It wasn't very pleasant." She didn't look at him when she spoke. Then she looked back down at the paper and continued.

"Hickory dickory dock. The hands fell off the clock."

Dr. Pickens heard a fusion of images here: Ruth's

hands were like the hands of the clock, and both were useless in fending off her attacker.

"Run from the man and get away. My legs are gone so I have to stay. The potty was warm and red. Hide the mess on the bed."

Here Ruth was unable to move, her legs pinned by the man's. Dr. Pickens had already heard Ruth refer to her childhood use of the word *potty* for the genital area, which the man had tried to penetrate, drawing blood.

"I hate him he feels like a railroad track. Sounds like an engine go away and not come back."

Ruth had told Dr. Pickens that her parents always warned her to avoid the railroad tracks, and the sound of the man's heavy breathing reminded her of a railroad engine.

"He turned into two with a worm like a bat. My insides came out I don't know where I'm at."

Here the man's penis became erect, and Ruth either threw up or bled.

"I'm dead as dead in a dress of white. I can't stand thinking I wish it was light."

And again she dissociated to escape the pain and terror of the assault.

"I want this to be the end. I wish I could go and bring back a friend. I saw my mother and ran to give her a hug. She yelled at me and covered me with bugs. I hugged her tighter and tighter still. She wouldn't look and never will. Patty cake patty cake baker's man. Burn the weenee in the pan. Opened my eyes and what did I see. A giant monster killing me. Because I cried and no one knows. I can't get air into my nose."

Ruth again referred to her mother's rejection. And the man, Dr. Pickens realized with revulsion, had held

Ruth's nose during the assault, forcing her to open her mouth.

"I shut my eyes so I can't see. My face is not there or it soon won't be. It hurts so much but I won't tell. So I can stay and not have to go to hell."

Ruth expected to be punished for the assault.

"A rotten kid is what he said. Please don't it hurts so much I now am dead. My teeth are gone and in their place. This giant snake all over my face."

Ruth glanced at Dr. Pickens to monitor the expression on his face, and this time his impenetrable repose reassured her. She resumed, reading slowly but steadily; the poem no longer rhymed. "I can't even yell I'm dying. I hope I die all the stink and noise and hurt on my nose and teeth. My teeth are gone. I want to be a clean little girl in my clothes. The book is blacker and all the pages are full. I hurt all over. I want my daddy. My back is gone with my legs and my hands. I'm all gone soon. Bad stuff to eat in my mouth. It is rotten and nasty and I want some air and my daddy. . . . I want my mother to hug me but she won't. All this in my mouth to eat. I can't eat it. I need to throw up. I am choking to death. I don't know. I can't look. All the bad smell. It stink and mean giants. I need to die. The mess is in my hair. I don't feel good. Now he won't pat my hair. I hate him. I wish he would die too. I wish I had my hands. I want my daddy. I'll get a whipping for throwing up in the bed. I can't help it. I'm a bad bad girl. I am dead."

With these words Ruth relived the feelings that had overwhelmed her when she couldn't dissociate. Several times while Ruth wasn't looking, Dr. Pickens had wiped tears from his eyes. He had never heard such anguish in a session. In the past he had listened to older children who had been forced, in stilted tones, to testify against adults for sexual abuse, and to younger children who had only a limited ability to describe what had happened to them. He had also talked to adults who reflected on childhood sexual abuse from a grown-up perspective. But Ruth's verses were the clearest and most articulate expression of a child's actual feelings that he had ever heard.

"That must have been horrible for you," he said softly.

"Yes, it was," Ruth said. She was in tears, but she wasn't sobbing. They were both wordless for several minutes.

"It's time for us to stop now," Dr. Pickens said, "but do you want to sit here for a while? You can stay in another room until you feel ready to leave."

Ruth shook her head. "No, thank you," she said. "I'll be fine."

As always he rose, walked her to the door, and opened it for her to leave.

9

DURING THEIR NEXT FEW SESSIONS, AS DR. PICKENS
had hoped, Ruth talked about the emotions and memories that the poem had evoked. But she found the
conversation strenuous, and although she was increasingly forthcoming about her anger toward her mother,
she continued to apologize for her. "Her life was so
tough," Ruth repeated.

Dr. Pickens reiterated an analogy he used with other
patients who defended their parents. "That may be
true," he said, "but in terms of what you experienced,
it didn't make any difference whether your mother's
actions were purposeful or not. It's like someone
being hit with a baseball bat. The amount of damage is
the same, regardless of the perpetrator's motivation."

Ruth nodded. The comparison helped her understand that while she need not blame her mother, she
could still feel bad about her childhood. She didn't say
anything however, for she believed that no matter
what she said out loud, her poem had captured what
she felt in her heart.

In a subsequent session Ruth remembered her hair. Before she was four she had pretty blond curls, but sometime later she began to imagine that something horrible had gotten into her hair, dirtying and spoiling it. Worse, like many baby blondes, Ruth's hair turned dark, and the curls disappeared, which as a child Ruth imagined was a terrible punishment for allowing all that bad stuff to get into it. "It was semen," she now told Dr. Pickens. "And that must be why," she added, "I still wash my hair so often."

At home Ruth wrote another poem, which she brought in a week later. From this point on, Ruth read aloud during almost every session, and her therapy focused on the content of her poems.

Again she took more than half a session to start reading her next poem and more than one session to finish it.

"I don't want to be a rotten girl," she read. "Peed in my hair and no more curl. I'm in a hole with all the fire. Get his hands and hold them with wire. He made the fire on top of my legs. It hurts and hurts I cried and beg. He is in the far away graveyard. My daddy killed him he hit him hard. I can't drink his pea I can't spit it out. Please come and get me with candy all about."

She stopped and looked down, holding on to the piece of paper tenuously. "Go on," Dr. Pickens suggested.

"I can't," Ruth said.

"Take your time."

A few minutes later she tried again. "I want my mother to put me in my bed cause it's clean. I'm on fire because the giant was mean. He's growing horns like a bull with the cows. Kill him dead and make him a pig and a sow. Rubbed me with his fingers before he made me dead. I'm all gone away but he left my head. I see pictures of dead persons all around. I know they're dead cause they don't make a sound."

She stopped and began to cry. "I can't read any-more," she said.

"Okay," Dr. Pickens said, "but tell me how you feel now."

Ruth wiped the tears from her face. "I'm fine," she said. "You must just think I'm the worst crybaby in the world, carrying on like this."

"Why would I think that?" Dr. Pickens asked.

"I don't know," Ruth mumbled.

"Is there anything I have said or done that would suggest I feel that way?" Dr. Pickens asked.

"No. I guess not," she said.

"Maybe you're expecting me to be like your mother. You remember that she was ashamed of you for crying, and so you think I will be too."

Ruth nodded.

"For instance," he said, "do you remember what you told me about the time you swallowed the poison on the paint brush?"

"Yes," she said.

"It was normal to cry in such a situation. And what you've just described was much more painful and sad."

"I guess it was," Ruth said, looking relieved.

"I'll read the rest of it now," Ruth told Dr. Pickens the following Thursday.

"Okay," he said, trying not to set a tone of approval or disapproval, as he felt Ruth's parents had done. "Whenever you wish."

Ruth paused for a moment, then she began. Again

she could only speak or read for a few sentences without stopping. "I hate him I don't want his nasty potty in my face. I can't stand the smell I'll die in this place. I'm bad and I screamed cried and am bad with this potty in my mouth is full I want my daddy please, somebody get my daddy to chop off his potty and get my hands I can't stand my hands to be gone. They're still gone and I can't find my hands. I saw them but they're off. I can't scream now I'm too sick of his pea. I can't stand this I am dead and I hate everyone. I'm glad I'm dead and I can't stand to burn up like this anymore. . . . It is so cold but I am on fire."

Once again Dr. Pickens asked Ruth how she felt. "Not too good," she admitted.

Dr. Pickens also felt sad, visualizing the brutal assault and the helpless little girl, and again he fought back the impulse to cry. He wanted to hold that little girl and comfort her. He also wanted Ruth to know that the consequences of her abuse as a child could be altered for her as an adult. In one corner of Ruth's psyche the little girl had been suffering alone and forever, but Dr. Pickens knew that Ruth would be released from her fear and anger if she could lift the repression of her true feelings and alter her perception of herself as a bad person.

Ruth was beginning to understand this too, and she left her session that day with conflicting feelings of pain and hope. When she walked outside, where the day was sunny and soft, as nice as a Kansas spring could be, Ruth could still hear her own words, "I'm glad I'm dead." But she thought, what a lovely day, and how odd it is that the world can be beautiful.

Ruth had a dream. She was a little girl riding a tricycle much too fast on a sidewalk, which ended, and she fell off the seat and had to go to the hospital. There she met Dr. Pickens, who was extremely nice. He was wearing a pretty red necktie, and Ruth told him how much she liked it. "Do you really?" he asked, and when she nodded, he took a pair of scissors, cut it off, and gave it to her.

This dream, which Ruth brought into her next session, led to a conversation about sexuality, a topic that Ruth never imagined she would ever discuss with anyone other than Ed, and especially not with another man.

Dr. Pickens had already concluded that Ruth led a relatively normal sex life, although she disliked oral sexual activity. "That's one thing no one will ever do to me," Ruth told Dr. Pickens passionately. Given Ruth's history, he found her reluctance understandable, and he told her that she was actually quite fortunate to have escaped from the sexual trauma of her childhood so relatively unscathed. Still sexual intercourse and fantasies often left Ruth feeling guilty. During her marriage the issue of sexual enjoyment had been problematic, as she had previously mentioned to Dr. Pickens the few times they had discussed Ruth's sexuality.

Dr. Pickens had frequently encountered transference of sexual feelings in psychotherapy, but because Ruth had been brutalized and had lived in a sexually repressive family, she seldom gave vent to her sexual feelings. When they did occasionally emerge, however, Dr. Pickens tried to point out the possibility of viewing such feelings in positive ways.

Ruth, however, was surprised whenever she heard him mention sex, because she rarely felt that anything she said had such overtones. She was aware that they disagreed about any sexual feelings she might have toward him, but rather than discuss it openly, she always preferred to drop the subject. The one time he asked her outright if she was having sexual fantasies about him, she thought, oh, Dr. Pickens, dig you! You're the last person on earth I'd want to sleep with! Her actual reply was cool. "Not that I'm aware of," she said. In her opinion, psychiatrists thought about sex far too much.

"I'm going on vacation in a few weeks."

It was now almost summer, and Dr. Pickens handed Ruth a slip of paper on which he had written the dates he would be away from the office. Ruth looked at it with alarm. She had forgotten that, like anyone else, he took time off. What if I go nuts and he's not here? she thought. What am I going to do?

"What are your feelings?" he asked. "You seem upset."

No kidding, she thought, but only nodded.

"Tell me why," he said.

She considered the question, but rather than answer it directly, she unearthed childhood feelings of abandonment. Whenever Faye had left the house, Ruth always told herself that her mother would never return. "One day she went to Kansas City," Ruth said, "and so my dad took us over to Grandma Smock's. I remember crying the whole time we were there. My dad didn't help much either. Why didn't he soothe me or tell me it was just for a little while?"

"Do you think I won't come back?" Dr. Pickens asked.

Ruth shook her head. "I used to have this horror that my mother would die in a car wreck and I'd be alone forever."

"What is that fantasy about?"

"Well, I guess I was afraid of being left alone."

"Or perhaps you had mixed feelings toward your mother, including both anger and love," Dr. Pickens said. "On the one hand, you needed her, but on the other, you were angry at her, and that anger resulted in the imaginary car accident."

Ruth tried to absorb all this; sometimes he told her more than she could immediately understand. "Are you telling me I wanted my mother dead?" she asked.

"I'm asking you to consider that possibility," he said. He also drew a parallel between her former thoughts about her mother and her present ones about him. "You were angry at your mother for not giving you support when you were afraid, and now I'm abandoning you too, and so you're angry with me. That sets up the same sort of dilemma you had with your mother; you don't want me to leave, but at the same time you're angry that I might."

At first Ruth couldn't believe she had wanted her mother dead, but as she considered it more, she became uncertain. No one in her family had ever had a car wreck, and no one ever talked about one. "Well," Ruth said, "maybe the little girl thought she had been injured and her mother didn't help her. So maybe the little girl wanted her mother to be injured too."

"Do you think that could be?" Dr. Pickens asked.

Ruth thought it over. "I don't know," she said. "But," she added, remembering his vacation, "what if something happens while you're gone?"

Dr. Pickens took back the slip of paper, wrote on it, and gave it to her. Ruth looked down and saw the name and telephone number of a different psychiatrist.

"I'll tell this doctor about your situation," he said, "and if you need to talk to someone, you can always reach him."

Ruth felt better, but she never called the other doctor. She did fret while Dr. Pickens was away, however. She knew now that it was true what they had said in Richards when she was a child, that your head would never be the same if you went to a psychiatrist. But it was dawning on Ruth that this wasn't necessarily a bad thing.

10

"YOU'VE BEEN COMING IN HERE A YEAR NOW," DR. Pickens said. It was early fall, several weeks after he had returned from his vacation.

Ruth had been assiduously marking the time on her calendar. "Really?" she asked. "Have I?"

"I'd like to ask the court to cancel its commitment to treatment order," he said. "We both know you're here voluntarily. I think the court will be willing to acknowledge that."

"Fine," she said. She was elated. For months she had wanted to see him on her own accord rather than at the insistence of the authorities, partly for the sense of freedom, but also to let him know the extent of her commitment to therapy.

"There may have to be a court hearing," Dr. Pickens added.

"Well, that's okay," Ruth said, but her mood plummeted. The notion of an argumentative public forum over her sanity petrified her. She didn't voice this worry, however, fearing that Dr. Pickens might find it a manifestation of weakness. But the hearing never materialized. The judge simply granted Dr. Pickens's request, and beginning in October 1982, Ruth was no longer beholden to Wichita.

Throughout 1983 and 1984 Ruth wrote poetry at home to read during her sessions. She never deliberated on the content; each evening she simply sat down at a table and let whatever filled her mind flow onto the paper—a process somewhat comparable to the Poet's, Dr. Pickens told her. Ruth then ignored the poems until therapy, for she felt incapable of dealing with their feelings without support.

Of those feelings, rage came foremost, and much of it was aimed at adults: "The adults should control their brief moment of passion and ecstasy. If they don't want to produce one like me. Think of their careless fuck. This great fun might end at bad luck."

She was also angry at the man who had assaulted her and at men in general: "To keep the snake out of her mouth and face. She searched for herself a secret hiding place. She could keep a knife clenched in her teeth and then. She could use it on all wicked men."

But most of all Ruth was angry at her mother: "I was trouble right from the beginning. But somehow my memory fails to recall my sinning."

Dr. Pickens asked Ruth why she had never told her mother about the neighbor. Her first reaction was that the very idea that she could talk about the man had never entered her mind. Then as she explored the subject over many more sessions, other issues arose. For one, Ruth had believed the man's threats. She told Dr. Pickens about a recent recollection in which she was playing with her doll at her grandmother's house when the neighbor came by. The moment she saw him, she started to run, but he caught her and took her off to the side of the house. Then he grabbed the doll, pulled off its head, and said, "This is what happens to people who don't shut up." Ruth guessed that if she told, the man would take off her head too.

Another childhood fear had plagued her. If Ruth told her mother, maybe she would approve and turn Ruth over to the man forever. Throughout the last few months Ruth had been dreaming of headless chickens running around in circles after Faye had axed their necks. Both Ruth and Dr. Pickens agreed that as a child she had identified with the dead birds and had felt similarly helpless in the face of her mother's power.

Uncovering these associations led to two other possibilities. Faye had repeatedly told Ruth that God knew everything and marked it all down in a large book—which resembled, in Ruth's mind, the poetry book given to her by her aunt. So God already knew about the assaults and hadn't stopped them. Instead, he wrote about them and approved.

Finally, Ruth as a child had come to believe that her mother could read her mind. Faye used to look at her and say, "I know exactly what you're thinking." Ruth believed her, and so she assumed Faye was aware of the abuse. She had also learned to control her thoughts at a young age, for she never knew when her mother was listening in. But no matter which scenario Ruth imagined, the outcome was identical: she lost. It was no different than if the notion of telling her parents had never occurred to her, as she had first assumed. Everything led to nothing.

After Ruth read her poems, Dr. Pickens used them to discuss various issues; in particular, he encouraged her to consider the anger beginning to surface in much of her writing, along with its positive implications.

"When you were the Poet, you took all that anger and turned it against yourself," he pointed out. "Now you're letting it out. As a result you no longer see yourself as a bad person, and you're no longer filled with the need to hurt yourself."

Ruth nodded quietly. For years she had only blamed herself. Now for the first time in her life she was able to become angry at others—at least in her poems. Still she didn't want to agree with Dr. Pickens aloud. She felt insecure talking about her progress. But Dr. Pickens didn't expect Ruth to accept his every word consciously. He knew that she always reflected on his interpretations following therapy and quite often acted on them too; this acceptance was apparent in her willingness to discuss certain feelings and to deal with them in greater depth—especially the anger that more and more she was uncovering within.

"I've been seeing a blue rock," Ruth said in the winter of 1983, and she shuddered. Ruth didn't know how many incidents of abuse had taken place, and she was too anxious to let them all loose simultaneously, but sometimes the episodes surfaced through other memories. She feared the rock stood for something sinister. Three days earlier, as she had entered the tub to take a shower, she stepped over a blue rock. But when she bent down to pick it up, there was no rock, and she was panic-stricken.

Now, in session, she saw the blue rock flash in her mind again.

"What about it?" Dr. Pickens asked.

"I don't know," she said, and then stared at her lap for a few minutes. "It would be nice to curl up into a little ball," she added. "I'm not feeling good."

"What do you think is happening?" Dr. Pickens

asked. He watched her posture shift into a slightly fetal position.

"I don't know."

"Let your mind roam. Tell me whatever you're thinking."

Ruth suddenly remembered a dark place where something was dangerously wrong. "It's the storm cellar near our house," she said, "where we went in case there were tornadoes. We also kept canned goods down there, since it was cool and out of the way."

Ruth felt sick. "Oh, God," she said, and stopped talking. Dr. Pickens waited a full minute before encouraging her to continue.

"Well," Ruth said, "the little girl's aunt had given her a blue rock. It was like a paperweight, and once when the little girl was playing, the man came over and picked it up and told her that she had to come with him or she would never get her blue rock back.

"So she followed him into the storm cellar, and then he did it to her again. The little girl floated off to heaven, and the girl who was left in the cellar thought that her teeth were going to fall out.

"Later when the little girl threw up, the man picked up a jar of tomatoes and broke off the bottom and put it down on top of her vomit. Then he left. The little girl watched all the red juice flow from the tomatoes down the drain along with the vomit, and she wanted to be dead too, because if she was dead, then no one could hurt her anymore."

Ruth stopped talking. Dr. Pickens noted that she had been able to tell this story with fewer pauses than usual and had finished it within one session. She still needed to shift the story into the third person to recount the abuse, but Dr. Pickens never expected her to replace fully the little girl with herself in their sessions, nor was he convinced it was necessary, as long as Ruth recognized the truth in her heart.

On February 1, 1983, Ruth drove to Towne East, the mall where the stabbing had occurred four years earlier. She had considered never returning, but malls were an integral part of her life, and Towne East was one of the most convenient. After an hour of shopping for linens, Ruth, loaded with several large parcels, walked through the automatic doors and nearly fainted. In the parking lot, where there should have been cars, she saw only snakes: hundreds of oily reptiles hissing and writhing over the concrete. She stared, terrified, as the snakes moved closer and closer. But somehow she retained enough control to guess that she was hallucinating, and she forced herself to turn around, walk back inside the mall, and look for a pay phone. She fumbled in her purse for change and called Ed. "I can't find the car," she told him honestly. "Can you come help?" She had no intention of going outside to look.

"I'll be right over," he said.

A few minutes later Ed pulled into the lot and met Ruth at the phone. When she walked back outside with him, the snakes were gone. "I'm sorry," Ruth said. "I feel so silly."

"Happens to everyone," Ed said, and he walked her to the car.

She didn't tell Ed what she had seen in the lot; she was afraid it might frighten him more than it did her. She did mention it to Dr. Pickens, however, but they disagreed over the incident's significance. To Dr. Pickens the snakes were phallic symbols; to Ruth they were images representing fear. As ever, Ruth's major disagreement with Dr. Pickens concerned sexuality.

She continued to feel that he viewed the world through a sexual prism, but she never dared to say so.

Ruth showed up at her next session early enough to watch an attractive young woman trudge out of the office. She thought the woman looked unusually depressed, and so after Dr. Pickens ushered her inside, she asked, "What's wrong with that girl?"

"What are your thoughts?" Dr. Pickens asked.

Ruth immediately realized that he wasn't going to answer her question about another patient. Dr. Pickens could see in Ruth's face the emotional consequences of his refusal: first she felt anger toward him, next she feared dealing with that anger directly, then she whipped it around and directed it at herself and in turn felt foolish. This made her think of herself as a little girl, and she momentarily hated that girl too. "After all," she said to Dr. Pickens, "don't you think the girl was partly to blame for what happened?"

"Why do you say that?" he asked.

"Well, at first I liked all the attention the man gave me," she said. "I was pleased he wanted to spend so much time with me. He made me feel special. He thought I was pretty and he liked my hair, and my mother never said those sorts of things. But I was a fool to trust him."

"But here you are identifying with your mother again by finding a way to condemn yourself," Dr. Pickens said. "The fact is it wasn't your fault. Have you ever heard of the Stockholm syndrome?"

Ruth shook her head.

"People who are taken hostage," he explained, "often become dependent on their captors, which can lead to a sense of identification with those who have the power to kill or spare.

"It's not unsimilar to the situation with your mother," Dr. Pickens continued. "She was the parent who took primary responsibility for raising you. You were so dependent on her that you locked into her negative view—since the alternative was to be abandoned by her. It must have seemed better to share her negative view than to fight her over it and risk losing her."

Ruth listened and nodded, but she feared she was being unjust to Faye, so she changed the subject. "Well, I bet you wouldn't hug that little girl," she said.

"Why not?" Dr. Pickens asked.

Ruth wanted to answer that the little girl was unlovable, something that she could once have said easily but was now much more difficult. "Well, would you?" she asked.

"The little girl doesn't have a body anymore," Dr. Pickens said gently. "She's inside you. You feel I would have hugged her then. Well, you're the only one who can touch her directly now."

Ruth thought about this for only a moment before dismissing it.

For several weeks before Christmas Ruth had been making a ceramic nut dish in the shape of a walnut with a squirrel on one side. It was a gift for Dr. Pickens, and at her last session before the holiday, she handed him a brightly wrapped box. "Merry Christmas," she said.

Dr. Pickens smiled but shook his head. "I can't accept a gift from you," he said. He was surprised, but not in the manner Ruth had hoped. He thought he had told her his policy concerning gifts: he accepted them only when he felt it was in the patient's best interest to do so. In Ruth's case, where he suspected that she was highly vulnerable to exploitation, he had no intention of taking anything.

He did ask her to open it, however, so they could explore what she wanted him to have. After she took off the wrapping paper, he looked at the gift quizzically. "It's a nut dish," Ruth said.

"I see that now."

"It'll remind you of me," she said. "You know, ha, ha, from your nutty patient Ruth." She laughed, but she noticed that as usual he didn't.

Now Dr. Pickens was certain that he was right not to accept the gift, for he didn't want to provide her with any implicit acceptance of her view that she was nutty. Ruth accepted his decision, but inwardly she seethed.

On the first session after Christmas Ruth showed up with a new poem. "I don't know if you will like this one," she said.

"Go ahead and we can see," he replied.

"Fine." She seemed nervous, but it was, Dr. Pickens noted, a different sort of edginess. As usual Ruth wasn't eager to start once she had said she would read.

Pickens waited; Ruth was silent. Finally she began. "I let go of a shy modesty of my secret soul. Should have kept this buried like a mole."

This poem, Dr. Pickens realized, didn't pertain to a childhood memory, and the language was more mature than in the previous poems.

"A little gift I brought to you," she read. "Seems this was not the proper thing to do. My apologies to you for being so bold. My mistakes were counted as twofold."

Dr. Pickens was impressed; Ruth previously had allowed a few critical comments to slip out, and some

229

occasional sarcasm, but she hadn't yet admitted any full-fledged hostility toward him.

"The first was for appearing here with a present," she continued. "The second was revealing to you its content. I doubled my errors in your stand. By sitting there with a nut dish in hand. Your response of 'I don't accept gifts' gave the bearer of one a lift. I thought of something I'd like to unveil. But it would also surely fail. A plaque for your wall made of pure gold. My message to you on it would be told: 'I am a great doctor, I'm exceptionally smart. I go by the book and I've got no heart.' "

Ruth looked up at Dr. Pickens briefly, then back down at the paper. She was embarrassed. But he felt that in the context of therapy, Ruth had taken another leap forward. "It sounds as though you are feeling anger toward me," he said.

"I guess so," she said. "Maybe." She tried to laugh, to make it seem slight.

He then asked her if she would talk about her impression of him, but she found it impossible to elaborate on what she had said in the poem.

"Can you see that you created a difficult situation for me?" he asked. "I don't believe you are nutty, yet if I took the gift, wouldn't that imply that I do? But if I turn it down, then you assume I'm rejecting you."

"Uh-huh," Ruth nodded, and sighed with relief. Besides her anger, she had brought into the session her fear that Dr. Pickens would respond to her anger in kind. Instead he smiled, which puzzled her.

Ruth brought in another sequence of dreams; in them she experienced various versions of entrapment. In one an unhappy little girl in a glass house was trying to hide something. Ruth didn't know what the girl wanted to conceal, but the girl could see many adults with big eyes and big teeth laughing at her.

Ruth guessed his question before he asked it. "How do you feel about that dream?" Dr. Pickens inquired.

"Bad," she said, but she refused to say more.

"What else?" he asked.

"Trapped," she said. "There's no way out."

"None?"

"None."

"Well," he said, "I can see why you would think you were trapped. You were feeling exposed as a child, and this reflected your fear that your mind could be read. The house was your mind, and everyone could see what you were thinking. Now with your feelings coming out in therapy the same way, that exposure would be damning or punishable in the same way."

Ruth considered the interpretation but said nothing. He continued. "When you were a child, you felt the powerlessness that accompanies childhood. As I've said before, you aren't a child now. You're an adult. You have choices you didn't have then. And you were totally alone then; you didn't feel free or safe. You couldn't share those kinds of feelings with anyone else. Now you have me to help you with them."

Thank God, she thought.

Ruth continued to arrive early at Dr. Pickens's office; she enjoyed watching the other patients leave and often fantasized about their problems. She still found the attractive and depressed young woman the most interesting, particularly since her mood was noticeably lightening. The woman occasionally smiled at Ruth now and once even mumbled a greeting. Ruth longed to ask Dr. Pickens for her story, but she knew questions about his other patients were against the rules.

Another time, in the parking lot, a patient cornered Ruth by her car. "You have a beautiful complexion," the woman said.

"Thanks," Ruth said.

"Do you use Mary Kay cosmetics?" the woman asked. Ruth noticed that the car on her right was plastered with Mary Kay stickers. She tried to get away.

"I want an appointment to come see you," the woman said.

Ruth politely declined.

"You can't get away from me!" the woman yelled, "I'll get your license plate number!"

Ruth did ask Dr. Pickens about this woman, but he wouldn't comment. Ruth was disappointed, though not surprised. Then she realized that she felt reassured, for his silence indicated he wouldn't talk about her to anyone else either.

One Saturday afternoon in February, while Ed was out walking Ginger, Ruth was reading a magazine and listening to her music, lost in concentration. She took a moment to rest her eyes, and then she shook slightly. Some sort of movement occurred within her head, and once again her brain began performing without her conscious intent, but too quickly for Ruth to become frightened. Instead of a dark curtain descending over her mind, this time one went up. A lost memory materialized, and suddenly Ruth was staring three years into her past, at the stabbing incident at the Towne East mall. She was seeing perfectly clear pictures: There I am in the parking lot, she thought. I'm opening the car door, and now I'm struggling. Her memory duplicated the story she had told the police exactly, except for one detail. She was alone. Her assailant was inside her head. She was hearing the words, "You have to do it," and she was looking down at her hands —holding a knife. "You have to do it," the voice said. So she stabbed herself three times as hard as she could, and yet she felt no pain. Then she got into the car and drove out of the lot, and she didn't feel anything until she turned into the traffic. While she was driving, the attack recast itself in her mind, and by the time Ruth had reached the phone at the gas station a few minutes later, she thought it had all happened as she told Al Thimmesch: a man had assaulted her in the parking lot.

Ruth now knew what she had never fully understood before: she had truly been the Poet. She still insisted that the Fort Scott assault had taken place, that someone had both called her the night of Ed's hospitalization and had sent her the old newspaper article, and that an unfamiliar man had approached her on the street. Other people, including Bernie Drowatzky, had heard male voices on the phone, and Ruth couldn't have lit the Christmas wreath herself while she was sitting in the basement with Ed. Ruth also felt the knife left in the phone company lobby had to have been a stranger's prank, since by that time many people were watching the building's entrances carefully and would have noticed Ruth carrying a large knife. Someone, maybe one man or maybe more, had been playing a game with her.

Ed, who continued to struggle with his wife's history, still believed in Ruth's original version of the kidnapping, and even Ruth herself sometimes wondered whether it might have happened as she told the police. She couldn't understand how she had found her way to Twin Lakes or why the episode seemed so vivid. But these other memories didn't return to her now. Regardless, Ruth felt real comfort knowing that she had stabbed herself. It gave her, for the first time, a tangible connection to the Poet, and that made her feel less fractured.

11

THE THIRD WEEK OF MARCH 1983 WAS PARTICULARLY dank, but Ruth was in a good mood. As she walked past the receptionist in Dr. Pickens's office, she gave her an unusually cheerful greeting before starting to climb the stairs.

"Oh, Mrs. Finley," the receptionist called after her. "Didn't Dr. Pickens tell you?"

"Tell me what?" Ruth asked.

"He's not coming in today."

"No," Ruth said, "he didn't tell me."

"That really surprises me," the receptionist said. "He's usually so good about that sort of thing."

Ruth turned around silently, walked out the door, and drove home. She felt confused and upset.

At the next session Dr. Pickens welcomed her as usual. At first Ruth was afraid to mention the incident, but finally she said, "You didn't tell me you weren't going to be here on Tuesday."

Dr. Pickens was puzzled. He had told all his other patients, and assumed he had told Ruth too. If he hadn't, he knew she would feel hurt, and he regretted that.

Ruth thought, he likes his other patients enough to tell them, but he doesn't like me. What she said was, "It's probably because you wanted to see me so bad, you couldn't find the strength to tell me!" She forced a laugh.

Dr. Pickens smiled.

"But I know you didn't tell me," she said, no longer laughing.

"The truth is I don't remember," Dr. Pickens said. "But I think I did."

"No, you didn't," Ruth insisted. "Did other patients come in that day?"

"Not that I know of."

"So you told everyone but me."

"I have to admit, I don't remember if I told you or not."

"You didn't," Ruth said. "You didn't."

Rather than argue, Dr. Pickens asked her how she felt. Ruth couldn't respond honestly. She was afraid to admit her fear that he didn't like her. Instead that night she wrote a poem.

She brought it in the next session. "I have to read this," she announced.

"Fine," he said.

"You may not feel that way when I'm done," Ruth said.

Dr. Pickens encouraged her to continue.

"All right, then," she said. As always she paused before she began. "The atmosphere quickly faded from warm to cold," she read. "When I thought I was the only patient you hadn't told. Thoughtless and uncaring—a forgetful jerk. You carefully hide your guarded smirk."

Ruth read this line fearfully, afraid of his reaction, but Dr. Pickens was proud of her. Rather than make excuses for him, as she had always done for her mother, she was confronting him as directly as she could and raising a legitimate concern.

"Your line about caring is a big crock of shit," Ruth read. "You snow the weak with your knowledge and wit. I thought you were very sincere and kind. As I sat before you and dissected my mind. I see myself as the most insignificant one you tend. So my fantasy of being your favorite back into hiding I'll send."

Ruth had once admitted to Dr. Pickens her fantasy that she was his favorite. He had told her in turn that this was a natural desire, the equivalent of a child's wishing to be her parents' favored child.

"I've irritated your subconscious so you conveniently forgot," Ruth read. "But this only confuses me and thickens the plot. My first reaction was you'd never again see me. I'd never come back and then I'd be free. . . . But then I decided I'd again show my face. And we could discuss this together my leaving this place. I'll return to myself and forever be still. I'm sick of everyone and I've had my fill."

Dr. Pickens didn't tell Ruth that if indeed he had forgotten to mention his absence, the reason was probably the opposite of what Ruth feared. He may have been so engrossed in their last session that he simply forgot. Ruth was acting like a raging child, he thought, and although some anger was appropriate to the situation, the intensity of Ruth's was due to its origins in her past.

"I can understand why you might feel this way," he said. "And it's important we sort out the issues you've raised."

"I just did," Ruth said. Still, they talked about

whether or not Dr. Pickens had forgotten to tell her of his absence. Because he couldn't remember, he refused to admit he had erred. "Actually," he said, "it doesn't really matter whether I did or didn't forget. Understandably you expect me to be certain about something so important."

"It would be hard for someone not to be upset," she said.

"Yes," he said. "But the issue is whether any of the reasons you've suggested for why you think I forgot are accurate. For instance, do you have any evidence that I resent you or had any harmful intent?"

Ruth considered the question, but she didn't want to respond. She knew the answer was no.

Dr. Pickens also realized that Ruth was facing another issue. When she had read her poem about the rejected gift, she feared her anger might precipitate an equally angry reaction from him. That fear was still present, yet Ruth had been able to confront him anyway. "You're not as afraid of your anger as you used to be," he told her, "if you can admit it openly to others."

For the second time since Christmas Ruth, who idealized Dr. Pickens, had expressed anger toward him. She left the session feeling better than when she had come in; it took her some time to understand why.

In succeeding sessions Ruth and Dr. Pickens worked on her shifting attitudes toward herself and her mother. Although Ruth's sense of autonomy was growing and her self-image was improving, she was afraid she would never truly understand herself, and without such insight another Poet-type incident could occur. Still, when Dr. Pickens went on vacation that summer, Ruth felt confident enough to wish him a good time and relax while he was out of town.

When he returned in August, they resumed their sessions, focusing primarily on Ruth's self-esteem. In the late fall Ruth read another poem.

"In the night I awake with a start," she said. "Feeling cold with a fast beating heart. And see the picture in my mind unfold. Watch with envy the little girl you hold."

Here Dr. Pickens noted that Ruth, because she wasn't yet fully willing to accept her past and needed to use the third person for distance, was continuing to fantasize that he had a daughter. But these lines represented significant progress, because Ruth was also imagining that Dr. Pickens could have been a loving parent to her as a girl. And her fantasy that a different parent might have loved her meant, he thought, that she no longer felt totally blameworthy for her mother's rejection.

"I would like to push her away from your touch," Ruth continued. "I feel in my heart this would mean so much. But to my mind how strange it seems. I hold you in awe even in my dreams. Your little girl will not have to surrender and be afraid. Your endurance rewarded by the bond you've made."

The bond was between Dr. Pickens and the little girl within Ruth.

"To have no control over the events in your life. And seem to be the opponent of man can cause you strife. But you might even value her a little more than if she were a boy. She'd not deny the painful consequences of being a broken toy."

The reference to a boy derived from Ruth's conviction that her parents preferred males. Her reference to being a broken toy in part recalled her assailant, who had threatened her by pulling the head off her doll. Dr. Pickens also heard in it an allusion to a theme expressed by many women in therapy who at moments of concentrated insecurity described themselves as broken males: castrated, defective, substandard. This self-image wasn't a core aspect of feminine identity, he felt, but an unconscious burden borne by some women because of their childhood experiences.

"I see life as a game where men win and women lose. A symbol of man's pleasure is whomever they choose." Ruth talked often about her anger toward men, but that anger was always ambivalent. She had had a closer, more secure relationship with her father than with her mother, yet Ruth was also angry at him because he had failed to rescue her.

"Your little girl will eternally embrace. Knowing you care by the look on your face. A faint voice not crying in her brain. Men are powerful and will strike again. Not in passion, terror, nor fear. Your little girl can tell who to be near."

These lines pleased Dr. Pickens. Ruth was saying that the little girl was now able to differentiate between good and bad people—an important step, particularly considering the incident when Ruth had comforted the crying man only to have him attack her once more. She had often mentioned that this act had made her feel foolish and that, even as a child, she should have known better. In turn Dr. Pickens repeatedly told Ruth that the inability to discriminate between good and bad people is a natural part of childhood; that was why laws existed to punish wrongful acts against children.

"She will be strong under the critics' stare. And of their presence she will become unaware. She'll carry no indelible marks on her side. Because she ran to you and cried and cried.''

Again Dr. Pickens heard proof of positive changes. Ruth was now willing to admit that hope was possible. She wasn't totally damned and abandoned.

"My mother told me I could take it and come back for more. Not to be afraid and quit checking the door. And when my friends said they could not with me be seen. She thought this was fine and certainly not mean. In fact her reply was to reverse the facts. If it had been someone else in this act. I might not want to associate with them for a spell. Now I wish everyone had gone to hell.''

Ruth had felt bad that Wichita had shunned her after she confessed to being the Poet, but at the time she understood that reaction. If the situation had been reversed, if the Poet had been someone else, she would have done the same. Now she was willing to admit that she could find empathy for someone else's misfortune, and she was more consciously outraged at the people who had been so judgmental of her.

"But if your little girl seemed helpless, confused and insecure. You would not look on her as being impure. You'd get your hands dirty to get her clean. You'd not just stare and seem so mean. So terrible the scene I should have cried. But cut myself off from my body and then I died.''

In these lines Dr. Pickens heard Ruth's overview of her therapy and her fantasy of how things would have been different if he had been her parent. As those feelings developed, they were beginning to replace her self-imposed guilt. She wasn't responsible for being unloved or for being abused. Any fault lay with others.

"With you she reexperienced her flesh being torn away. She chattered to you until there was nothing to say. She told you her blood was the brightest she'd ever seen. You kept listening with your mind caring and keen. I had to look at the iron red hot at last. . . ."

The iron, Dr. Pickens assumed, was the one that had been part of the incident in Fort Scott.

"But on man's hands no stain I can see," Ruth continued. "His madness weakens and he is free. But they are not innocent of the crime. Do they forget it with the passing of time. But your little girl your hand can clutch. And as I see you I know I can't touch. When my soul is tempted to all of this hide. Out slides the merits of suicide."

Although Ruth still felt that suicide represented the only true escape, the one time she had seriously considered killing herself was during the month of her confession, when her childhood memories were trying desperately to push their way to her conscious mind and Ruth was equally desperate to stop them. Suicide seemed to be the sole means at her disposal.

Ruth and Dr. Pickens seldom discussed incidents that were related to the Poet unless in reference to a poem. Ruth felt no desire to mention them, and Dr. Pickens no need. One issue on which they could never agree, however, was the genesis of the Poet. They both thought that Ed's apparent heart attack was one factor. Ruth felt that the man who had sent her the *Fort Scott Tribune* article and later approached her on the street was the other.

Dr. Pickens, however, considered the BTK Strangler of key importance, which Ruth denied because she remembered feeling indifferent to the killer. Dr. Pickens assumed that Ruth was telling him the conscious truth but that subconsciously she had feared BTK, so much so that his similarity to her assailant had begun to force her memories to come forth from the past. As these memories caused increasing anxiety, Ruth needed more than the vague threat of BTK to explain them; she needed her own assailant. The emergence of the Poet in turn gave Ruth the illusion that whatever danger she was feeling was imminent; it hadn't yet happened. Thus she undid her history, saving herself from having to admit she had been sexually abused as a child. In writing the poems, she was also able to express her fears, anger, and self-hatred.

"You keep check on your little girl's face," Ruth continued. "And rescue her when she lost her grace. . . . And when she wished for you to be there. She knew you were because you cared."

Ruth glanced over at Dr. Pickens for his reaction. "There are some very hopeful feelings in that poem," he told her.

She nodded. "I guess so," she said. She hadn't realized the poem was positive until the last few lines.

They next briefly discussed the ending. "I guess I think it might have been different if you had been there," she said.

"You are continuing to move away from blaming yourself," he said.

Ruth nodded, but she was thinking once more about how different her life would have been if he had been her father. Again she wondered if he had a daughter. Then her mind wandered back to the little girl. "I really want you to hug her," she said, but her tone of voice suggested to Dr. Pickens that as much as this remained her fantasy, she knew it was impossible.

"The little girl doesn't exist physically anymore," he reminded her. "There's only one person who can reach her directly."

"Right," Ruth said, for whenever she expressed that wish Dr. Pickens responded similarly. But she couldn't imagine doing such a thing herself, hugging that horrible, dirty little girl, and so she didn't consider it. Instead she preferred to discuss how much she wished the abuse hadn't happened.

"And I want you to make it that way," she told Dr. Pickens. "Why can't you make it all disappear?"

"But it did happen," he responded. "This is a very painful reality that can't be changed. Repressing the truth as a child enabled you to cope. Ever since it has caused you problems, culminating in the Poet."

"Uh-huh," Ruth said. "I'm sure, of course, that you're right." She frowned and turned her head away.

"What are your feelings?" he asked.

Ruth struggled to tell the truth, because she was aware that he already knew the answer. "I think," she said, "that it would be hard for someone not to be real upset with you."

Dr. Pickens realized that her comment was as strong an expression of anger as she could make without poetry. Over the last few months he had noticed that Ruth was growing increasingly angry at his inability to change the past, and they now discussed that anger in the larger context of the need to deal with irrational feelings.

Overt abuse isn't the only means by which children can be impaired, Dr. Pickens explained. Substantial damage can also result from other psychological factors, such as in this case the inability to deal with irrational feelings. Once again Dr. Pickens used the analogy of patients and children, which Ruth found condescending—it reminded her of her vulnerability and his power—but helpful. Most parents are hated by their children at times, he continued, because all kids detest the word *no,* and childhood is filled with noes. Most of the time the no is for a good reason, but good reasons seldom make a difference to a child. Loving parents respond appropriately to the child's hatred in ways that help her work through those feelings, creating a secure environment in which the child can say, "I hate you," without being afraid that her parents will hurt her in return. However, the child of unloving or abusive parents is alone with both the hate provoked by abuse and the normal, irrational hate of youth.

Likewise, Dr. Pickens explained, a patient required a therapist to accept that same kind of rage and not return it in kind or act defensively. Ruth felt angry that Dr. Pickens couldn't erase her unhappy childhood, but she was slowly beginning to realize that her ability to express such anger toward him was one more constructive step in her therapy. She had never been able to admit anger openly before; she could do so here because she felt safe.

In her next session Ruth mentioned an issue that now became an integral part of her therapy: whether or not to tell her story publicly. "Don't you think Wichita deserves to know what happened," she asked Dr. Pickens, "after all the trouble I caused?" But Dr. Pickens suspected that Ruth wasn't telling him the entire truth. He felt her real concern derived from her own needs, although she had difficulty saying so. Ruth wanted to alter her public image. The Wichita media had covered the Poet objectively, but no one had ever reported any explanations. Ruth, who projected her sense of her own badness into that void, assumed others did the same.

Over the previous year Ruth's fear of public appearances had diminished, yet she still felt people stared at her. "But I can't go up to everyone and tell them I was raped," she said, "or that I developed a dissociative disorder and that I didn't know what I was doing when I was the Poet."

"What would you like to do?" Dr. Pickens asked.

"I don't know," Ruth said. She thought about the different people in the media who had already made her offers. Many of them were movie producers, whom Ruth was finding increasingly rude. "Ruth," one executive from a well-known company had said, "someone as strange as you is a natural for television." Writers had also called, wanting to collaborate on articles or books, and Larry Hatteburg, a news producer at KAKE-TV, had been phoning every six months to ask if Ruth wanted to appear on local television. Ruth had said no to all of them, but if she relented, KAKE would be her first choice. Larry Hatteburg was a well-known personality in Wichita; if she could trust anyone, it would be Hatteburg. Still a part of her assumed that any response to her story would be highly condemnatory. "Don't do it," Ed said when she asked his advice. "You'd be making a mistake. Why drag all this up again?"

Dr. Pickens understood that Ruth's choice was difficult. But he thought she might need to tell her story to achieve closure. The Poet incident had been so visible that in order for Ruth to feel vindication for herself as a child, public vindication for Ruth the adult might be necessary. Furthermore, Dr. Pickens realized that patients often pretend that therapy isn't the real world, and while such an illusion can be beneficial in creating a nonjudgmental environment, it can also create a gap between what is felt and said inside therapy and what is experienced outside. He believed that Ruth's self-integration could be greatly aided by a positive public reaction to her story.

The more they discussed the issue, the more Ruth became aware of the intensity of her ambivalence. Dr. Pickens let her know that he would help her sort out these feelings; whatever she decided, he would support her.

That's not what I want, Ruth thought. She wanted him to make the decision for her.

12

WICHITA'S MAJOR CITY STREETS ARE AS FLAT AND UN-
bending as the interminable highways that flow into
them from the prairie. On the corner of two of the
longer ones, Pawnee and Greenwich, on the sparsely
populated southeast side of town, were a decrepit
house, a vacant lot, and the only store in the area to
sell kilts, bagpipe replacement parts, and cold pork
pies. Called the Royal Scottish Company, it was
owned and operated by a short, tough-spirited immi-
grant from Edinburgh named Emma Dillinger, wife of
R. K. Dillinger. The *R* stood for Royal, thus the name
of the store.

Emma had come to Wichita in 1981 to marry R. K.
Three years later, before the store opened, the couple
were thinking of buying a new house and were touring
a show home in a development near McConnell Air
Force Base when, looking at a living room fireplace,
Emma wondered out loud if anyone had priced the
cost of another fireplace in the basement.

"It's seven hundred and fifty dollars," said a

woman standing nearby. It was Ruth. She and Ed had decided to leave their old house on East Indianapolis —not because of bad memories, they told friends, but because Ed had always wanted a fireplace, a second bathroom, and a two-car garage, all of which these houses had. And, although neither had mentioned it, both Ed and Ruth were happy to try life in a new home.

"Seven fifty's not bad," Emma said. "Maybe we can knock a few dollars off." Starting to chat, the couples took an immediate liking to each other. "I'd like to pal around with that guy Ed," R. K. told Emma. "He'd make me look good." R. K., not as bald as Ed, was losing his hair nonetheless. Ruth and Ed liked the Dillingers too, and when both couples purchased development homes in the same cul-de-sac, they became friends.

Emma had arrived in Wichita as the media coverage of the Poet was subsiding, although some of her co-workers at Wesley Hospital, where she worked as a medical transcriptionist, continued to talk about a remarkable patient who had recently left. Emma found the story sad, but she soon forgot about it.

Emma herself was an unusual woman, with unrestrained opinions, a forceful personality, and a rhythmic Scottish inflection in her voice. She certainly wasn't typical of her friends prior to therapy, Ruth told Dr. Pickens.

In the summer of 1984 Ruth took a day off from work, and Emma dropped by. "There's something I have to tell you," Ruth said.

"What is it?" Emma asked.

"Have you ever heard of the Poet?" Ruth asked, and then she explained. It took her fifteen minutes to finish the story. "Well, I'll be damned," Emma said.

Ruth hadn't wanted to tell, but a mutual friend of theirs was applying for a position in Dr. Pickens's office, and Ruth feared that the woman would find his notes about her, although Emma reassured Ruth that a psychiatrist's files were always confidential. Nevertheless, Ruth now had an intimate friend in whom she could confide.

With Ruth's permission, Emma told R. K. about the Poet the next day. R. K. felt bad for Ruth, but he had a classic poker face; his nature was so unflappable that Emma felt she had never once surprised her husband —not, however, that she stopped trying.

As the couples' friendship grew, they began to confide even more in each other. Still Emma and R. K. never brought up the Poet, and Ruth mentioned it only occasionally. But one day Emma saw Ruth drive home early. When she walked down the street to chat, she found that Ruth had been crying. "I've just been through a real bad session," she said.

"Do you want to talk about it? Or do you want to be alone?" Emma asked.

Ruth said she wanted to talk, but not about therapy. So they talked about everything else, and finally Emma said, "Ruth, it's okay to cry now and then."

"I know, Emma," Ruth replied. "I just don't like to do it."

Faye Smock's mental health was starting to fail. Back in the mid-1970s, a few years after her husband had died, Faye broke her arm falling on a sidewalk in Nevada, Missouri, where she and Carl had moved after retiring from the farm. As soon as Jean heard about the accident, she invited her mother to stay with her and Bill in Wichita while she recuperated. Faye accepted, and throughout her three-week convalescence Jean and Ruth fussed and fretted about her health, which was, however, good, as Faye repeatedly pointed out.

But a month after Faye returned home, Ruth's phone rang. "Hello, Ruth," Faye said. "This is your mother. I've sold the house. Can you find me an apartment?" Ruth guessed that Faye wanted to move to Wichita so that her family could stop worrying about her. The next Sunday morning Ruth and Ed drove the Oldsmobile around town until they found a place large enough to house the furniture Faye insisted on keeping —her dining table and chairs, her cedar chest, and her sewing machine. A few weeks later Faye moved in.

Faye was aware that Ruth had been the Poet and that she was now in therapy, but Faye never asked any questions. Nor did Ruth consider confronting her mother about her memories. She knew Faye wouldn't respond. Still the two saw each other frequently, and Faye remained remarkably healthy until one day in late 1984 when she told Ruth that she feared her brain had stopped telling her what to do. At this point Ruth decided to spend part of every weekend with her mother, helping her with small chores and shampooing her hair.

Faye was reading her Bible and study guides daily, but she was having trouble with almost everything else, including the television remote control. Faye called her daughter regularly. "Hello, Ruth? I can't find my show," and Ruth, who knew the remote by heart, would explain to her mother which buttons to push. "It's pretty remarkable," Ed said, "that her remote operates all the way from over here."

When Faye became increasingly incapable of keeping track of time, Ruth placed a small strobe light in her apartment that went off at dinnertime, reminding her to eat. Ruth carefully explained the light's purpose to her mother, who thanked her. But Faye called every day the next week. "Hello, Ruth? There's a strange light in my apartment. What is it doing here?" Ruth drove over, removed the light, and hired a telephone service to remind Faye about dinner. Faye thought the woman who called was the nicest person on earth, and Ruth never mentioned that she was paying for the service.

One late Sunday afternoon Ruth was rinsing her mother's hair when a thought struck her. Here she was, looking after her mother, who was totally dependent on her. It was a reversal of their situation fifty years earlier, and at that moment Ruth looked down at her hands. They were strong, and they were wrapped around her mother's neck, which looked as frail as a chicken's. I could strangle this woman right here, Ruth thought. She pictured her hands tightening around Faye's neck until her mother suffocated and fell over dead on the floor. Then Ruth shivered. With considerable effort she shook the fantasy out of her mind, dried her mother's hair, and helped her with dinner.

Still these fantasies made Ruth feel guilty. Didn't they verify her failure as a daughter? "I've been thinking a lot more about my mother," she told Dr. Pickens nervously in her next session.

"Yes?" Dr. Pickens said.

"It's funny, you know, how roles reverse. She used to take care of me, and now . . ." Ruth tapered off into silence.

"What thoughts do you have?" he asked.

She had wanted to say this directly for months. "Sometimes," she began, almost whispering, "I have horrible feelings toward her."

She looked at Dr. Pickens, who nodded for her to continue. "And I guess I've been thinking," Ruth said, now relieved that the subject was being aired, "it wouldn't be hard to, well, to kill her. Isn't that terrible?"

"Why is it so bad just to think something like that?"

"Well . . . ," Ruth said. She didn't finish. The answer seemed obvious.

"As a child," Dr. Pickens said, "you confused thoughts with actions, and saw them as similar. All children do, and so do many adults. But they're not. For instance, if you were angry with me and momentarily wanted to hit me over the head with that lamp, that wouldn't hurt me. If you actually did hit me, it would. There's a big difference between the two."

Ruth looked at the lamp, and for a brief moment she did want to hit him. He was always so right. Then she realized that of course she never would. She also understood that despite her fantasies, she was never going to hurt her mother either.

Once again she began to fantasize about how much better her life could have been if Dr. Pickens had been her parent, and she tried to trick him into talking about his family, mentioning the subject nonchalantly, as if it hardly mattered. She told another story about Faye and then asked, "You wouldn't have treated your own daughter that way, would you?" She waited for a response, but none came.

"How do you think I would have treated a daughter?" Dr. Pickens finally asked.

Ruth was crying.

"What are the tears about?"

"If you had raised me," Ruth said, "none of this would ever have happened. You wouldn't have been

253

angry. Everything would have been different than it was with my mother."

Hearing what she had said, Ruth immediately became self-conscious over her anger toward her mother. Dr. Pickens had already noticed that when Ruth remembered an incident in which she felt Faye had been hurtful, she often felt guilty, which automatically launched her into the refrain that she herself was totally culpable for her situation and that everyone in Wichita had a right to despise her. Now she was doing it again. "I did such a terrible thing," she said. "I'm a horrible person." But Dr. Pickens found that these often-repeated diatribes were increasingly more cant than conviction. Ruth's negative self-image was continuing to erode.

As Ruth read her latest poem in the winter of 1985, Dr. Pickens knew that her therapy had achieved at least a measure of success, for in it he heard a positive overview of their relationship.

"When I think of what the little girl wanted from you," Ruth read, "Most of all what she wished for you to do. To pick her up all crumpled and torn. And understand why she was so forlorn."

The poem went on to describe her fear, her pain, and how she was a "hollow body with empty hands" until Dr. Pickens "rescued her from the dark night."

Like many, the poem was long—almost two thousand words—and it concluded: "She wanted you to wash her clean and keep her warm. And hug her tightly and tell her there would be no more harm."

At this point Ruth's tone changed and her posture tightened. "But suddenly you dropped her and told her this was absurd," she read. "She surely thought you'd forgotten what you heard. She wanted you to squeeze her—she'd not had enough. But you had turned on her and told her life was sometimes rough. She followed after you but you did not see. You were sickened of her frantic plea. She must have been dreaming about what she'd found. But awakened suddenly as she hit the ground. She wanted you to think it rare. A child was born—but was not anywhere. She wanted you to find her she was so sad. She wished you would not think of her as bad. She searched for you but then she knew. Her childish ways it was time she outgrew. But just the same I dread the day. When I remain and you fade away."

"This poem," Dr. Pickens said when she had finished reading, "shows that you are capable of operating at two levels."

Ruth asked him to explain.

"For one," he said, "you can reexperience your childhood feelings. But at the same time you're getting perspective on them. You understand our relationship and how painful it can be. It's like a kid getting a shot to prevent disease: it hurts, but the child knows it's good for her."

The poem's last lines also raised a topic that they hadn't yet discussed but that slowly became Ruth's next major issue: the termination of her therapy.

The subject came up again several weeks later. Ruth had been considering it for some time and had feared mentioning it outside of verse. But now that she did, she spoke as if she were just making an offhand remark at the end of an hour. "Well," she said, "maybe this is as much therapy as a person needs." Dr. Pickens raised his eyebrows but said nothing, so Ruth dropped the subject.

Two weeks later, after reading another poem and analyzing it, Ruth abruptly brought up termination again. "Well, I guess that's about it," she said, out of any context. "We could be winding this down now, don't you think?" She kept her language as ordinary as possible because she knew that too much emotional content set off alarms.

"What are your thoughts?" Dr. Pickens asked.

"Well, there doesn't seem to be much more for us to work on," she said.

"Do you really feel it's the right time for us to stop?" he asked, looking right into her eyes.

Ruth met his gaze with difficulty, but she knew it was necessary to prove her point. "Yes," she said firmly. "I do."

"We can discuss it then," he said.

Dr. Pickens now had to discover whether Ruth was truly ready to end therapy or if she was using termination as an excuse to flee from some other recollections hovering near the surface. They talked about the issue for the next several sessions, after which Dr. Pickens decided that Ruth was indeed ready to terminate, for several reasons. First, her depression and anxiety had dissipated to the point where, as far as he could tell, they no longer interfered with her life. Moreover, he felt she had reexperienced her repressed memories enough to discuss them repeatedly in the first person and recognize their significance. Ruth now understood, although not consistently, that the abuse was not her fault and that it hadn't taken place because she was a bad child. And she saw her mother in a realistic new perspective. While she genuinely loved her mother, Ruth was able to admit that Faye hadn't been a consistently empathic parent and that she, Ruth, wasn't responsible for her mother's shortcomings.

Dr. Pickens knew that Ruth had also become much more assertive in her day-to-day life, which was a significant accomplishment. In the past she had not only denied her own assertiveness but had considered it a negative trait in others. Finally, Ruth herself wanted to terminate, which Dr. Pickens felt was an important step in establishing her own therapeutic independence.

They spent the following several sessions discussing a date for termination. Ruth ultimately selected September 30, 1985, four months away, and almost exactly four years after she had been committed. But the closer she came to quitting, the more painful she found the concept. Over those four years she had been able to tell herself that if she ever really lost her mind, Dr. Pickens would be there to save her, and she didn't want to lose that safety net. His presence soothed her, and she feared that without him she might regress to her previous emotional state. Sitting in the waiting room before her sessions, she now stared enviously at the other patients who came and went. They would continue to see Dr. Pickens, while she was being sent off alone into the world.

In August Ruth suggested they reconsider termination. "Maybe this should be put off another year or so," she said.

"Why do you feel that way?" Dr. Pickens asked.

"Well, it sounds good." Then she changed her mind again. "Oh, maybe it is time," she said, laughing nervously. She felt as if she could hear a little girl's voice protesting the loss of someone who could hug her and make her feel good. But then she thought that maybe it wasn't a little girl speaking; maybe it was the adult Ruth. She wanted Dr. Pickens to hug her too.

Anxiety over termination now competed with Ruth's desire to tell her story to Wichita as her primary topic in therapy. Specifically she feared that while she would always remember him, Dr. Pickens felt no real need for her and wouldn't care enough to remember her. She finally told him how much she envied his ongoing patients and added that she was afraid he would like them more than he did her.

In response Dr. Pickens shared with Ruth his vision of the patient-therapist relationship, which again involved an analogy to the child-parent relationship. "The therapeutic relationship is unavoidably more intense for the patient than it is for the therapist," he said. "A child has only one biological father and mother, whereas parents can have more than one child. Children always need parents. Parents may love and want children, but they don't need them to survive and mature. Therefore children and patients are vulnerable in ways that parents and therapists aren't. The child needs her parent to care for her in ways that she can't return. This parallels aspects of the therapeutic relationship."

Ruth found some of Dr. Pickens's explanations slightly long-winded, but she nodded. By this time in her therapy she could follow his thoughts, consider them, and agree.

"For instance," Dr. Pickens said, "suppose you give an enraged child under the age of five a button and tell her that if she pushes the button, she'll blow up the object of her rage. At some point almost all children will push that button, which is one reason why three-year-olds aren't given that button."

Ruth looked at him until she realized he was waiting for her to express some form of understanding. She nodded again, and he continued. "But children need to feel that, no matter what, if their parents had that same button, they wouldn't push it. And in a way parents do have that button: they have the power to do real damage to their children. When you get in touch with such childlike impulses toward me, you tend to assume I'll feel the same way toward you as your parents did.''

Ruth smiled cautiously. She grasped everything he said, and her fear over termination lessened, but she still hurt. "It's scary," she said. "How does someone know if they're really ready?"

"Part of what you're dealing with," Dr. Pickens said, "is a recognition that everything isn't going to be tied up in a neat package when your time is over, and that must hurt. But one of your goals here has been to achieve autonomy—to learn how you can live as independently as possible. So you'll continue to grow, but you'll do it without me.''

Ruth then disclosed another benefit she had derived from therapy: the terrible headaches and stomach-aches that had plagued her for so many years had disappeared. Dr. Pickens was pleased. He told her that traumatized children and adults typically converted psychological anguish into physical pain and that insight into such trauma often provided a remedy. He seldom suggested this to patients directly, however, because he found that they didn't profit from the knowledge or sometimes actively resisted the suggestion and became angry. But now that Ruth had brought up the matter, he agreed with her conviction that the pain was gone.

13

OVER THE PAST FOUR YEARS ED HAD SEEMED TO AP-
prove of her therapy, Ruth thought, since he never
criticized it. But in his heart Ed's discontent had
grown. He had originally acquiesced because Ruth
had unquestionably needed help and because the court
had mandated it. No one had told him, however, that
therapy would take so long, and it seemed to him a
crutch without which Ruth couldn't live. "Aren't you
ever going to stop?" he asked her one day. "You can't
do this for the rest of your life, you know." He reminded her that they could use the money for other
things, such as a new car or an overseas vacation. But
Ed was worried for himself as well. He was wary of
the bond that had grown between Dr. Pickens and his
wife, and he felt excluded from their relationship.

Ruth didn't comment the first time Ed voiced his
impatience. She was afraid to say aloud that her termination had already been arranged before she felt totally confident in taking the step. The next time Ed

complained, however, she did reveal that the sessions with Dr. Pickens would soon be over.

She also told Ed about her childhood sexual abuse. She had discussed with Dr. Pickens her need to talk to someone outside the sessions, and Ruth knew Ed should be the first. Over several sessions she had speculated about how he might respond, but she was unprepared for his actual words. "That's too bad," he said, and picked up a newspaper. "Did you see this here about the mayor?" he asked.

Ruth looked into his eyes and saw nothing to suggest that she should continue the conversation. Still, she gave it another try. "It was terrible, what happened," she said.

Ed put down the paper. "I think I'm going to have to mow the lawn tomorrow," he said, "even if it gets too hot." Then he walked out of the room.

Ruth reported Ed's reaction to Dr. Pickens during her next session. "I guess he didn't want to deal with it," she said.

"How does that make you feel?" Dr. Pickens asked.

"I think I'm angry," she said. "But Ed has stood by me through everything. It's hard to get too upset. The thing is, I can't blame him." But then she thought, sure I can. I can blame him all I want.

Nonetheless she continued to worry. "I think he's feeling neglected," she said.

"Perhaps," Dr. Pickens suggested, "this would be a good time for Ed to come in."

A few days later Ruth and Ed were eating dinner in silence. Ruth kept thinking that it wouldn't hurt to ask; finally she spoke. "Hey," she said, "would you like to come in to a session?"

Ed was surprised. "Do you really want me to?" he asked.

Ruth nodded.

"Well, I guess then I will," he said.

On August 19 both Ruth and Ed drove to Dr. Pickens's office. During their session Ruth told Ed more about the abuse, and Dr. Pickens explained the process of dissociation that had created the Poet. Ed listened patiently, keeping silent until near the end of the hour. "I still don't understand how I could have missed spotting the Poet," he said.

"It's really not that surprising," Dr. Pickens said. "If Ruth could hide it from herself, she could easily hide it from you too."

Dr. Pickens went on to discuss the psychology of child abuse. But Ed wanted to talk about the Poet. Why hadn't he noticed? Was something wrong with him? Dr. Pickens found himself disliking Ed's insistent point of view. He had hoped Ed would be less curious about his own relationship to the Poet and more interested in what had happened to Ruth. He also wanted Ed to give Ruth his full support. Without that kind of empathy Ed was unwittingly recreating the same sort of relationship Ruth had endured with her mother, and Dr. Pickens hoped she could be spared that. Yet Ed only wanted to discuss his own potential culpability.

Afterward, in a rare fight, Ruth accused Ed of being antagonistic toward both her and Dr. Pickens. Ed denied it. In fact, Dr. Pickens didn't feel that Ed was hostile at all. Given the range of patients' spouses whom he had met in therapy, Dr. Pickens found Ed only distant and resentful, and he believed that he was somewhat angrier at Ed than Ed was at him.

Ed himself knew only that he was uncomfortable. In their session Dr. Pickens had told him that Ruth was disappointed by his reaction to her stories of childhood abuse, and Ed interpreted this as an appeal that he be more emotional. But I was brought up to be like John Wayne, he thought. I don't show my emotions; no one in my generation does. He hoped Ruth still remembered that. Ed was pleased that therapy had helped his wife, but at times he felt more left out than she ever guessed.

Ruth also told her sister. She didn't quite mean to, but one warm late-summer afternoon she was drinking frozen daiquiris by Jean's back yard pool when the combination of the sun and the liquor loosened her tongue and she talked a little about the abuse. Ruth had already implied something had happened to her as a child, so Jean wasn't surprised. Still Ruth didn't go into great detail, and instead the two sisters discussed their childhood and their mother for the rest of the afternoon. Ruth told Jean that she wouldn't go public with her story while Faye was alive; that much she felt she owed her. It would be difficult enough to denigrate Faye's memory after she died, Ruth said, but to bring her any humiliation while she was still living seemed unnecessarily cruel. And the last time Larry Hatteburg had called from KAKE to ask Ruth if she wanted to appear on television, she had said no.

On September 30 Ruth woke up feeling both wistful and expectant. She got up, dressed, ate breakfast, and then returned to the bedroom, where she slipped out of her blouse and skirt and put on her favorite dress, which was bright red with a small ornamental bow near the neck. It was her last day of therapy.

Ruth was diffident at the session's start and didn't

want to talk. Finally Dr. Pickens asked, "How are you feeling?"

"I don't know if I want to stop," she said.

"How do you feel?"

"Very sad," she admitted. "For a while I didn't want to come in here at all. I even thought about canceling."

"What was your fantasy?" Dr. Pickens asked.

"I was afraid that you might have forgotten this was my last session," she said, "and that when it ended, I'd get up and leave, just like always, and then I'd never see you again."

"Do you think that's going to happen?"

"I guess not," Ruth said, "since we're talking about it." She started to cry. "I'll miss you," she said. She wiped her eyes with a tissue.

"I want you to know that it has been a pleasure to know you and to work with you," Dr. Pickens said.

Ruth was elated and embarrassed by what she perceived to be a sincere compliment.

"I'd like to give you a little gift," she said, and then added self-consciously, "Well, of course I'd like to give you a little gift, since it's right here with me."

She handed him a box. "If you don't like it, you can just give it away to a charity or something," she said.

He took the box and looked at it. "Will you take it?" she suddenly asked, concerned.

"Do you think I will?"

She nodded. "Yes."

He opened it. Inside was a ceramic tableau of a boy on a bench and a girl sitting on a little rocking chair. "Yes," Dr. Pickens said. "I can accept it."

Ruth's heart leaped. She had truly feared he might say no again. "They're called 'The Orphans,'" Ruth said, and then they talked about why Ruth wanted him to have this particular image. "I think it'd be good to leave orphans with you," she said. "You'll take such good care of them."

"Thank you," Dr. Pickens said, and they talked a little more about the gift until Ruth's session was over.

"It's time to go now," Dr. Pickens said.

Now Ruth truly cried; it amazed her that after all her tears she could generate still more. "Right," she agreed. But she wasn't ready, so she waited a few minutes before standing up.

Dr. Pickens walked her to the door and extended his hand. "I wish you the best future possible," he said.

"And you too," Ruth said. She put her arms out tentatively to hug him but was poised to drop them if he backed away. Instead he reached out and embraced her.

"Good-bye," Ruth said. She looked down at the floor. "You've been, you know, one of the most important people in my life." She was thrilled that they had hugged.

"I appreciate your saying that," he said. She didn't move.

"Are you okay?" he added.

"Yes."

"Are you sure?"

Ruth thought about it. "No, I guess I'm not," she said. She sat down in a chair next to the door for another minute until she felt composed. Then she rose once more, he opened the door for her, and she left.

Ruth passed the receptionist quickly so the woman wouldn't see her tears. Ten minutes later, while on the road, she had to pull her car into a parking lot to wipe her eyes with a tissue. Then she went home, cried again, made dinner, and sat quietly with Ed watching television. Ed knew she had terminated therapy that day, but he said nothing about it, only asking if she felt okay. Ruth said yes. And that night she slept more soundly than she could ever recall.

Ruth was still visiting with her mother each weekend. The next Sunday as she was combing out Faye's hair, she suddenly said, "I'm out of therapy."

Faye remained silent for a moment. "Well, I know that's been hard on you," she said, and Ruth nodded.

That was it. Ruth thought later that she could have continued the conversation herself. For instance, she could have said, "No, actually, I enjoyed some of it." But she didn't. She couldn't talk freely to her mother, and she now realized she never would.

Over the next few months Faye's health continued to deteriorate, and although Faye didn't like the idea, Ruth and Jean were forced to consider a nursing home. They were convinced that once Faye actually checked into a home, she would be fine. They had to trick her into entering one, however, by telling her they were just taking her out for a short walk. That walk led to a nursing home across the street, and once she settled in, Faye didn't mind at all. But after only a week neither Ruth nor Jean was happy with the home, as they found the staff neglectful. One afternoon Ruth was standing in the hallway near her mother's room and she heard two attendants talking to each other. "Do you like ice cream?" one asked. When the second woman said she did, the first attendant replied, "Well, then, take Smock's. She'll never know if she ate it."

Ruth walked straight to the front desk and complained—the new, bold Ruth, she thought. A few days later, she and Jean moved Faye to a better home.

On March 4 Jean called Ruth at the phone company.

"I have a premonition," she said. "I'm going over to see Mother. Do you want to come?"

"No," Ruth said. "I'll go at six." But that afternoon Jean phoned again, in tears. "You've got to come over now," she said. "Mother's not going to make it much longer."

"I'll be right there," Ruth said. First she called Carl, and then she drove to the home, where she found her mother thrashing about in her bed, lapsing in and out of consciousness. Ruth wondered whether her mother was in great pain or was perhaps reliving a terrible memory. Her mouth suddenly broke into a horrible grimace, which confused Ruth because she had always believed that people died looking pleasant and contented. Then the nurse said that Faye's pulse had stopped. She was gone.

Ruth sat still and stared at her mother's distorted, spent face, and she felt a surge of sympathy for the hard life that had just ended for Faye. She had been born without advantages, she had raised a family during the Depression, she had made the best out of nothing, and Ruth wondered if her mother had ever dreamed about what might have happened if the times had been different. Faye was an intelligent woman; she had been a schoolteacher in Missouri, and then had moved to Seattle, where she became that city's first female postman, only to be called back home by her family when they needed her.

Another thought struck Ruth. She remembered an incident many years before, when her own children were young, and she and Ed brought them to the farm in Richards. There Bruce, seeing cows for the first time, burst into tears. Faye quickly scooped him up into her arms and soothed him. "You just tell Grandma why those cows scare you so," she said, and

Bruce replied, "Why, look at their eyes! They're so big, and they look right at you." Faye smiled, and in a few minutes she had Bruce laughing and petting the cows. Now Ruth thought, sitting by the bed, "Mother, those times when I was crying so hard, why couldn't you have picked me up like you picked up Bruce, and why couldn't you have asked me why I was crying? Because maybe I could have told you."

Then Ruth turned to Jean, and they hugged each other.

The funeral home's staff was unable to come get Faye for several hours, and so the nurse bathed her body, dressed her, and put her back in bed looking so alive that when Carl showed up, he poked her to make sure she wasn't asleep. "Don't do that," Ruth said.

"Just checking," Carl said.

A few weeks earlier they had decided to move Faye into a semiprivate room, and Jean and Ruth had studied the other residents, looking for a suitable roommate before selecting a small, timid woman. Now as they sat in the hallway waiting for the funeral attendants, that woman was shrieking at an innocent, elderly man who she thought was trying to rob her. "Get away from me," she howled, "or I'll shoot your balls off!" Ruth, Carl, and Jean burst into laughter.

Faye's funeral was held in Nevada, Missouri, and she was buried in Richards. Ruth was filled with sorrow. The excuses that had sometimes seemed so feeble in therapy, that despite everything Faye had done her best, now had a ring of truth. Ruth grieved and mourned, and she hoped that all the anger that had surfaced so violently over the last few years was being laid to rest along with her mother. If only, she thought, something weren't twitching in the back of her mind, like a mosquito bite she couldn't reach.

14

On a warm Indian summer Saturday in 1986 Ruth was sitting in her back yard, floating between wakefulness and sleep, alternately leafing through a magazine and dreaming of a tremendous tornado tearing across the prairie. She glanced at the magazine and drifted off again; she flinched at the image of the storm and woke clearheaded. Thank God, she thought. She often dreamed of tornadoes, which she had once assumed was peculiar, but Dr. Pickens had assured her that he repeatedly heard tornado imagery in midwestern dreams.

Half an hour later Ruth was still mulling over the storm's meaning, amused at the notion that she had become one of those people who analyzed their dreams, when a piece of paper suddenly flipped over the fence from a neighbor's yard. Ruth stood up, shook off her stiffness, and walked over to retrieve it. But as she bent down to pick up what appeared to be an old envelope, something curious caught her attention—a smell. It wasn't the paper. What was it? Ruth sniffed, like her dog Ginger trying to identify an important odor. A moment later she knew what it was: corn! Suddenly Ruth's mind flooded with images of corn husks, corn kernels, corn debris. She felt cold and frightened, and she trembled. Then the smell and the images evaporated. Ruth walked inside the house, lay on her bed, and wept.

A month later she was down in the basement searching for a photo album when she opened a storage closet door and saw, instead of old clothes and files, corn, exactly as she had seen in the back yard. Ruth slammed the door shut and ran upstairs. She had been certain her visions were all over. What was happening to her now? What was wrong? She thought of Dr. Pickens and wondered what he would say, but she decided that the proper course of action was to go on with her life and hope for the best. Apart from these two incidents, her life had become unexceptional, and for that she was truly grateful. She was enjoying her work at the telephone company, she and Ed were socializing with friends more frequently, and she had actually made a few new ones. At home Ed was startled when he voiced an opinion and Ruth occasionally disagreed or even argued; therapy had helped her verbalize her convictions. The change made Ed uncomfortable, but their marriage was solid, and Ruth remained grateful that while Ed wasn't uniformly supportive with his words, he loved her.

So Ruth ignored her visions and instead, now that Faye had died, brooded over telling Wichita her story. She still sensed while she was shopping or eating out or just driving in her car that other people were watching, and she wanted to correct what she perceived to be their severe judgment. By November 1986 Ruth was so anxious over her indecision that she called Dr.

Pickens for advice. She had planned just to chat on the telephone, but when Dr. Pickens's receptionist answered, Ruth realized she wanted to see him in person. She missed him.

Dr. Pickens's immediate schedule was so crowded that the receptionist could offer only a fifteen-minute session. Ruth accepted it and went to the office on November 26. She didn't mention the corn because, as she told herself later, she forgot. Instead she asked if she should talk to the media. If so, with whom should she meet—the newspaper or the television people? What should she tell them? Or should she let someone make a movie? What about those real-life television programs? Dr. Pickens expressed his continued interest in her welfare and reaffirmed that he would support any decision she reached. But the decision, he repeated, was hers.

"Nice seeing you again," Ruth said when she was leaving, as if she had been visiting a friend. She realized later that, in a way, for her it had been exactly that.

She returned to Dr. Pickens's office one more time, on December 16, to discuss the media again. The easiest choice was to do nothing, and so Ruth decided once and for all to keep her story private. When she walked out of the office that afternoon, she felt confident she was saying good-bye to Dr. Pickens forever.

In the late spring of 1987 Ed was scheduled to take a weekend business trip to Topeka, and he expected Ruth would want to accompany him, for she had yet to spend a night by herself in the house since his sudden collapse ten years earlier. But given the success of her therapy and her burgeoning sense of self-confidence, Ruth decided she could handle the two nights alone. It made her feel healthy, she told Ed, to know that she could take care of herself.

Ruth spent her customary Saturday afternoon working on her ceramics until six o'clock, when she started to fix herself a sandwich. Then the telephone rang. She had been expecting to hear from her son Bruce, but the caller was Ray Weller, the local businessman who had continued to help Ed and Ruth with their finances. They had come to rely on his advice.

Weller asked if he could drop by for a visit. He and Ed had been discussing a business proposal, and he wanted to fill Ruth in on the details. She saw no particular reason for this, but Weller insisted, so Ruth gave in. When he showed up an hour later, she offered him a cup of coffee and they sat down on the living room sofa, where he presented her with several folders on investment programs for retirees. Weller, who was married and had three grown children, dressed formally for Wichita; that night he was wearing a light gray suit with a blue and red striped tie. Whenever she saw him, Ruth thought of a television weatherman.

Ruth glanced through the folders and shrugged. She told Weller that while she appreciated his effort to keep her informed, Ed was the professional accountant and the family financial overseer. "Well, then, I guess that's about it," Weller said.

"Guess so," Ruth said, and she stood up. So did Weller, and they walked to the door together.

"Nice to see you," Ruth said. "Good-bye."

"You know, Ruth," Weller said, "you are certainly looking good these days."

He didn't move. Ruth stood by the door, wondering what he was thinking. "You don't mind if I give you a kiss, do you?" he asked.

Ruth stared at him, speechless.

"Well, I guess you don't then," he announced, and tried to kiss her on the lips. Ruth was shaken. She slipped away from him and ran out the door, shutting it behind her. However, it had just started to rain, and her clothes were becoming drenched. So she composed herself, walked back inside the house, and held the door open for Weller to leave.

"Come see us again," she said, giving away no emotion.

Weller stared at Ruth for only a second. "Super," he said, and walked quickly toward his car.

After he left, Ruth paced the house. The episode unnerved her. A few years earlier her hairdresser, Jerry, had also made a pass at her. While having her hair cut, she had mentioned her address. "Why, that's not far from me," Jerry said. "I could come over to your house some noon."

"You already have a lady friend," Ruth replied. "You don't want to see me."

"I didn't say I wanted to have an affair with you," Jerry said. "I just want to come and fuck you."

Ruth switched hairdressers and didn't think about Jerry again. But Ray Weller's actions infuriated her. It wasn't simply what he had done but what he knew. Because of the Poet incident, Ruth felt she had no credibility: who in Wichita would ever take her seriously? No one, she thought bitterly. Weller was aware of that too. He was a well-known businessman and Ruth a well-known lunatic.

When Ed called from Topeka the next morning, Ruth told him about Weller. "Now that's bad," Ed said. "That's really bad." He struggled to say more, but he couldn't find the words. Like Ruth he was angry, but neither of them could imagine an appropriate course of action.

Over the next week Ruth's rage surged, and she started to dream about revenge. But this time she wasn't going to write a poem, nor was she going to hurt herself. She wanted Weller dead. Through a friend Ruth had heard of an ex-convict who claimed to take care of this sort of thing. How would he kill Weller? Ruth wondered. What was the best means? She started imagining rifles and knives and pistols, obsessing over them endlessly until one morning she found herself standing in her kitchen with a peach pie in the oven, holding a piece of paper containing the ex-con's telephone number in one hand and the receiver in the other, ready to dial. She couldn't remember how she had located the man's number, or who had told her about him, or even walking over to the telephone.

Now she became scared, for once again she was performing actions without her conscious knowledge. She then did something she had learned from therapy: she went to Ed, and together they talked about a disturbing emotional issue, Ruth's mental health. They both decided she should call Dr. Pickens.

The day before Ruth's appointment she reached into a kitchen cabinet for a can of soup and momentarily blanked out. She didn't lose her balance, and the dizziness passed quickly, but in that brief second images of corn had appeared once again.

Since Ruth's last session, Dr. Pickens had relocated his practice to Twenty-first Street, a mile from his previous office. Ruth liked the new building more, although she wondered if she was simply accustomed to the idea of therapy. She found the office nicer too; it was better lit, with brighter carpeting and a modern couch. As before, Dr. Pickens had placed only a few nondescript decorations on the walls.

Dr. Pickens himself, Ruth decided, looked no different except for his mustache, which was trimmed. But she didn't want to stare.

Dr. Pickens had thought about Ruth frequently over the last year, particularly when he heard stories in the media about sexual abuse or when he was driving through Ruth's neighborhood. He didn't call her, however, because he felt his presence in her personal life would cross critical boundaries. A relationship between doctor and patient outside the office could encourage unrealistic expectations on the patient's part, such as, in the extreme, a patient who tells her doctor that if they could have an affair, she wouldn't require psychological treatment. A patient needed a therapist to be a professional rather than a personal adjunct to her life. The line was difficult to sustain, and Dr. Pickens was familiar with several doctors who he felt transgressed on both sides—some who became overly intertwined with their patients' personal lives, and others who unequivocally forbade patients to talk to them outside the office.

"What led you to set up this appointment?" he asked.

"Well," Ruth said, "I've been kind of upset. I just thought, you know, I might come in and well, you know . . ."

Dr. Pickens waited.

"Well," she said, "I've been thinking about some things." She laughed, "I mean, everything's okay. It's just . . ." She stopped again.

After several minutes Dr. Pickens asked, "Is there anything you'd like to say?"

Ruth nodded but waited a few more moments before

finding the words. "I want to kill a man," she said. Then she told Dr. Pickens about Ray Weller. "Ed doesn't really know how to help. I don't think he understands how angry I am. How could Ray do such a thing? And who would ever believe me, after everything I did?"

She talked more about the incident, slowly repeating the details. "Maybe I should come back into therapy for a while," she said. "It bothers me I could get so mad. I'm, well, too mad."

She stopped, then resumed. "Also, this weird thing happened a while back. It was like before, when I was seeing things."

"What were you seeing now?" Dr. Pickens asked.

"Corn." Ruth could barely say the word, and she didn't want to pursue it.

After she hadn't spoken for a while, Dr. Pickens said, "There may well be some unfinished business we didn't get to the first time, things that further therapy could clarify." He guessed that her excessive anger pertained to another memory rather than to Ray Weller.

"This time it might be more helpful if you came in three times a week, rather than twice," he added. "Also, I think you might try the couch now."

Ruth hadn't expected the second round to differ from the first. "Sure," she said. "That's okay." But she was flustered. What did all this mean, how much would it cost, and most of all, why the couch? She had noticed it immediately and then pretended she hadn't. She felt a couch in a psychiatric office was a cliché for spoiled people who wasted money complaining about nothing.

But after further thought she realized that she might not mind lying down. If she faced the ceiling, she wouldn't have to look at Dr. Pickens. As much as she valued therapy, she disliked watching him while she talked: she felt too self-conscious. But she also wondered if these changes meant she was crazier than before.

Dr. Pickens guessed her thoughts. "I think," he said, "the intensity of your feelings indicates the repression was too strong for us to have uncovered all of it before."

"Okay," Ruth said. That sounded a little scary.

"And the couch can help," he continued, "because it fosters regression. So can the increase in the number of sessions."

Ruth wondered why they hadn't used the couch the first time. Then she remembered: Dr. Pickens didn't have one. He explained later that he had started to use it in his new office only when one patient's therapy clearly required it.

They had three sessions together before each took a summer vacation, and the therapy resumed in mid-August. Once again Ruth relied on poetry to express her emotions, first writing verses at home, and then discussing the feelings they evoked after reading them aloud to Dr. Pickens.

Ruth, a veteran of four years of psychotherapy, quickly acclimated to the couch. There was, however, one strong disadvantage in not seeing Dr. Pickens. During the long silences that still pervaded her sessions, she wondered if he was awake. She felt that she was so dull that she had to be putting them both to sleep. On days when she was sure he was bored, she listened closely to his breathing. Was it steady or irregular? Was it the breathing of someone who was asleep or someone who was fully conscious? Now and then when he was particularly quiet, Ruth would suddenly ask, "Are you there?"

"I'm right here," he would answer. Ruth's question, he felt, was another example of her negative transference. When she couldn't see his face, she instantly suspected that, like her mother, he wasn't there for her emotionally. He told her this, and she thought how sad it was that Faye's grip had survived her death.

As in the old office, Ruth couldn't see the clock, but during one late August session she assumed that at least three minutes had passed since Dr. Pickens had shown any signs of consciousness. Suddenly she sat up on the sofa to see if he was awake. There he was, his eyes wide open, and the only emotion she saw on his face was astonishment. On the other hand, he felt that his expression was composed and the only astonishment was on Ruth's face, because he wasn't asleep.

"Just checking," she said.

"What did you expect?" he asked.

"Oh, nothing," Ruth said, but he knew what she meant, and she knew he knew.

A month later Ruth was on the couch, and she could hear herself counting again, which she hadn't done for over a year. She quickly guessed she was holding back something very unpleasant and fought it by launching into what she referred to as her "babbling."

"Everything at work's good," she said. "Ed's job is taking a lot of his time. We heard from Bruce this weekend. He's doing so well. His wife is real sweet, and she has a wonderful boy. The new house is turning out great." Ruth trembled; she was scared.

During the next session she added laughter to her

babbling, speaking at length about nothing of significance, erupting into fits of giggles and then talking again, while all the time thinking, Dr. Pickens must think I'm a real screwball.

"What are you feeling?" he asked.

"I'm fine!" Ruth said. "Things are great! Who cares? Life goes on!"

For the next few minutes Ruth couldn't speak. She became dizzy and had to grab the couch for support. "Oh, no," she said. "No, no, no."

Dr. Pickens waited.

"This can't be happening," Ruth said. Her body was rigid. "I'm going to take off. I don't have anything to hold on to. I just can't stand this. Oh, my God!"

Dr. Pickens moved his chair closer to the sofa. Ruth still couldn't see him, but his hand, which he now extended from behind her, was visible. "It may help you to keep in contact with the present by holding on to me," he said softly.

Ruth was startled. Dr. Pickens had never voluntarily offered to touch her before. She burst into tears and grabbed his thumb so tightly she thought she was going to squeeze it off. Then she cried louder.

"Don't touch me!" she said in her fantasy.

Dr. Pickens, aware that she was talking to someone inside her head, suddenly thought of science fiction, picturing Ruth as a time traveler alive in two worlds, her mind in the past, her body in the present—and her only hold on the moment his thumb.

"It's just," Ruth said quickly, "it's just that the little girl is in the corn crib." She stopped talking for a minute, and now could tell her story only in small pieces. "The man comes in . . . he holds her down . . . he hurts her. Oh, God, he does it again." Then her mouth froze shut.

A few moments passed.

"You can pull your hand away, or you can hang on," Dr. Pickens said. "Whichever you'd like."

Ruth was sobbing. She didn't want to let go, but finally she loosened her grip, and he leaned back in his chair. This was the first and only time Dr. Pickens had touched a patient during a session. Physical contact between therapist and patient ran counter to his training, and he had touched Ruth only because he guessed that her pain had put her in palpable danger of losing her connection to him, the present, and reality.

Ruth didn't mention the episode during their next session. But the week following she settled down on the couch quickly and laughed to cover her anxiety. "That was pretty funny, huh?" she asked. "My grabbing your hand like that and holding on to you and telling you not to touch me." Then she frowned. "You probably think I'm silly."

"Why would I think that?" he asked.

"I just thought you would," she said.

After a silence, he asked the usual question. "What are your feelings about this?"

Ruth checked herself. What she was actually feeling was gratitude. She had been extremely moved that he had let her hold his thumb. She truly believed that she had touched the fringe of her sanity and she wondered if fighting this kind of horror had first caused the Poet to emerge. But she didn't tell Dr. Pickens any of these thoughts; frank expressions of appreciation felt overly intimate, and she feared his reaction and more so his rejection. Instead she changed the subject and complained about an incidental problem at work—anything, she thought, to avoid the real issue.

During the next session, however, she did say that

holding on to his hand had made her feel better. It made her nervous to do so, but she wanted to voice her gratefulness.

On September 10 Ruth left the phone company and drove to Dr. Pickens's office without any particular agenda for her session. She felt relatively untroubled and calm. As she turned into the parking lot, however, she wiped her forehead and was surprised to feel moisture; she hadn't noticed she was perspiring lightly. Confused, she walked inside and sat down, feeling increasingly worse, and by the time Dr. Pickens opened his office door, misgivings and apprehension had overwhelmed her. She guessed what this meant—a memory was loose—but rather than let it emerge, she took a deep breath and relied on her well-practiced ability to talk about everything except what she wished to discuss. The couch allowed her a wider range of nervous movements than the chair, and she had never appreciated it more than now.

"Is it time to go yet?" Ruth asked.

"No," Dr. Pickens said. "You've been in here only a short time."

"Right," Ruth said. She stopped speaking.

"What's on your mind?" he asked.

"Oh, nothing," she said. But the pain inside her head was burning a hole in her defenses, and she sensed she was falling through that hole against her will. Suddenly she felt three-and-a-half years old.

She kept silent.

"What are you thinking about?" he asked.

Ruth couldn't answer for a few minutes, but when she did, her voice was high-pitched and shaky. "The little girl. She's in the barn lot."

"Who's in the barn lot?" he asked.

Ruth swallowed hard. "I am," she said. "And my dad's with me, and so's my granddad, and so's the neighbor. My dad's going somewhere in a wagon, so I turn around to wave good-bye. But when I look back, my granddad's going into the house. He's leaving me alone with the neighbor. Why is he doing that?"

Ruth stopped. Her recollection from the session in which she had held Dr. Pickens's thumb, blurted out in one sentence, had returned in more detail. "Why's he doing that? Don't leave me here!" Ruth's voice faded. "The little girl and the neighbor are all alone now. Just the two of them."

"Who?" Dr. Pickens asked.

"Me. I'm alone with the man."

She stopped again, shivering. "I'm looking at him," she said, "and he has this terrible leer on his face. My first thought was to run but he was standing between me and the house. I didn't know where to go, and so I ran as fast as I could inside the barn and up the hayloft ladder. But the man was faster, and he ran up to the girl and laughed and just grabbed her foot and pulled her down.

"Oh, the little girl just knew what was in store for her now. She could feel all the pain even before he touched her. She cried and cried, and she started kicking and lashing out, but he had her under his arm in that awful way he used to carry her, like she was a chicken or something. Then he put his hand over her mouth, even though his hand was all dirty and disgusting, so that she wouldn't make any noise.

"This time it's too much. It's like this time she can't deal with it anymore. She's giving up. She's dying."

Ruth was sobbing. "Oh God, oh God," she cried.

"It's okay," Dr. Pickens said. "You're okay here.

You're safe. This is a memory. This isn't happening now.''

Ruth nodded. But what was the difference between a memory and reality when the memory caused this much hurt? "Then he got her to the corn crib," she continued, "and he put her down on the floor and took off her coveralls. She was holding on to the fasteners to try to keep him from undoing them. But he just yanked her hands away and undid them."

Ruth squirmed on the couch and brushed her hair with her fingers. "There's corn in her hair," she said. "There's corn everywhere, and it's all dirty down here. It stinks." She stopped, and when she began again, her voice was so faint that Dr. Pickens could hardly hear. "Then he was doing whatever it was that he used to do to her teeth," she said, "and then this little girl's mouth was full of this dirty, stinking thing. This time she didn't throw up, though. But he wasn't ready to let her go. He straddled her on the floor, and now they're looking at each other, eye to eye. This had never happened before. Never. Then he put her coveralls over her face, and he went and hurt her."

Ruth stopped, allowing herself to cry for a few minutes and wipe her tears with a tissue. "This is why it's too much now," she said. "Something's wrong with the little girl. Oh God, it's because she tried to fly away but she can't, she can't do it. She didn't want to stay, but she had to. She didn't know why, because she knew she could escape if she flew into the clouds, but she couldn't. She couldn't do it."

Ruth's eyes were clamped shut. "The little girl felt nothing but pain, and she heard nothing but noise," she said, then stopped.

"What are you feeling now?" Dr. Pickens asked after a few moments.

She heard his voice, but it sounded distant. "I'm afraid," she said.

"That's understandable," he said, keeping his tone composed and steady. "What you went through was terrible. But there's nothing to be afraid of here. Nothing at all."

"Isn't there?"

"No," he said firmly. "Nothing at all. You are totally safe here."

Ruth considered his words. They made her feel calm enough to continue. She thought, his voice is like his hand. I can feel it.

"The little girl thought she was going to die," she said. "Why couldn't she fly into the clouds? She figured she should just die, since she didn't want to be with the man but she couldn't get away. Why couldn't she fly away this time?

"Then he was gone. Now she's lying there, on the corn crib floor, with her coveralls hiding her face. She didn't remove them. She just lay on the ground crying, trying to keep quiet because she thought the man might be hiding nearby. But all she heard was her own sobs.

"The little girl was sure that everyone hated her now. No big person would ever help her, and this meant no big person ever liked her. If she had been a good girl, God would have helped her. But he didn't. She wanted to die."

"You," Dr. Pickens said.

"Right," Ruth said. "I wanted to die. I hoped that if I just stayed still long enough, I could die."

Ruth paused, then returned to the third person again. "She just wanted to be dead," she said. "Dead."

"How do you feel?"

"Horrible. This was the worst. This time she might as well be dead."

Ruth cried, and Dr. Pickens waited until her sobbing relented. Then he asked, "Where is the little girl right now?"

"She's still there, lying on the barn floor, and the coveralls are over her face," Ruth said. "Nobody is helping her. Oh God! No one is helping her. She's just there, all alone."

"Okay," Dr. Pickens said. "Now who is the little girl?" He was guiding her recollections more actively now than he had at any other time in her therapy. But Ruth didn't respond. She knew, but she didn't want to say so.

"Who is the little girl?" Dr. Pickens repeated.

"I am," Ruth said through her sobs. "I am the girl."

"Tell me again," he said. "You talked about the little girl. Can you tell me the end of the story again but now saying 'me'?"

Ruth considered his suggestion. "Yes. I guess so." She paused.

"Whenever you're ready," he said.

"Okay," she said. "I thought I was going to die. Why couldn't I fly up into the clouds, like before? I didn't want to be with the man, but I couldn't fly away, and I didn't understand it. This was the worst of all. The other times I could leave. I can't leave this time. I'm still there."

Ruth stopped again.

"The man left," she said when she could speak again. "I'm lying on the corn crib floor with my coveralls over my face. I don't want to take them off. I just want to stay in the dark and cry."

Now more than ever Ruth understood why she disliked recalling her memories in the first person. "At this point I just knew that everybody hated me and that everyone wanted to see me get hurt," she said. "There wasn't one big person who would help."

She stopped talking. She was fidgeting and her body ached.

"Where are you now?" Dr. Pickens asked.

"She's on the crib floor." Ruth smelled the corn and she felt the crib's scratchy surface.

"Who?"

"I am."

"What would you like to do?"

"Well, I want you to do something," Ruth said.

"What?" Dr. Pickens asked.

"I want you to pick her up and hug her. I want you to go and make the little girl feel better. I want you to tell her that you're sorry for what happened and . . ."

"What else?" he asked.

"I want you to help her get cleaned up and dressed," Ruth said. "And then I want you to take her out of the barn. Tell her this will never happen again. Tell her that she's safe."

"You've asked me this before," Dr. Pickens said. "And I've told you that I can't touch the little girl because she no longer has a body. She's inside you. But can you do that yourself? Can you do those things for her? The little girl needs you."

"I don't want to," Ruth said.

"Why?"

"It doesn't seem right. One can feel sorry for other people, but one shouldn't feel sorry for oneself."

"But do you think that I could ever do those things you ask?" he said.

Ruth dreaded the question she knew was coming, but the gentleness in his voice reassured her.

"Do you?"

"I guess not," she said.

"Who can do those things?"

"I don't know," she said.

"Don't you?"

When she didn't say anything, Dr. Pickens continued. "The horrible events are in the past. The little girl exists within you. Only you can touch her. You are the one who can help yourself."

The thought so repulsed Ruth that her mouth flooded with the taste of bile. Me? she thought. Yeah, she replied to herself. That'll be the day. But she didn't speak a word, and neither did he. Another moment passed.

"Are you still there on the floor with your face covered?" Dr. Pickens asked quietly.

Ruth wanted to say, "No! The little girl is dead and gone and forgotten. Now everyone is happy because she can't be hurt anymore and she won't cause any more trouble." Instead she nodded imperceptibly.

"What would you do if you saw another little girl in so much trouble?" he asked.

"Another little girl?" Ruth said. "If it were another girl, I'd help her. I'd do everything I could to let her know I was sorry and that I cared."

"Then what about this little girl?" he asked. "She can't fly away now. Her wings of dissociation are broken. So can you help her? Can you do that for yourself?"

Dr. Pickens had asked Ruth this question before, and she had always been able to reject it. Now she couldn't. She thought it over. Nothing had changed, and yet she felt everything had. The sadness within her welled.

"If you can do that," Dr. Pickens said, "you are

touching and accepting that part of yourself that you thought was unlovable.''

Ruth heard what she had said a minute before, that she could help another little girl, but now she realized that she could help herself too. An unfamiliar emotion replaced her sadness. What was it? She knew the word before she could fear it. It was compassion—compassion for herself.

Now Ruth traveled back in her mind to the past once again. But this time, instead of watching from a safe distance, the adult Ruth walked into the barn where the little girl lay sprawled out on the floor, sobbing and helpless.

''I'm there,'' Ruth said softly. ''My God, I'm right there in the barn! Oh, it's horrible in here. It stinks, and it's filled with the smell of the man.''

She stopped and drew in a deep breath. ''Now I'm kneeling down next to the little girl on the barn floor. And oh, look at her, she's so unhappy, just lying there, all alone and crying and thinking that she's hateful and dead.''

Ruth stretched her arms out to touch the little girl. ''I'm taking the coveralls off her face,'' she said, ''and I'm wiping the tears off her dirty cheeks. She's watching me, and she looks so happy because she knows I'm not going to hurt her. You see, she thought that everyone in the world wanted to hurt her and make her unhappy.''

Ruth's arms extended around the little girl's body. ''I'm holding her in my arms now, and we're hugging each other, and we're crying together.'' She looked directly into the little girl's eyes. ''I'm so sorry this ever happened that I can't stand it,'' she said. ''But you're not alone. There is someone who loves you.''

The little girl smiled and told Ruth that she felt much

better. Ruth was so happy to hear this that she hugged the girl again, trying to give her an entire lifetime's worth of love and support. Then they held on to each other as long as they could, not speaking, just touching and crying. When she couldn't hug anymore, Ruth said good-bye to the little girl and returned to the present, while the little girl went back to her childhood.

Ruth was crying softly. Guessing that she had taken up more than her allotted time, she sat up, tears streaming down her face, and thought, I have been in this room forever.

"Would you like to stay on the couch for a while?" Dr. Pickens asked. Ruth was grateful for his presence. Her time with the little girl had seemed so real that his words sounded remote, making her fear that she had become lost in her own mind.

"Isn't the hour up?" she asked.

"Yes," he said gently. "But if you need more time, you're welcome to take it."

"Just a moment," she said. After a minute had passed, she stood up.

"Are you sure you want to go?" he asked.

"Yes," she said. "I'm ready."

He opened the door for her and said good-bye.

Ruth stepped outside. She had arrived at the building only an hour before, but the day had changed; the light had dimmed, and the various sounds in the parking lot were hushed and distant. She looked for the car through her tears. "Be calm," she told herself. "Just get in the car and leave." She drove back to her office and sat quietly at her desk, keeping apart, working without thinking. Later she couldn't remember a single moment from the phone company, but she replayed the therapy session over and over in her mind so that she would remember it forever.

The session moved Dr. Pickens as well. He had never experienced anything as powerful in his career, and he felt both proud of himself and happy for Ruth. This memory, and the resulting moment when Ruth was able to hug the little girl, were her therapeutic turning points. But he knew that she still had more work, not only on her past, but on her eventual termination, as well as on her continuing ambivalence about telling her story to Wichita.

During the next few sessions Ruth continued to talk about that last assault. "It was the worst," she said. "This time it was so awful even the little girl couldn't do anything about it. She couldn't even fly into the clouds."

"Maybe that's why you were able to go back and help yourself this time," Dr. Pickens suggested. "It was when you needed help the most."

Ruth thought this over and decided it made sense. "Do you think there are more memories inside?" she asked.

"What's your understanding of it?" he asked.

"I don't think there are," Ruth said. She wasn't sure why she said this, but she was certain of its truth. And she was glad, for despite that session's significance she felt no desire to relive its intensity. The connection between herself as an adult and as a child had been made, and now she wanted to focus on her present life. She also discovered another by-product of her last recollection: she no longer wanted to kill Ray Weller. That anger had faded. When Ruth thought about Weller now, he just seemed like a jerk.

15

RUTH'S PRIMARY ISSUE THROUGHOUT THE REST OF the fall was, as Dr. Pickens had suspected, her conflicting attitudes about taking her story to the media, which she had turned into an all-or-nothing proposition. Dr. Pickens sensed that he could help relax that stance by proposing intermediate steps. First, he moved her from the couch back to the chair because he felt that Ruth no longer needed the regression facilitated by the couch. Next, he asked her if she wanted to invite her brother into a session to gain some experience discussing her past. Ruth considered the idea for a few days and then agreed. Carl came in a week later.

The session was difficult for Ruth, and she let Dr. Pickens do most of the talking. Then Carl too started to remember. For instance, during the Depression the Smocks and their neighbors used to trade help; no one could afford hired hands. Carl recalled his father trying to leave Ruth at the neighbor's house while he went off to work, but Ruth screamed and cried so loudly that Faye couldn't quiet her. Carl also remembered the time when he and Ruth were playing in the barn lot with Stubby and the neighbor came by but Stubby refused to let him near.

Carl was struck with another memory from a half-century earlier: an unusually angry Faye was talking to his father while holding something in her hand. She showed it to him, and his father's response was, "He'd never do something like that." Then the two started to whisper, and Carl heard no more. But immediately thereafter the neighbor disappeared from the Smocks' life. This conversation had occurred just before the fall planting season, which indicated that the neighbor's sexual assaults on Ruth had lasted only that one spring and summer.

Later Carl and Ruth discussed their father's inaction, and they both decided they couldn't blame him. He had no proof, and the law in rural Missouri was minimal. Still Carl wondered if his father had considered a confrontation. "I'd sure have shot the son of a bitch," he told Ruth. Carl decided to track the neighbor down himself, but he discovered that the man had died several years earlier. His wife was still living in a Fort Scott nursing home, however, and Carl wanted to confront her, but Ruth talked him out of it. "It might kill the old gal," she said. "It's not worth it."

"I don't give a goddamn," Carl said. "I want her to look at you and say nothing happened."

Ruth refused, and Carl dropped it for a while. A short time later the wife died too. "I want vengeance," Carl said. "How about letting me dig up that son of a bitch's grave, and I'll hang his bones over the railroad overpass on Highway Fifty-four?" Ruth still said no.

* * *

Dr. Pickens next suggested that Ruth talk to her sons. She consented, but first she asked Dr. Pickens to call and prepare them for what she knew would be an intense conversation.

Dr. Pickens called Bruce and his brother and said, "When she tells you about the incidents, keep in mind that a part of her has the same sense of vulnerability she had when she was three years old." Bruce wasn't sure what Dr. Pickens meant until Ruth called him ten minutes later. "Hello, Bruce?" Ruth said. "This is your mother . . . ," and she broke into sobs as she told him an abbreviated version of what she had learned in therapy. Her voice was high and shaky, and Bruce thought she sounded like a scared kid.

That night he lay awake in bed, thinking about his mother. He was glad she had found an explanation for her behavior; he was sorry it had involved so much pain. But he wanted to know more, so the next morning he called Ruth and asked direct questions, which Ruth answered honestly. Then she asked him questions too, about his own life, and he answered as honestly as she had. Ruth was delighted to find a sympathetic ear in her own family, and soon she and Bruce were calling each other frequently, communicating openly about their emotions and not, as in the past, simply reporting on the day's events. Their relationship changed from stilted to tender, and perhaps this was, Ruth thought, the nicest reward of therapy.

Dr. Pickens also asked Ruth if she might try once more to read the *Eagle-Beacon* articles about the Poet, which Ruth still feared were hostile and inaccurate. But on February 10 she brought them in and this time read them straight through without crying. "What do you think?" Dr. Pickens asked.

"You know," Ruth said, "they're not so bad." It

hadn't occurred to her that the articles contained only facts.

Having taken these steps safely, Ruth was now more inclined than ever to go public with her story—as long as Dr. Pickens accompanied her. He consented because he knew she needed support; he compared her to a child forced to testify about sexual abuse without an adult present for guidance. But before Ruth and Dr. Pickens decided which medium to approach, KAKE-TV's Larry Hatteburg made his annual call to see if Ruth wanted to appear on television. Ruth then asked him to talk with her and Dr. Pickens in a therapy session. He agreed, and he proposed his concept of a one-hour documentary featuring live interviews and dramatic recreations. Ruth and Dr. Pickens were impressed that Hatteburg's main interest was in the child's story; others had expressed interest only in the Poet. After discussing his proposal between themselves, they decided to work with him.

It was only now, after Dr. Pickens had consented to support her in front of a television camera, that Ruth felt he had fully accepted her. Ed, however, remained unremittingly against the program. "Why do you want to dredge up all this stuff again?" he asked.

"Are you saying you don't want me to do it?" Ruth asked.

"It's your decision," he said. "I'd prefer it if you didn't." Hatteburg produced a series of programs called *Hatteburg's People,* in which he talked with unusual Kansans. Ed feared that this kind of television would trivialize Ruth's story, placing her in the same category as the woman who raised caterpillars in her home or the man who turned old barn wood into art. Ruth, emboldened by Dr. Pickens's support, disagreed.

Hatteburg doubted that Ruth would feel comfortable in KAKE's studios, so he rented an expensive show home and interviewed Ruth and Dr. Pickens in its living room. Ruth was anxious, but when the cameras started rolling, her nerves steadied, and by the third and final hour she was almost enjoying herself. Then every day for the next month Ruth checked the newspaper, looking for a program listing. Finally, in May she called Hatteburg. "Were we that bad?" she asked.

"You were fine," Hatteburg said. "It's a good show." Ruth then asked if she could see it, but Hatteburg refused. "It'll be on in a few weeks," he said.

The program aired on May 26, 1988, and ran without any commercials, partly because of KAKE's commitment to the subject, but also because no one believed an advertiser would sponsor it. "Good evening," Hatteburg said at the show's start. "Tonight KAKE news presents a special report, a very personal look at a Wichita woman and her secret." Next KAKE managing editor Randy Brown reminded viewers of the ominous atmosphere in Wichita during the Poet's existence, due to the BTK Strangler. Then the two narrators recounted the story of the Poet from the first telephone call to the house at East Indianapolis to Ruth's confession. The camera next moved in on Ruth herself, who looked healthy and attractive in a pretty pink dress. She talked about the dissociation that created the Poet and about the sexual abuse of her childhood. While she spoke, the camera caught her nervous mannerisms by continually returning to her hands, which were anxiously twisting a handkerchief. At home, sitting with Ed, Ruth watched, nervously critical of her words and appearance.

KAKE dramatized the attacks with visually ambiguous black-and-white reenactments accompanied by a frank narration. Ruth could barely look at these segments; Hatteburg hadn't told her how her childhood would be filmed.

Then Dr. Pickens explained the Poet's behavior, and Ruth expressed her embarrassment about what she had done as the Poet. "I think one of the reasons we're in front of the camera right now is because you wanted to correct that negative image," Hatteburg said.

"I'm sure there are people," Ruth said, "[who] wondered, what on earth is wrong with her? . . . Maybe if I explained my life a little, they would understand, because I've changed my opinion of myself during therapy. I don't think I'm a bad person, like I did. I understand that this little girl had her problems, that she just was kind of put on hold and then acted up a little."

Hatteburg looked slightly embarrassed. "This is a hard question for me to ask because of everything you've been through," he said to Ruth. "The Poet was not real. How do you know that what happened to you when you were three and a half was actually real?"

Ruth had expected this question. She answered, "I think [with all] the details I remember, I'm sure they were real. But people would have to be their own judge."

Hatteburg turned to Dr. Pickens. "What proof do you have, Doctor? What would you say to answer that criticism?"

"I also might add," Dr. Pickens said, "that Mrs. Finley has been in therapy for a total of approximately five years. . . . You don't do that as a lark. It's expensive, it's painful, it's difficult."

Hatteburg interrupted. "Is the Poet dead?" he asked.

"Oh, I think so," Ruth said. "I would say yes, wouldn't you?"

"Yes," Dr. Pickens said. "Definitely."

At home watching the program, Ruth sighed.

Hatteburg changed the focus of the program from Ruth to the issue of child abuse. "There is help available," he said. "If you are being abused, or if you know someone who is, here are some people who can help." He then gave numbers for the Sedgwick County Department of Mental Health and the police department's exploited and missing children's unit, and the program ended.

"What did I mean by that?" Ruth had wondered throughout the program. "Why did I do that?" Now that it was over, she was deprecatory, not of Hatteburg but of herself. Was this what other people saw when they looked at her? Ed, however, felt so relieved that the program hadn't hurt or disparaged Ruth that he grabbed the phone and called Hatteburg. "Larry, you did a super job," he said.

Over the next few weeks Ruth and Ed received a stream of positive calls from friends and strangers. And at KAKE, where Hatteburg expected the program's explicit dialogue to generate at least some unfavorable feedback, the telephones had been silent until the hour's end. Then the switchboard couldn't handle the volume, which was overwhelmingly favorable and included dozens of viewers calling to relate instances of abuse from their own childhoods. Many of them had never talked about it before.

The response both pleased and confused Ruth. In the past she had equated the media solely with trouble, because she felt it brought shame on all those caught in its spotlight, including herself. Worse were the people who voluntarily exposed their embarrassing private lives on television talk shows, proving themselves either foolish or self-seeking. But Ruth felt the KAKE program had helped her considerably. She no longer felt cloaked in disgrace. Anyone who chose to dislike her now did so fully informed, and Ruth could cope with that. When she heard about the calls to KAKE, she guessed that her story was helping people who had suffered as she had. Again, therapy taught her to rethink her perspectives. There was little in life that could be reduced to simple answers, and strangely enough, Ruth realized, that truth applied to the media as well.

Emma Dillinger watched the program alone. Ruth had told her about her childhood, but nonetheless Emma was upset. When R. K. came home later in the evening, she was lying awake in bed. "How was it?" he asked. "Tragic," she replied.

Joyce and David Middleton also knew about the show in advance, but Ruth hadn't filled them in on the details. Joyce cried. She also wondered how any parent could not have known what was going on. There had to have been some blood. Joyce couldn't understand Faye Smock's indifference.

Jean cried too, and both she and Carl were proud of their sister. After the show aired, they found people openly sympathetic and willing to talk about the Poet for the first time. A few days later Jean and Ruth were shopping at a women's boutique on Kellogg when the store's owner heard Ruth's voice and said, "Oh, you're Ruth Finley!" To Ruth's slight embarrassment, the woman hugged her.

Bernie Drowatzky had retired from the Wichita Police Department and was now working as a police officer in Kaw City, a small town in northern Oklahoma, but his television received KAKE. He and his wife, Dora Ann, watched Ruth tell her story, and they both felt vindicated. "The times I was around Ruth, she was so convincing she had to believe the things she was telling us," Drowatzky said. "She never slipped, not once. I would have picked up on her if she had been faking."

But neither Mike Hill, now Sedgwick County sheriff, nor Richard LaMunyon agreed with Drowatzky. Hill never saw the program, but later, when someone told him about Ruth's therapy and her account of her actions as the Poet, he shook his head. "Nah," he said. "No way." And though LaMunyon, still chief of police, did see the program, he didn't change his mind either. "She was not Ruth Finley, then the Poet, then Ruth," he told the press. "That is irrational. She knew everything she was doing." Nor did LaMunyon believe Ruth had been assaulted at Fort Scott. That incident, he was sure, was also self-invented, but for what reason he couldn't guess. "The lady has problems," he said. "I just don't know what they are."

The entertainment industry called Ruth too—producers, agents, packagers, television talk show hosts, even a movie star. Now that the story had a happy ending, the pitching was more frantic than ever, and Ruth listened politely to them all.

"Ruth, Ruth, Ruth," said one young man calling from Hollywood. "You can't say no. You're coming in here tomorrow, and I'm going to take you out to a terrific lunch, and I'm going to give you a big fat check. What do you say to all that?"

"I'm in Wichita," Ruth said. "I can't have lunch with you."

"Where are you?"

"Wichita," Ruth said. "Kansas."

"Wichita? Kansas?" the man asked. "What the hell are you doing in Wichita, Kansas?"

"I live here," Ruth said.

"Then why did you call me?" the man asked.

"I didn't call you," Ruth said. "You called me."

The man immediately denied it, but a moment later Ruth heard him swear at his assistant over the miscommunication. Then he hung up. In another call a young agent wailed that his boss would fire him if Ruth didn't let him handle her rights. A day later a well-known producer screamed, "Just who the fuck do you think you are, lady?" when Ruth refused to say yes. "You know something?" Ruth told Ed. "These people from Hollywood remind me of the Poet."

Before they taped their interview for the documentary, Ruth and Dr. Pickens had selected a date for Ruth's final session: June 30, 1988. For the remainder of her therapy they discussed Ruth's reaction to termination and her newfound confidence that she could, although not always happily, take over from Dr. Pickens the role of custodian of her psyche. He had been telling her for years that therapy lasted long after the actual sessions, which she understood. But she still feared the end of their relationship because she sometimes felt she had nothing in her life to take its place.

Another subject that arose was Ruth's changing character in her day-to-day life. For instance, she had recently gone to the mall and bought a bench for her vanity table, she told Dr. Pickens. After bringing it home, she read in the newspaper that the bench had been on sale, although the salesgirl hadn't informed her. Before therapy she would have moaned to Ed about being cheated and dropped it there. But now she went back to the store, demanded the better price, and got it. Ed was floored. It was a small matter, Ruth said, but to her it was important.

Ed's thinking had also changed. "I think therapy has done you some real good," he told her. They both felt it had helped their marriage and their communication. After years of silence Ed began talking to Ruth about his own upbringing, which hadn't been as pleasant as he had once implied. His father, Elmer, had been an alcoholic, and Ed's childhood memories were fraught with traumatic incidents, which Ed now described for Ruth. These conversations, candid and painful, helped the couple achieve new insight into each other's life.

"There's something I have to tell you," Dr. Pickens said at the end of a session. "I've accepted a job in St. Louis, and I'll be moving there at the end of the summer."

Ruth had been about to get up from her chair. "Really?" she asked casually. Inside, her heart sank. "Isn't that nice," she added. She didn't want him to know how much she cared—until the next session, when they talked about it at length. Termination was now their sole topic.

"It's one thing if you're still in Wichita," Ruth said. "But St. Louis?"

"You can always call me," he said.

"It's not the same thing," she said. In making her decision to leave therapy, Ruth hadn't reckoned on Dr. Pickens leaving town. One farewell was reparable, the other felt much too final.

301

On June 30, 1988, Ruth went in for her last session. She expressed anxiety over her sense of being left on her own, but she also said that she was happy that her therapy had been so rewarding.

"I guess I'm sort of lucky," she said.

"Why?" Dr. Pickens asked.

"You came to Wichita a few months before I started therapy," she said. "And you're leaving a few months after I'm ending it."

Dr. Pickens was pleased. "Much of your pain has been due to bad luck," he said, "but I think you're right. My arrival here was good luck. Otherwise this type of therapy wouldn't have been available for you." No one else in Wichita practiced psychoanalytic psychotherapy, and Dr. Pickens believed strongly that while another therapy might have helped uncover the abuse, none would have been as effective in helping Ruth cope.

Dr. Pickens and Ruth had often talked about the relationship between luck and life. Frequently patients wondered how such horribly traumatic incidents could have happened to them when they were so young; typically they blamed themselves. "But if therapy is successful," Dr. Pickens told Ruth, "a patient reinterprets such a situation as having been born into bad luck, rather than believing she was the cause.

"Children tend to view good and bad in life on the basis of reward and punishment," he continued. "They see a direct correlation between outside forces and themselves. But adults eventually accept the haphazard reality of good and bad fortune in their lives, whether they like it or not."

"Yes," Ruth said. "That sounds true." And she meant it.

Before she left, Ruth read from her last poem:

Thank you for helping me see as a goal
Having the little girl melted into me and being
    whole . . .
I can't be rescued except in my mind
But that's only possible because you have been so
    kind . . .
My heart feels it might break on this sad day
As I leave here and you go away
But my heart is also happy inside
That I gained my freedom and also some pride
In my mind when the need may arise
I'll be with you and I'll shut my eyes . . .
In my heart your spot will always be there
Close to a little girl who felt you did care.

Ruth's time was over. She cried, and on her initiation, she and Dr. Pickens hugged and said their final good-byes. Two months later Dr. Pickens moved back to St. Louis, where he set up a new practice.

Ruth and Ed settled into the conventional, stable life Ruth had craved so urgently for so long. Her health was good, her marriage remained strong, and she felt happy. In the spring of 1991 she retired from the phone company, and she filled her days with friends and family, including two new grandchildren and a step-grandchild. Occasionally she became lost in thought about her past, but now, when she remembered herself as a little girl, it was with sympathy and affection. And although she kept all her poems from the therapy sessions in a box in the basement and read them from time to time, she never felt the urge to write another line of poetry again.

AFTERWORD

AND ACKNOWLEDGMENTS

I FIRST MET RUTH FINLEY IN THE SUMMER OF 1988, A few months after Larry Hatteburg's documentary aired on KAKE-TV. A friend in a child abuse support center in the Midwest had told me about an unusual story being discussed in her peer group; the story turned out to be Ruth's, and immediately after our conversation, I called Wichita information for her number. When I reached Ruth, I asked if she would let me write about her for a national magazine. Like many other callers, I was also interested in the movie rights. Ruth, however, was noncommittal, refusing to say yes or no—an emotional defense about which I later learned much more. Nonetheless, after several other calls that were neither encouraging nor discouraging, I flew out to Wichita to meet with her and Ed in person. Because we got along well with each other, Ruth agreed to the article. She also consented to a movie, but was relieved when, after several years of development, that project collapsed.

Still Ruth refused to let anyone write a book. At first

305

she thought she might do it herself, but she found the task overwhelming and so tried collaborating with a journalist. When that failed too, she retreated again into her privacy. My magazine article, published in the fall of 1988, caused still another round of calls from movie and television producers with offers, and although many of them were well-meaning, their total effect was to frighten Ruth once more.

Meanwhile Ruth and I talked occasionally on the phone. As we did, she related pieces of information about her therapy, never more than a fragment at a time, but their totality made me realize how little of Ruth's story the article had captured. Every year I asked her if she would let me write a book that would include all these details, and every year she said no. Then in 1991 she changed her mind, and shortly thereafter I flew to Wichita once more and we began to work together.

By nature resolutely private, Ed was opposed to the book. But once his wife had agreed to the project, because he is also fair, Ed felt he should cooperate too. His unflagging assistance was invaluable, as was that of Bruce Finley, who diligently guided me through the family history and located many otherwise lost documents. (The older Finley son, however, didn't wish to be interviewed.)

Ruth herself was astonishing. Going over her therapy, she said, was not unlike reliving the actual sessions, and some of it was enormously stressful. Many times our interviews started with a few hopeful sentences, and then there were tears, and then we shut off the tape recorder and talked about other matters. Over the last few years Ruth has become an avid devotee of current events, and often when she couldn't talk about her therapy, we instead discussed politics, sports, and movies.

Between these conversations, at chance moments when Ruth suddenly felt comfortable, we were able to reconstruct the most difficult parts of her therapy, except for the critical session described in the book's final chapter. Ruth couldn't talk about that at all. So instead, whenever possible, she jotted down notes, which she gave to me. I rewrote them, and then she rewrote them again, until finally we had the session on paper. This book wouldn't exist if Ruth hadn't been willing to relive two horribly painful experiences: one when she was a child and was so badly abused, and the other when she was the Poet.

Once Ruth had consented to the book, Dr. Pickens agreed to help reconstruct the therapy sessions from his point of view, and his remarkable insight and effort eventually resulted in over fifty tapes of material. The descriptions of these sessions are an attempt to recreate hundreds of hours that took place many years ago and in which few notes were taken; they represent my best estimate of events as described, read, corrected, and approved by Ruth and Dr. Pickens. For the most part their memories were identical. They differed solely on the timing of certain discussions, and their only ongoing disagreement concerns the relationship of the BTK Strangler to the genesis of the Poet. Dr. Pickens continues to believe that BTK's presence in Wichita was a primary trigger; to this day Ruth is unable to recall having any feelings about BTK and doesn't understand Dr. Pickens's interpretation.

(BTK has never been apprehended, nor has he ever attempted to kill again. Since serial killers rarely cease committing homicide without some external interference, the police are baffled and they assume the man has either died or has been incarcerated in a prison or a mental hospital in another state. Or, as Mike Hill conjectures, perhaps BTK found such a sexually gratifying and permissive partner that he no longer felt compelled to murder. There is still another possibility. In the mid-1980s Richard LaMunyon had one of his usually infallible gut instincts about a suspect, but he was unable to prove his case absolutely and his suspect was never charged.)

Not counting the inexorable weather, Wichita has changed significantly over the last dozen years. "The city's going to hell in a wheelbarrow," says Bernie Drowatzky, who is glad to have retired to a rural Oklahoma road where half his neighbors are ex-policemen. Violent murders have become common throughout the city, and the problems of urban America, which once seemed incidental, are now rampant. "Wichita used to be a friendly small town, but since the gangs and drugs, it has become an unfriendly big town," Larry Hatteburg says. "Before if you had a major crime like the Poet or the BTK Strangler, people were astonished. Now drive-by shootings occur nightly." And, in 1991, when large-scale antiabortion protests turned Wichita into that summer's national synonym for protest and violence, the city's sense of remoteness changed forever.

Richard LaMunyon is no longer chief of police; he quit in 1990 when he was offered a higher-paying job as the executive director of Wichita Greyhound Charities. Then, in 1992, late in the race, he entered the Republican primary for Congress. He lost, but considering how little money he spent for how many votes (including Ruth's; she holds no grudge against him), he expects to run again. LaMunyon still believes that Ruth's actions as the Poet were conscious and deliberate, and he has bet me that Ruth will run into the law again. Yet despite his knowledge of this book's theme, LaMunyon devoted countless hours of his spare time to recreating the police's investigation of the case, and the account of it in this book depends heavily on his recollections, as well as on those of his gracious wife, Sharron. Also invaluable were the others on the case: Mike Hill, who ran once more for sheriff of Sedgwick County, and won; Bernie Drowatzky and his wife, Dora Ann (Drowatzky ran for sheriff of Kaw City and was not as fortunate as Hill); Jack Leon (now a Wichita police captain); Kerry Crisp (currently Director of Security and Fire Protection for Boeing); Mark Hephner and Richard Zortman; and Dr. Donald Schrag.

I am indebted as well to Ruth's friends and family, especially Carl Morris Smock, Jean and Bill Jones, Joyce and David Middleton, and Emma Dillinger. Also very helpful in Wichita were Larry Hatteburg and historian Dr. Craig Miner, as well as the staff of the Wichita Public Library, along with my local friends, Scott and Kelley Christensen.

Many of the above provided me with transcripts, tapes, and other supporting evidence, particularly Ruth's confession and the KAKE docudrama. Some of these documents have been reproduced verbatim in the book, except when they were illegible or when for clarity's sake I was forced to amend them or, particularly in the case of Ruth's confession, shorten and edit them. In no case, however, has their meaning been altered. Ruth and Richard LaMunyon provided me with the Poet's letters, and Ruth and Dr. Pickens gave me copies of the poems written during Ruth's therapy. The Poet's punctuation and spelling were erratic, and several symbols have been changed for readability, especially the ampersand, which was most often represented by a dollar sign or a zigzag. Finally, four identities have been disguised in the book: Ruth's childhood neighbor in Missouri; Jack Sartin, the television producer; Jerry, Ruth's hairdresser; and Ray Weller, the Finleys' financial adviser.

Over the last few years many generous friends have read sections of the manuscript and offered excellent advice, including Sally Arteseros, Betsy Beers, Suzie Bolotin, Richard Flagg, Dan Frank, David Hickman, John Homans, Hillary Johnson, Fran Kiernan, Susan Lee, Laura Marmor, Steve Randall, Jim Stewart, and Will Swift. At Simon & Schuster I am grateful for the help provided by my editor, Fred Hills, along with Burton Beals, Julie Rubenstein and Leslie Ellen. I am also grateful to Carolyn Reidy, for her patience, and to Jack Romanos, for more than a decade of friendship and support. My agent, Richard Pine, has been inestimably helpful as well, as were, in the initial stages of this project, Kathleen Finn and Gordon Freedman. Most of all, I am thankful for the unwavering love and guidance given to me by Ted and Barbara Flicker.

Ruth too read the final manuscript, but she found the task difficult. She feels embarrassed and exposed, and her wish is that she won't be judged too harshly. She also worries that readers will misinterpret her past feelings of anger toward her mother, for today she says she wouldn't have traded Faye for anyone else. Still Ruth has persevered, because she has come to believe that the desperate sense of isolation and hurt among child-abuse victims can be relieved by an awareness of other people's stories. That is why she changed her mind and allowed the book to be written, and I hope, as do Ed Finley and Dr. Pickens, that she is correct.

Gene Stone
November 1993

Quimby Library

51519
51519
RC 569.5 .M8 S76 1994 / Little Girl Fly Away

DATE DUE		
JAN 0 5 2009		
MAR 1 9 2012		

QUIMBY MEMORIAL LIBRARY
Southwestern College
P.O. Box 4788
Santa Fe, New Mexico 87502